URBAN INFRASTRUCTURE IN TRANSITION

NETWORKS, BUILDINGS, PLANS

Edited by

Simon Guy
Simon Marvin
Timothy Moss

Earthscan Publications Ltd, London and Sterling, VA

First published in the UK and USA in 2001 by
Earthscan Publications Ltd

ISBN: 1 85383 689 3 paperback
        1 85383 694 X hardback

Typesetting by PCS Mapping & DTP, Newcastle upon Tyne
Printed and bound by Creative Print and Design Wales
Cover design by Susanne Harris

For a full list of publications please contact:
Earthscan Publications Ltd
120 Pentonville Road
London, N1 9JN, UK
Tel: +44 (0)20 7278 0433
Fax: +44 (0)20 7278 1142
Email: earthinfo@earthscan.co.uk
http://www.earthscan.co.uk

22883 Quicksilver Drive, Sterling, VA 20166–2012, USA

Earthscan is an editorially independent subsidiary of Kogan Page Ltd and publishes in
association with WWF-UK and the International Institute for Environment and
Development

A catalogue record for this book is available from the British Library

Library of Congress Cataloging-in-Publication Data
Guy, Simon.
    Urban infrastructure in transition : networks, buildings, plans / Simon Guy, Simon
    Marvin, Timothy Moss.
        p. cm.
    Includes bibliographical references and index.
    ISBN 1-85383-694-X (hardcover) — ISBN 1-85383-689-3 (pbk.)
    1. City planning—Environmental aspects—European Union countries. 2. Public
    utilities—European Union countries. 3. Sustainable development—European Union
    countries. I. Marvin, Simon, 1963- II. Moss, Timothy, 1959- III. Titles.

    HT169.E8 G88 2000
    363'.094'091732—dc21

                                                                            00-046597

This book is printed on elemental chlorine-free paper

CONTENTS

PART 1 INTERPRETING INFRASTRUCTURE

PART 2 RECONFIGURING NETWORKS

PART 3 TRANSFORMING BUILDINGS

PART 4 CONNECTING PLANS

PART 5 RE-INTERPRETING URBAN INFRASTRUCTURE

LIST OF FIGURES AND TABLES

FIGURES

TABLES

ABOUT THE CONTRIBUTORS

Susanne Balslev Nielsen is a civil engineer working as assistant professor in the Department of Planning (IFP) at the Technical University of Denmark. She has a PhD in urban ecology and the transformation of technical infrastructure. Since 1997 she has researched and taught on urban ecology and planning at IFP with a particular research focus on new planning practices and public participation for sustainable infrastructures.

Morten Elle, PhD, MSc, is Associate Professor of technical urban ecology in the Department of Planning (IFP) at the Technical University of Denmark. He is author of the book *Urban Ecology of the Future*. His particular research interest is in the interrelationships between people, buildings and technical infrastructure and the development of novel methods of public participation. He is co-author of the Danish scenario-workshop method.

Simon Guy is Reader in Urban Development and Director of the Centre for Urban Technology in the School of Architecture, Planning and Landscape at the University of Newcastle. His research interests revolve around the social production of the material environment. He has undertaken research into a wide spectrum of urban design issues including the development of greener commercial office buildings, the role of architecture and property development in urban regeneration and the links between environmental building design and the provision of infrastructure services.

Simon Marvin is the United Utilities Professor of Sustainable Urban and Regional Development at the University of Salford. He has developed an interdisciplinary research programme examining the reconfiguring of urban infrastructure networks across the energy, water, telecommunication and transport sectors in the UK, Europe and developing cities. Key publications include *Telecommunications and the City* (with S Graham) and *Cities, Regions and Privatised Utilities* (with S Graham and S Guy).

Regine Mauruszat is an economist at the College for Administration and Law in Berlin. She was previously at the Institute for Regional Development and Structural Planning (IRS) in Erkner, near Berlin, where she researched a wide range of issues relating to regional development and planning, including green building, transport planning and spatial development in the state of Brandenburg.

Timothy Moss holds a DPhil in urban history. He is a research associate at the Institute for Regional Development and Structural Planning (IRS) in Erkner, near Berlin, where he has coordinated and conducted a number of national and international research projects on institutional dimensions to environmental change in urban and regional contexts. His special research interests are in the areas of infrastructure management, river basin management and EU strategies for sustainable urban and regional development.

Jesper Ole Jensen has a MSc in civil engineering. He has worked as a research assistant in the Department of Planning (IFP) at the Technical University of Denmark (DTU) on various projects on urban renewal, green strategies, the environmental performance of buildings and urban ecology. Currently he is studying for a PhD at the Danish Building Research Institute (SBI) with a project on housing, lifestyle and consumption.

Suzie Osborn was formerly a research associate at the Centre for Urban Technology in the School of Architecture, Planning and Landscape at the University of Newcastle. She is now working as a Local Agenda 21 officer.

FOREWORD

The commitment to sustainable development is clearly one of the most important features of the Treaty of the European Union agreed in 1997 at the Amsterdam Summit. Complementing and reinforcing the policies adopted at other levels of governance – local, national and global – the European commitment to sustainability will have considerable implications over the coming years. Many aspects of public policies, business strategies, institutions, individual lifestyles and behaviour will have to be reconsidered. Research clearly has a fundamental role to play in preparing and enabling the necessary transitions.

The European Union's current fifth Framework Programme on Research, Technological Development and Demonstration Activities therefore lays strong emphasis on improving the knowledge base, on developing new technologies and on devising appropriate tools to achieve sustainable development. Within this general scope the programme acknowledges the special importance of urban issues, grouped under the key action 'City of Tomorrow and Cultural Heritage'. Cities are not only the places where the vast majority of Europeans live and work, it is also there that the implementation of sustainable development policies is most urgent and particularly complex.

It is the merit of the EU-funded research project 'Sustainable Flow Management', upon which this book is based, to have pioneered an important, novel area of concern in EU research: the evolving and complex nature of urban infrastructures. In many respects the project anticipated the philosophy of the EU fifth Research Framework Programme: it is concerned with the interactions between economic, social and environmental policies and motives; it attempts to unravel the web of factors at play in the supply of vital services to urban citizens; furthermore, it recognizes and documents the difficulties of applying common policies to the extreme variety of situations that occur across the territory of the EU.

The project casts new light on a domain as yet inadequately understood and in doing so will hopefully generate further action-oriented research. More generally, the publication of the results will make a valuable contribution to the various European Commission initiatives aimed at promoting and supporting sustainable urban development.

Christian Patermann, Director
Research Programme Environment and Sustainable Development
European Commission

PREFACE

This book has grown out of a learning process set in motion by a joint research project on the management of urban technical networks. In the summer of 1995 a small group of researchers from various European countries and research backgrounds came together to discuss a common interest in utility services. While all the participants were, to a greater or lesser degree, engaged in research on the sustainable development of cities and urban regions, each had previously specialized in very different aspects of infrastructure management and worked within very different theoretical frameworks. The Danish team studied technical networks as instruments of urban ecology, advocating alternative environmental technologies. The British team had led debates about the urban and regional implications of utility liberalization and privatization and identified the emergence of new logics for infrastructure management. The German team worked on the restructuring of large infrastructure systems following unification. The issue that helped draw together a diverse team representing historians, sociologists, urban studies specialists, engineers and ecologists was a desire to understand how far urban infrastructure networks could be socially and technically reconfigured under new economic and environmental pressures.

The EU research programme 'Environment and Climate' (1994–98) presented the opportunity to pursue this common interest in utility services with a joint research project on their environmental impact (contract no ENV4-CT96-0249). The project, entitled 'Technical networks as instruments of sustainable flow management: a comparative analysis of infrastructure policy and planning in European urban regions', was designed to examine how utility services for water, wastewater, electricity and solid waste are managed and how changes in their management could contribute to achieving greater sustainability in urban regions. What 'Sustainable Flow Management' meant was deliberately kept open. The aim was not to define sustainability for the field of infrastructure management but to map different – even competing – pathways towards more sustainable forms of resource use as illustrated by empirical case studies of resource management in each urban region.

Working collaboratively within a common methodological framework and meeting regularly over a three-year period, the research team explored the changing social, technical, spatial and commercial contexts of infrastructure provision and use. One striking revelation emerging from an initial mapping exercise of the contextual framework of utility services was the extent to which infrastructure management is undergoing considerable transformation in very different urban regions. The new pressures for change include not just the privatization and liberalization of utility service markets but also the tightening of environmental standards, new forms of economic incentives, the high cost of network modernization, competition between a growing number of viable technologies, uncertainty over future consumption patterns and overcapacity in some networks. Although the intensity of these pressures varied considerably across regional and sectoral contexts it was clear that all utility managers – whether public or private, local or supra-national – are having to come to terms with new ways of working.

This book is about how these pressures are challenging dominant forms of infrastructure management of the past, how novel logics of infrastructure management are developing in response and what new openings for minimizing resource use and preventing pollution are being created through the emergence of new styles of infrastructure provision and consumption. Connecting the reconfiguration of networks to the transformation of buildings and the reinterpretation of urban plans, the book explores the environmental implications of urban infrastructure in transition.

Simon Guy
Simon Marvin
Timothy Moss
Newcastle, Salford, Erkner, November 2000

ACKNOWLEDGEMENTS

This book is based on an EU research project entitled 'Sustainable Flow Management', which was funded under the Environment and Climate Research Programme (1994–1998): Human Dimension of Environmental Change (ENV4-CT96-0249). The authors would like to express their gratitude to the European Commission for its financial support. The authors would further like to acknowledge the support of the following organizations involved in the research:

Institute for Regional Development and Structural Planning (IRS), Erkner near Berlin, Germany
University of Newcastle, Centre for Urban Technology, United Kingdom
Technical University of Denmark, Department of Planning, Denmark
ELIUS – Catherine Vei Spiropoulou Ltd, Athens, Greece

Thanks are due also to Bernd Schulze for the illustrations and Ines Fürstenberg for the layout.

Sustainable flow management

LIST OF ACRONYMS AND ABBREVIATIONS

AKTESP	Agreement, Knowledge, Technology, Economic, Social, Political barriers
BLUE 21	Berlin Association for Environment and Development
BMS	building management system
BUND	Association for Environment and Nature Protection of Germany
BWB	Berliner Wasser Betriebe (water utility)
CEC	Commission of the European Communities
CEGB	Central Electricity Generating Board (UK)
CHP	combined heat and power
CLD	Copenhagen Lighting Department
DH	district heating
DoE	Department of Environment (UK)
DSM	demand side management
EEO	Energy Efficiency Office (UK)
EMS	environmental management system
ESI	electricity supply industry
EU	European Union
FoE	Friends of the Earth
ICLEI	International Council for Local Environment Initiatives
JMWC	joint municipal waste company (DK)
KAB	non-profit housing association of Copenhagen
LA21	Local Agenda 21
LTS	large technological system
MIPS	material intensity per service unit
NEA	Neighbourhood Energy Action (UK)
NESA	regional electricity company in the Copenhagen area
NGO	non-governmental organization
PV unit	photo-voltaic unit
REC	regional electricity company
SCOT	social construction of technology
SenSUT	Senate Department for Urban Development, Environmental Protection and Technology, Berlin
TERC	Torup Ecological Rural Community (DK)
TMR	total material requirement
URCC	Urban Renewal Company of Copenhagen
VAT	value added tax
VEGA	waste company in Copenhagen
WDA	Welsh Development Agency

PART 1

INTERPRETING INFRASTRUCTURE

Credit: Timothy Moss

1   FLOW MANAGEMENT IN URBAN REGIONS: INTRODUCING A CONCEPT

Timothy Moss

INTRODUCTION: INFRASTRUCTURE SYSTEMS AND URBAN FLOWS

Water crisis in Yorkshire: During the summer of 1995 a severe shortage of rainfall in Yorkshire forced Yorkshire Water to tanker water into the region at a cost of £50 million. Freak weather conditions had destabilized the regional water network, causing Yorkshire Water temporarily to lose control of its management. The crisis had a lasting impact, however, in unsettling the complex social, environmental and technical relations that had shaped the way water was provided in the past. Customers rejected pleas by the recently privatized company to reduce water consumption, revealing an altered relationship between supplier and user after privatization. An independent inquiry subsequently set a new standard for measuring network stability, obliging Yorkshire Water to re-order its network to withstand worst-scenario drought conditions.

Planning a power plant in Copenhagen: In July 1996 the Danish Ministry of Environment and Energy rejected a proposal from the power companies serving the Copenhagen region to build a state-of-the-art combined heat and power plant ('Avedøre 2') to replace outdated electricity-generating capacity. The decision marked a milestone in Danish energy policy. For the first time, the environmental regulator had departed from the conventional supply-building logic, recommending instead a combination of demand management and decentralized generation where necessary. Against the arguments of the power companies SKpower and Elkraft that the new plant would reduce emissions substantially, generate electricity more efficiently and secure long-term supply, the ministry justified its rejection on the grounds that the plant exceeded predicted capacity requirements, countered national energy-saving targets and was less cost effective than alternative solutions.[1]

Competing waste-management strategies in Berlin: The fall of the Berlin Wall heralded a period of unprecedented uncertainty for waste-management planning in the Berlin region. A combination of major reform to national waste policy in Germany, sharp shifts in levels of urban waste, competing technologies of waste treatment and political differences has caused plans for managing the region's waste to be revised frequently over the past few years. Before unification West Berlin deposited its urban waste at low cost on East German territory. In response to calls from the new government of Brandenburg for Berlin to reduce the waste it deposited in Brandenburg by 50 per cent, three new incineration plants were planned by the city. However, as waste levels declined, more waste was recycled and resistance grew to the proposed plants, the plan was shelved by the new political leadership of Berlin's Environment Department and a mediation procedure was established involving all interested parties – a unique step in waste-management planning in Germany.

All three examples illustrate emerging problems that are challenging the way technical infrastructure systems in Europe are managed. In the case of Yorkshire it is a crisis of supply set against the backdrop of privatized utilities; in Copenhagen it is the upgrading of physical infrastructure under stronger pressure for environmental protection; and in Berlin it is the re-structuring of technical networks to take account of shifts in the regulatory framework, consumption patterns and technological solutions. The responses to each of these problems mark a departure from previous, established strategies for managing infrastructure systems. Yorkshire Water has had to win back customer confidence and re-order its physical networks to meet new drought specifications. Copenhagen's power utilities are having to practise demand side management instead of network expansion. Waste planners in the Berlin region are seeking flexible technical solutions (including waste reduction) to cope with planning uncertainties.

This book is about the transformation of infrastructure management in response to emerging new pressures and how this transformation is affecting the way technical networks shape material and energy flows in urban regions. Utility services for water, energy and waste influence the flow of a substantial proportion of the material and energy used in cities. They draw on external water and energy resources, distribute these in the required quality and form to consumers and dispose of waste products in and beyond the urban region. Power stations, water works and sewage treatment plants are key transformation and distribution points of anthropogenic material and energy flows, acting as nodes in a complex network. Cables and pipes are the lines which link these nodes, transporting large quantities of natural resources to and from the consumer. Infrastructure systems themselves require considerable energy and material resources to operate. Given their strategic importance in shaping the quantity and quality of urban environmental flows, technical networks offer enormous potential for minimizing the resource use and environmental impact of cities (BUND and Misereor, 1996, p225). Any efforts to make urban regions more sustainable will therefore need to exploit this potential better, understanding and using technical networks as instruments of sustainable urban and regional development.

In the past, strategies to improve the environmental performance of technical infrastructure systems have focused on technological efficiency and innovation, encouraged by state regulation and market incentives. The challenge to limit the environmental impact of utility services has been treated by urban planners and network managers primarily as a technical problem, to be solved via the application of the appropriate technology. However, recent difficulties in meeting the demand for natural resources, in financing network modernization and in planning infrastructure plant suggest that the root problem has as much to do with the way utility services are managed. It is becoming clear that existing structures, processes and logics of network management are often not conducive to resource conservation and pollution prevention. What is more, many instruments applied in the past to minimize resource use are not proving so effective under emerging new institutional frameworks of infrastructure management.

This introductory chapter first outlines the current process of transition in urban infrastructure, identifying recent pressures for change and indicating the implications of these changes for resource use and environmental protection. The following sections draw on the concept of flow management as an approach to sustainable resource use widely favoured in research and policy circles in recent years, demonstrating the value of the concept for understanding environmental flows and raising questions not answered adequately in the flow-management literature which have guided the research work presented in the book. The chapter then introduces the three urban regions where the case studies in Parts 2, 3 and 4 were conducted and concludes with an overview of the book's structure.

EUROPEAN URBAN INFRASTRUCTURE IN TRANSITION

The dominant logic of network management

Until recently, infrastructure management in Europe has been dominated by a public service ethos to provide adequate and secure services available and affordable to all (see Figure 1.1). The overriding aim has been to build supply capacity and extend the physical networks in order to meet rising demand, maximize connection levels, avoid supply bottlenecks and satisfy higher performance standards. The predominant logic, or rationale, of 'expand and upgrade' has over the last century encouraged the development of large-scale, centralized infrastructure systems of extensive physical networks drawing on increasingly distant natural resources (Guy and Marvin, 1996; Guy et al, 1997).

Under this supply-driven logic there has been very little interest in shaping the intensity, time or place where demand is routed. Most utilities in Europe have in the past enjoyed a territorial monopoly over local services which has enabled them to plan long-term investments and distribute costs evenly among all consumers within their service area. Consequently, there has been little social or spatial differentiation in the treatment of consumers: prices for services in the past varied – if at all – only between commercial and household customers (Guy et al, 1996, 1997). Interaction between service providers and

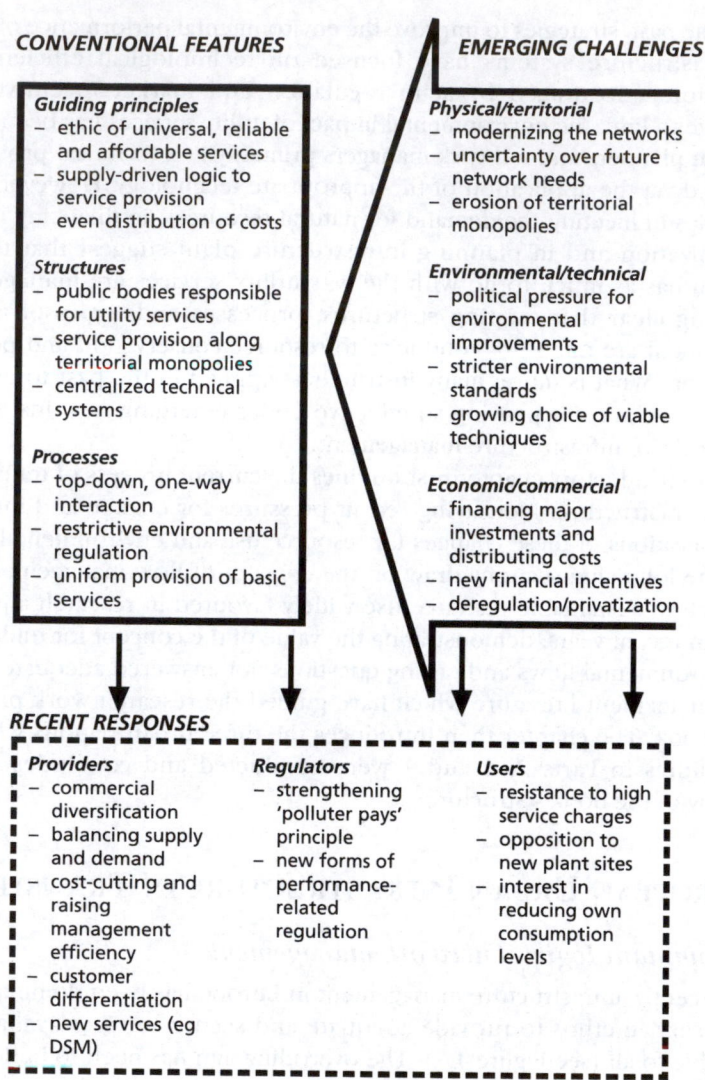

CONVENTIONAL FEATURES

Guiding principles
- ethic of universal, reliable and affordable services
- supply-driven logic to service provision
- even distribution of costs

Structures
- public bodies responsible for utility services
- service provision along territorial monopolies
- centralized technical systems

Processes
- top-down, one-way interaction
- restrictive environmental regulation
- uniform provision of basic services

EMERGING CHALLENGES

Physical/territorial
- modernizing the networks
- uncertainty over future network needs
- erosion of territorial monopolies

Environmental/technical
- political pressure for environmental improvements
- stricter environmental standards
- growing choice of viable techniques

Economic/commercial
- financing major investments and distributing costs
- new financial incentives
- deregulation/privatization

RECENT RESPONSES

Providers
- commercial diversification
- balancing supply and demand
- cost-cutting and raising management efficiency
- customer differentiation
- new services (eg DSM)

Regulators
- strengthening 'polluter pays' principle
- new forms of performance-related regulation

Users
- resistance to high service charges
- opposition to new plant sites
- interest in reducing own consumption levels

Source: IRS

Figure 1.1 *Urban Infrastructure in Transition*

service users has been predominantly one-way and top-down; usually, the only contact between provider and user has been in the form of the monthly or annual bill. Environmental improvements have followed regulatory pressures set by national or European Union (EU) bodies and, until recently, were directed more at minimizing emissions than reducing resource flows. Although regulatory and funding mechanisms have contributed substantially to raising environmental quality in recent years, their effectiveness has been limited by the fact that they have been interpreted largely in technical terms, they are often unresponsive to local specifics, they are cost-intensive and regularly fail to influence planning processes early enough to affect the outcome.

Within this general picture of conventional infrastructure management there are significant regional and sectoral variations. These would appear to depend primarily on the degree of local government responsibility for utility services, the regulatory framework, the market structure of each utility sector and the dominant technique or techniques used. Whereas, for instance, in the UK prior to privatization, infrastructure services were provided by distinct national and regional public bodies, in Germany and Denmark they remain a municipal responsibility operated by a large number of, often minor, actors.

New challenges for utility managers

The traditional logic of infrastructure management, however, is coming under pressure from a variety of emerging challenges. These new demands or 'signals' include primarily: the liberalization of utility service markets, the tightening of environmental standards, the high cost of network modernization, competition between a growing number of viable technologies, uncertainty over future consumption patterns and over-capacity in some networks. Infrastructure management in Europe is, as a result, undergoing major transformation on several distinct, but interrelated planes. The pace and nature of this transformation process vary considerably according to regional and sectoral specifics – the different degree of privatization of utility services in the UK, Germany or Denmark is one clear example; the high degree of social subsidization in Greece is another. The important point, though, is that the emerging challenges are affecting all utility managers, whether public or private, local or supra-national, creating tensions with traditional forms of infrastructure management.

If we read these signals in terms of their impact on urban environmental policy we might expect to detect new opportunities for resource conservation and new obstacles to past environmental strategies. For instance, the current modernization of water, sewage, electricity or waste infrastructure offers the chance not only to improve environmental performance but also to limit resource consumption through demand side management, particularly where demand threatens to exceed existing capacity. Conversely, stagnating or unpredictable demand – as detected for sections of the water and electricity networks in Germany and Denmark – question the conventional supply-oriented logic based on steadily rising consumption. Here, though, the immediate effect may be in the opposite direction, maximizing under-utilized existing infrastructure.

Recent responses by the actors

Combined, these new challenges are changing the context of infrastructure provision, forcing network managers to rethink how resources and networks are managed (Guy et al, 1996, 1997; Guy and Marvin, 1996). An important task of this book is to illustrate how different actor groups are responding to these signals in the way that they provide, regulate or use utility services and what openings these responses are creating for more efficient forms of resource use. On the basis of recent experiences a number of key research questions can be formulated relating to each of the three main actor groups.

Utility companies: commercialization and customer differentiation
Under the new competitive climate, utility companies are cutting operational costs and improving management efficiency. In the case of the larger companies they are also diversifying and widening their commercial interests into other utility sectors as well as into other countries. A new logic of differentiation in the treatment of customers would appear to be slowly developing as utilities seek to capture or retain lucrative customers, resulting in more reciprocal and dense relationships between producers and select consumers (Guy et al, 1997). The salient questions here are:

- What new opportunities for minimizing urban environmental flows are emerging from the growing shifts towards commercialization and customer differentiation?
- How do pressures to limit investment costs and reduce service prices encourage utilities to use and sell less water or energy?
- What options are being created for integrating alternative environmental technologies into existing infrastructure networks as a result of new regulatory, technological and institutional pressures?

Regulators: searching for new environmental instruments
In response to the above trends the bodies responsible for regulating the environmental and economic performance of utilities are seeking new constraints and incentives capable of stimulating resource conservation and pollution prevention under the shifting framework. These may take the form of taxes on resource use (for example, on water abstraction, fossil fuels or landfill sites), performance standards (for example, on the quality and price of services) or measures to strengthen the 'polluter-pays' principle (for example, promoting the use of modern monitoring techniques). The key research questions here are:

- What limitations to conventional instruments of environmental regulation and funding by the state are being revealed by recent changes in infrastructure management?
- What new ways of shaping urban environmental flows are open to national or local authorities under the emerging logics of commercialization, cost efficiency and socio-spatial differentiation of services?

Users: reacting to price signals and technological opportunities
The users, or consumers, are also developing an interest in the utility services that, in the past, they took for granted. Some are registering their opposition to planned sites for new plant or to the rising cost of service charges caused by network modernization and customer differentiation. Many are seeking ways of reducing their own consumption levels and recycling waste, either for environmental reasons or to offset an increase in unit service charges. Some are themselves becoming infrastructure providers, operating their own decentralized heat and power plants, storm water infiltration systems or composting units. These recent developments beg the questions:

- To what extent are consumers acquiring new roles and responsibilities for resource use in response to recent shifts in the way utility services are provided?
- What (combinations of) factors are encouraging users to minimize their resource use?
- What obstacles – institutional, financial or socio-economic – continue to limit consumers' motives to install or use environmental technologies?

Flow Management: A Concept for Sustainable Resource Use

In order to appreciate the environmental implications of recent changes in infrastructure management it is helpful to set the research questions of this book in the context of a growing literature on the management of material and energy flows. The concept of flow management emerging within the broad debate on sustainability has served as a useful point of departure for the research work underpinning the book, providing background knowledge on the environmental importance of urban flows and demonstrating state-of-the-art approaches to their management at national and local level. It is used here as a backdrop for understanding recent scientific and policy approaches to shaping environmental flows and, at the same time, as a foil for raising important issues as yet inadequately addressed by the flow management debate which will guide the reader through the book.

The origins of the flow management concept

Scientific and policy interest in anthropogenic flows is rooted in the development of a more holistic approach to environmental protection since the 1980s. Whereas, previously, environmental policy was directed primarily at minimizing harmful emissions, the debate on sustainable development has focused attention on the damage to the environment caused by the over-use of natural resources as well as pollutants (Meadows et al, 1992; Jänicke, 1993; Schmidt-Bleek, 1994). Not only does the consumption of non-renewable resources deplete the world's finite material and energy stocks upon which economic and social development depend, but the use of both renewable and non-renewable resources causes environmental degradation during transportation, storage, processing and disposal. In recognition of this, environmental policy and research has been directed towards determining the scale of resource use and devising strategies for minimizing material and energy consumption. Most recently, the focus of scientific interest has broadened to consider the ecological quality of environmental flows rather than merely their scale (Hofmeister, 1999).

The concept of flow management

The concept of flow management has been developed through research and applied in practice to meet these growing needs. In contrast to previous ways of managing material use, which were shaped by economic considerations and technical limitations, flow management looks at the life cycle of materials or products systematically, with the purpose of optimizing resource use in accordance with both environmental and economic objectives (Frings, 1995; Friege, 1998). Central to the concept is the notion of flows of materials and energy passing through an economic system or production process. Once identified, these flows can be reduced, for example by improving resource efficiency, reusing resources or substituting non-renewable resources. Ultimately, the purpose of flow management is to de-couple economic growth from resource use, permitting economic and social development which does not overexploit the world's natural resources. The concept of flow management is, indeed, framed by the wider debate on sustainability. Significantly, the objectives of flow management are founded on the four 'management rules' for sustainable resource use widely accepted in the literature on sustainable development (Pearce and Turner, 1990; Daly, 1990; Enquête-Kommission, 1994; Rat von Sachverständigen, 1994; Frings, 1995). These are as follows:

1   The rate of consumption of renewable resources should not exceed the rate of their regeneration.
2   Emissions should not exceed the carrying capacity of the environment.
3   The rate of consumption of non-renewable resources should not exceed the rate of substitution by renewables or higher productivity of non-renewables.
4   The timing of anthropogenic impacts on the environment must respect the time needed for the environment to recover.

Methods of flow management

On the basis of these 'rules', what methods does the concept of flow management apply to approach the problem of unsustainable forms of material and energy consumption in practice? The literature describes several distinct phases of flow management. These consist in the first instance of *measuring and modelling flows*, that is, analysing the inputs and outputs of ecologically relevant material and energy flows through a specified system, whether a national economy, a production process, a branch of the economy or a region (Schmidt, 1995, p6). For individual companies or branches of industrial production, material flow analyses commonly take the form of life-cycle assessments or inventory analyses (Enquête-Kommission, 1994; Schmidt, 1995; Umweltbundesamt, 1998). At a national level, studies of total material throughput of a national economy have developed and applied various methods of flow accounting and modelling, such as total material requirement (TMR), demonstrating the sum of domestic and imported primary natural resources (Bringezu, 1998b, p5; cf Schmidt-Bleek, 1994; van der Voet et al, 1995, pp91–92; Bringezu, 1998a). Most well-known is the concept of expressing the consumption of material resources in terms of the ecological space needed to accommodate (national) resource use, devised first for the Netherlands and since applied to other countries, including Denmark (Friends of the Earth Netherlands, 1993; BUND and Misereor, 1996).

On the basis of flow analyses, *targets* are set for *reducing flows* and their environmental impact. These can be based on desired environmental quality, ecological 'footprints' or scenarios for changing patterns of resource use. One widely discussed example is the call to increase resource productivity by the factor four (von Weizsäcker et al, 1998). Here, the state is ascribed a role in setting the regulatory framework for more resource-efficient forms of production, while commercial actors are encouraged to focus on key substances or products (de Man, 1995, pp12–14). In Denmark, for instance, the Ministry for Environment and Energy is applying the concept of ecological 'footprints' as a policy principle for defining the limits of consumption and has launched several projects to help apply the concept in practice (Groth et al, 1998).

The third phase is then to devise *suitable strategies and instruments* to achieve the objectives. These could involve measures to improve vertical or horizontal cooperation between production plants (Frings, 1995; de Man, 1995) or – at the government level – financial incentives to minimize resource use. Currently, considerable efforts are going into developing indicator systems to identify important material and energy flows, such as the material intensity per service unit system (MIPS) developed by the Wuppertal Institute and eco-accounting indicators used in EU certification of eco-management (Bringezu, 1998a; Grießhammer, 1999).

A preliminary appraisal of the flow management concept

Conceptual studies and practical applications of flow management have, within the past decade, made a substantial contribution to raising awareness and deepening understanding of material and energy flows. Specifically, the value of flow management today lies in:

- quantifying changing patterns of resource use in terms of material and energy flows;
- analysing flows for select systems (for example a product, a chemical component or a production process);
- relating resource use to resource availability and environmental impacts (for example in a region);
- pinpointing critical areas for flow management (for example inefficiencies in a product's life cycle); and
- developing techniques, methodologies and economic incentives to minimize resource use.

These important advances in knowledge, however, give an incomplete picture of the processes and structures involved in managing material and energy flows. The concept of flow management appears to offer little help, for instance, in explaining why the problem situations in Yorkshire, Copenhagen and Berlin outlined above arose and why the various actors responded in the way they did. Yet both problems and responses of this kind are having a major impact on patterns of resource use. How far, then, does the debate on flow management provide us with explanations for the management of material and energy resources within technical infrastructure systems? What important issues does the concept of flow management answer or address inadequately? In the following section we develop research questions for this book out of a reflection of the gaps in the flow management literature for explaining new openings for resource efficiency in the field of urban infrastructure, building on recent research and policy demands for greater recognition of the socio-spatial dimensions to resource use.

TAKING FLOW MANAGEMENT FORWARD: RESEARCH QUESTIONS ON URBAN INFRASTRUCTURE IN TRANSITION

How do space and locality frame infrastructure management?

The literature on flow management has, in the past, focused primarily on national economies and production processes rather than on local or regional contexts. In the case of national flow accounting, regional differences are generally not considered and studies of industrial metabolism tend to ignore sub-national spatial dimensions. There is, however, growing recognition of the need for more local or regional approaches to flow management, given the complexity of resource flows, the strong interdependence of resource use with regional development and the need to involve local decision makers. Initial steps have been made to research the metabolism, or material through-flow, of individual regions and sub-regions (Baccini, 1996, 1997; Baccini and Bader, 1996; Hanaki et al, 1997). Owing to the difficulties in specifying system boundaries and collecting data, many studies of regional flow management have concentrated on setting out methodologies for analysing and modelling regional flows (Hofmeister and Hübler, 1990; van der Voet et al, 1995; Tjallingii, 1995; Hofmeister, 1997). Nevertheless, rough estimates have been made of the regional dimensions of energy, water and waste flows, illustrating the degree of spatial dependency of each resource flow (Adam, 1997). In practice, several cases illustrate how the flow management concept can be applied effectively to minimize a region's resource flows (see Figure 1.2).

What is still underrepresented in the literature on flow management, though, is an understanding of how far patterns and strategies of resource use are locally or regionally specific and, if so, why this is the case. What kinds of local factors – environmental, economic, social, technical or institutional – frame the problems of regional infrastructure management, the way these problems are perceived by the actors and the options for solving them? This book seeks to provide a better understanding of these local forces.

How is infrastructure management socially shaped?

In the past, literature on flow management has paid little attention to the social relations that influence the way material and energy are used. The emphasis has been on establishing models and instruments for action rather than investigating human factors shaping resource use. It is rarely asked, for

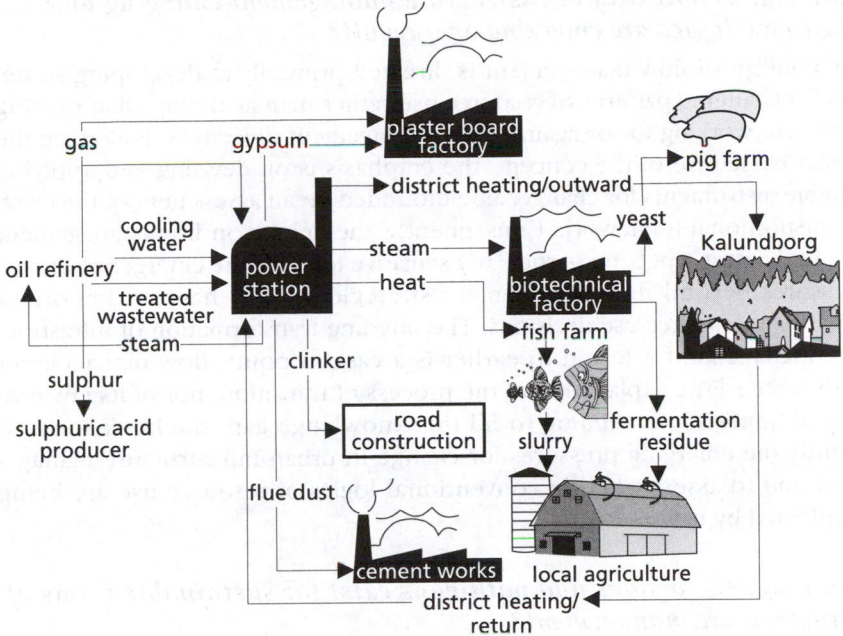

Source: Bringezu, 1998a, p174

Figure 1.2 *Kalundborg (Denmark): a Well-known Example of Regional Flow Management*

instance, who the actors behind the flows are, what motives they pursue, what influence they possess and how they interact with one another. Similarly, little attention is given to the institutional framework within which these actors operate; that is to say, the organizational structures, norms, regulations and market forces that frame actors' use of natural resources.

The absence of the actors in flow management studies has been criticized by de Man and others (de Man, 1995; de Man and Claus, 1998). He points to the crucial importance of actor engagement and cooperation in achieving the objectives of sustainable flow management and argues for analyses of actor networks, motives and influence as a preliminary step of flow management procedures. However, de Man's interest is limited primarily to actors in production processes determining micro-economic strategy and, to a lesser extent, the state setting the macro-economic policy agenda. In the case of infrastructure management, where a growing number of actor groups are becoming involved and acquiring new responsibilities, there would appear to be a real need to broaden the scope of actor analyses. This book will map the social organization of infrastructure management in selected urban regions, identifying the principal actor groups, their spheres of influence and forms of interaction with one another.

How is the context of infrastructure management changing and what new logics are emerging as a result?

The concept of flow management is directed primarily at developing strategies for changing patterns of resource use rather than analysing what existing forces are working for or against flow management objectives. Following the normative nature of the concept, the emphasis is on devising and applying suitable instruments for change, albeit founded on an assessment of the existing institutional framework. Consequently, the debate on flow management has, in the past, not been particularly sensitive towards the emergence of new pressures beyond flow management strategies, which have an important bearing on resource-use decisions. The ongoing transformation of infrastructure management referred to earlier is a case in point; flow management studies offer little explanation of the process of transition, nor of its environmental implications. Aiming to fill this knowledge gap, the book seeks to identify the emerging pressures for change in urban infrastructure management and to assess whether conventional logics of resource use are being supplanted by new ones.

What models, visions and pathways exist for sustainable forms of infrastructure management?

The flow management literature does not claim to develop a blueprint for managing material and energy flows applicable to any context. It is emphasized that each management step needs to be designed to suit its specific purpose (de Man, 1995, p8). Nevertheless, there is a generally accepted procedure for flow management. The phases of flow management entail – for individual companies, for instance – launching an initiative, preparing and conducting flow analyses, organizing cooperation with other companies relevant to material flow needs, introducing proposals and controlling their implementation (de Man, 1995; de Man and Claus, 1998). The tasks of state authorities are specified as improving information on flows, setting objectives and introducing the necessary regulatory and economic instruments to achieve these goals (Frings, 1995; de Man, 1995; de Man and Claus, 1998). The planning and management of flows is thus widely conceived as a linear process of clearly defined steps: a 'series of decisions' in de Man's words (1995, p17). While this rather deterministic approach certainly provides useful guidance in designing strategies for action, it encounters difficulties in situations where actors do not follow the inner logic of arguments to minimize resource use. In situations of growing planning uncertainty, as in the case of urban infrastructure today, it is proving increasingly difficult to plan along a linear model of decision-making and to follow rational choice logic. For this reason the book is interested in establishing what different kinds of resource-saving pathways and strategies are developing in response to the new challenges, rather than searching for a particular preferred model for sustainable flow management.

The Urban Regions Selected for Case Study

This book is founded on in-depth empirical studies of utility services for water, wastewater, electricity and solid waste in selected urban regions of northern Europe. There are several reasons for focusing on urban regions as the spatial frame of investigation. Firstly, the metabolism of cities is high; that is, they are characterized by a high level of material and energy throughputs. Material flows and processes – from accumulation, transformation and distribution to use and recycling – are highly concentrated in cities (Baccini, 1996, 1997). Secondly, extending the spatial focus to urban regions enables the book to transcend administrative boundaries and explore the interrelationship between cities and their surrounding hinterland, in terms of the interdependency of resource flows and of actors inside and outside the city (Haughton, 1997). The meso level of urban regions is, thirdly, more suitable for studying the management of infrastructure systems than either the macro level of national infrastructure policy or the micro level of individual consumers. The city and its hinterland of water and energy resources and waste-disposal opportunities provide the spatial frame for utility managers if not also the territorial scope for infrastructure planning (d'Alleux, 1993). The pipes, sewers and power cables of urban technical networks have long since extended into surrounding areas. From this derives a fourth argument for selecting urban regions: the ability to explore the links – existing and potential – between infrastructure management and spatial or environmental planning at a local and regional level. For these reasons the term 'urban region' is used loosely in this book to refer to the spatial sphere of influence of an urban infrastructure network.

Owing to the broad scope of the research, studying social, technical, environmental, economic and institutional factors affecting four different utility services (water, wastewater, electricity and solid waste), the number of urban regions selected for case study was limited to three: Berlin, Newcastle upon Tyne and Copenhagen (see Figure 1.3). Each of these regions has been chosen because it exhibits not only distinctive national characteristics of infrastructure management – for Germany, the UK or Denmark – but also specific regional features of wider interest to researchers and practitioners of utility services.

The *Berlin region* demonstrates the dense regulatory framework (particularly for environmental protection) and decentralized institutional structures of infrastructure planning and management characteristic of Germany, while also standing as an illuminating example of infrastructure systems in transition. What makes the Berlin region particularly interesting is the simultaneous emergence of multiple new pressures for change to infrastructure management. Following the reunification of Germany and of the two halves of the city in 1990, utilities from East and West Berlin have been amalgamated, technical networks have been reconnected and considerable investments have been made in upgrading and refurbishing the physical infrastructure. This has happened against the backdrop of sharp shifts in patterns of resource use, strong urban development pressures, major changes to the federal regulation of energy and waste management, recent privatization of the city's electricity

Source: IRS

Figure 1.3 *Location of Case-study Urban Regions*

and water utilities and demands to cooperate more closely with the surrounding state of Brandenburg. The overriding question for the Berlin region is how the key actors are responding to these multiple challenges and to the planning uncertainties they entail.

The *Newcastle region* has been selected as a good example of the regional impact of the recent privatization and liberalization of utility services in the UK. It illustrates the sudden transition from service provision by mainly national and regional public bodies operating territorial monopolies to an increasingly competitive marketplace of private utilities bound to serve their shareholders as well as their customers. Focusing on an urban region reveals how these new utilities attempt to secure their position in a regional market by means of mergers, new services and extending their commercial activities. In terms of resource use, the Newcastle region is of interest because of strong environmental demands locally to reduce harmful emissions by improving the physical infrastructure, and owing to the regional dimensions of water transfer to the neighbouring county of Yorkshire.

The *Copenhagen region* demonstrates some common recent developments of infrastructure management in Denmark in the form of a growing awareness of environmental problems and stricter environmental regulation, which together are putting pressure on utilities to upgrade their technical networks. The resulting financial burden, along with the partial liberalization of certain sectors, is threatening the existence of smaller municipal utilities. The chief interest of Copenhagen to a wider audience, however, lies in the emerging problem of overcapacity. As a result of past heavy investment in the physical infrastructure and stagnating or even declining levels of resource use, utilities are having to revise their long-term, supply-building strategies. Such a shift is hampered, however, by the centralized nature of the city's infrastructure systems, the interdependency between sectors (for example waste-to-energy technologies) and difficulties in integrating small-scale technologies into large-scale systems.

STRUCTURE OF THE BOOK

Exploring the complex interplay of institutional structures, emerging new signals and actor interests in infrastructure management demands a novel methodology. From a review of the science, technology and society literature, the following chapter develops a rationale for a 'socio-technical' approach to infrastructure management which guides the research throughout the book. It elaborates on this new 'way of seeing' infrastructure networks, in particular the need to understand their social and technical components not as separate compartments of consumption and production, but as forces that interact to shape infrastructure management. The chapter concludes with a description of the innovative methodology and vocabulary used in the book to analyse and describe these forces.

The following three parts provide the empirical substance to the book, presenting the results of case studies on major problems of infrastructure management in urban regions. Each case study is used to pursue an issue of key interest to research on infrastructure networks: for example, the integration of decentralized technologies in centralized systems, crisis management, or the social organization of utility services. The case studies are grouped according to different spatial levels of flow management critical to changing patterns of resource use: the physical networks shaping regional resource flows; buildings as nodal points between networks and in-house infrastructure; and plans for future forms of flow management at the city or urban borough level. In contrast to most previous studies of infrastructure systems, the book adopts a cross-sectoral approach to the analysis – covering energy, water and waste management – and draws transnational comparisons of the different contexts and changes to infrastructure management in the UK, Germany and Denmark. To assist comparison and analysis of the findings, the three case studies in each of the parts are framed by an introduction and a conclusion.

Part 2 examines competing solutions to a regional water resource problem as an illustration of the logics and signals currently shaping the way water and sewage networks are managed. Three emerging challenges to network management are explored with case studies: adjusting existing systems to accommodate shifting contextual factors (water recycling in the Berlin region); incorporating decentralized technologies into centralized networks (storm water infiltration in Copenhagen); and responding to a resource crisis (the Yorkshire drought). Each case study describes how the relevant actor groups view a local water resource problem, how their assessment of the problem shapes the solutions they propose and how each solution addresses intra- or inter-regional equity concerns, such as long-distance supply networks or downstream pollution. The spatial focus of this part of the book is thus on urban regions; the actor focus lies with the network planners and operators, rather than the users.

In contrast, Part 3 explores the micro-level of buildings to discover what factors shape the application – or non-application – of environmental technologies and practices. The conventional approach in analysing 'green' buildings is to measure their environmental performance, that is, how far the physical installations and the behaviour of the users reduce resource use and minimize harmful emissions. This part of the book°Δ looks, rather, at the process by which environmental technologies and practices are introduced in the first place, investigating what social contexts assist or hinder the application of individual measures. The emphasis is, therefore, on the actors responsible for planning, designing, investing in, installing and using infrastructure facilities for water, sewage, energy and waste in buildings and their motives for applying – or resisting – environmental technologies. The case study from Newcastle explains different ways of seeing green buildings, reflecting the different assumptions of individual actors and the different contexts within which they operate. The second case study – from Berlin – examines the social organization of green building, demonstrating the role and interests of different actor groups in introducing and using environmental technologies in the housing sector. The Copenhagen case study emphasizes the importance of location and existing physical infrastructure in shaping the design, planning and implementation of green elements in housing.

Part 4 investigates how far the new agendas of urban infrastructure management interconnect with local environmental planning. The development of urban infrastructure has, in the past, been shaped substantially by both spatial and sectoral planning. Since the 1970s, local energy and waste concepts have been developed to improve the environmental performance of localities and the 1992 Rio Conference on Environment and Development has given fresh impetus in the form of Local Agenda 21 (LA21) initiatives. The first chapter identifies the degree of connection between local environmental planning and the new emerging strategies of infrastructure management with a case study of electricity management in post-liberalization UK. The second case study – of Copenhagen – explores interconnection from another angle, taking LA21 as an example of a new form of local planning to examine linkage between debates on resource use in LA21 and in infrastructure management. The third case study identifies widely diverse plans and visions for sustainable flow management within the confines of a single city with a case study of LA21 initiatives in Berlin.

The final part draws general conclusions from the research. These comprise, in the first instance, the principal findings on the management of technical networks; that is, how infrastructure management in Europe is undergoing transition, how new logics of infrastructure management are emerging as a result and how these influences are 'reconfiguring' infrastructure networks. A subsequent section highlights the scientific interest and novelty of these findings, demonstrating how the book's socio-technical approach to understanding infrastructure management takes forward debates in the literature on sustainable urban development, flow management, the liberalization of utility services and the development of large infrastructure systems. The contributions to scientific knowledge refer in particular to the social organization of technical networks, the need to rethink the spatial scales and understand the local context of infrastructure management, the existence of competing pathways along which infrastructure management can develop and the need for a new approach to planning infrastructure systems. A final section formulates the findings in terms of future challenges for research and policy making.

NOTES

1   Two years after the initial rejection, however, an 'Avedøre 2' plant is under construction. Elkraft submitted a fresh proposal which the Minister for Environment and Energy felt obliged to accept. The design of the new plant is, though, quite different from the initial proposal, offering substantial environmental advantages through the replacement of a number of old plants.

REFERENCES

Adam, B (1997) 'Wege zu einer nachhaltigen Regionalentwicklung. Raumplanerische Handlungsspielräume durch regionale Kommunikations- und Kooperationsprozesse', *Raumforschung und Raumordnung*, vol 55, no 2, pp137–141

d'Alleux, J (1993) 'Räumliche Entwicklung unter dem Diktat von Umweltqualitätszielen', *Ökologisch nachhaltige Entwicklung von Verdichtungsräumen*. ILS-Schriften, no 76, pp7–25

Baccini, P (1996) 'Understanding Regional Metabolism for a Sustainable Development of Urban Systems', *Environmental Science and Pollution Research*, vol 3, no 2, pp108–111

Baccini, P (1997) 'A City's Metabolism', *Journal of Urban Technology*, vol 4, no 2, pp27–39

Baccini, P and Bader, H P (1996) *Regionaler Stoffhaushalt. Erfassung, Bewertung und Steuerung*, Spektrum, Heidelberg

Bringezu, S (1998a) 'Ausgangssituation, Ziele und Planungselemente für ein integriertes Ressourcenmanagement', in H J Kujath, T Moss and T Weith (eds) *Räumliche Umweltvorsorge. Wege zu einer Ökologisierung der Stadt- und Regionalentwicklung*, edition sigma, Berlin, pp157–177

Bringezu, S (1998b) 'Comparison of the Material Basis of Industrial Economies', in S Bringezu, M Fischer-Kowalski, R Kleijn and V Palm (eds) *Analysis for Action: Support for Policy Towards Sustainability by Material Flow Accounting*, Wuppertal Institute for Climate, Environment and Energy, Wuppertal, pp57–66

BUND and Misereor (1996) *Zukunftsfähiges Deutschland. Ein Beitrag zu einer global nachhaltigen Entwicklung, Studie des Wuppertal Instituts für Klima, Umwelt, Energie*, Birkhäuser, Basel/Boston/Berlin

Daly, H (1990) 'Towards some operational principles of sustainable development', *Ecological Economics*, vol 2, pp1–6

Enquête-Kommission 'Schutz des Menschen und der Umwelt' des Deutschen Bundestages (1994) *Die Industriegesellschaft gestalten – Perspektiven für einen nachhaltigen Umgang mit Stoff- und Materialströmen*, Bonn

Friege, H (1998) 'Stoffstrommanagement: Die Idee und ihre Entwicklung', in H Friege, C Engelhardt and K O Henseling (eds) *Das Management von Stoffströmen. Geteilte Verantwortung – Nutzen für alle*, Springer, Berlin/Heidelberg, pp1–9

Friends of the Earth Netherlands (Milieudefensie) (eds) (1993) *Action Plan Sustainable Netherlands*, Amsterdam

Frings, E (1995) 'Ergebnisse und Empfehlungen der Enquête-Kommission "Schutz des Menschen und der Umwelt" zum Stoffstrommanagement', in M Schmidt and B Schorb (eds) *Stoffstromanalysen in Ökobilanzen und Öko-Audits*, Springer, Berlin/Heidelberg, pp15–30

Grießhammer, R (1999) 'Am Anfang war das DDT', *Politische Ökologie*, vol 62, pp24–27

Groth, N B, Hedegaard, M B, Holmberg, T, Höll, A and Skov-Petersen, H (1998) *Land-use in Denmark 1995–2025*, Danish Forest and Landscape Research Institute, Hørsholm

Guy, S, Graham, S and Marvin, S (1996) 'Privatised Utilities and Regional Governance: The New Regional Managers?', *Regional Studies*, vol 30, no 8, pp745–751

Guy, S, Graham, S and Marvin, S (1997) 'Splintering Networks: Cities and Technical Networks in 1990's Britain', *Urban Studies*, vol 34, no 2, pp191–216

Guy, S and Marvin, S (1996) 'Transforming Urban Infrastructure Provision: The Emerging Logic of Demand Side Management', *Policy Studies*, vol 17, no 2, pp137–147

Hanaki, K, Matsuo, T and Ito, T (1997) 'Lowering the Environmental Impact of Urban Infrastructures', *Journal of Urban Technology*, vol 4, no 2, pp41–52

Haughton, G (1997) 'Developing sustainable urban development models', *Cities*, vol 14, no 4, pp189–195

Hofmeister, S (1997) 'Stoffstromanalyse und Stoffstrommanagement – Ein Beitrag zur Organisation einer nachhaltigen Raumentwicklung', in K-H Hübler and U Weiland (eds) *Bausteine für eine nachhaltige Raumentwicklung in Brandenburg und Berlin*, Verlag für Wissenschaft und Forschung, Berlin, pp43–58

Hofmeister, S (1999) 'Über Effizienz und Suffizienz hinaus', *Politische Ökologie*, vol 62, pp34–38

Hofmeister, S and Hübler, K H (1990) *Stoff- und Energiebilanzen als Instrument der räumlichen Planung*, Akademie für Raumforschung und Landesplanung, Beiträge 118, Hannover

Jänicke, M (1993) *Ökologisch tragfähige Entwicklung: Kriterien und Steuerungsansätze ökologischer Ressourcenpolitik*, FFU-Report 93–7, Berlin

de Man, R (1995) 'Erfassung von Stoffstromen aus naturwissenschaftlicher und wirtschaftswissenschaftlicher Sicht. Akteure, Entscheidungen und Informationen im Stoffstrommanagement', in Enquête-Kommission 'Schutz des Menschen und der Umwelt' des Deutschen Bundestages (ed) *Umweltverträgliches Stoffstrommanagement. Bd.1. Konzepte*, Bonn, pp1–65

de Man, R and Claus, F (1998) 'Kooperationen, Organisationsformen und Akteure', in H Friege, C Engelhardt and K O Henseling (eds) *Das Management von Stoffströmen. Geteilte Verantwortung – Nutzen für alle*, Springer, Berlin/Heidelberg, pp72–81

Meadows, D, Meadows, D and Randers, S (1992) *Die neuen Grenzen des Wachstums*, dva, Stuttgart

Pearce, D W and Turner, R K (1990) *Economics of Natural Resources and the Environment*, Harvester Wheatsheaf, Hemel Hempstead

Rat von Sachverständigen für Umweltfragen (1994) *Für eine dauerhaft-umweltgerechte Entwicklung, Umweltgutachten 1994*, Metzler-Poeschel, Stuttgart

Schmidt, M (1995) 'Stoffstromanalysen und Ökobilanzen im Dienste des Umweltschutzes', in M Schmidt and B Schorb (eds) *Stoffstromanalysen in Ökobilanzen und Öko-Audits*, Springer, Berlin/Heidelberg, pp3–13

Schmidt-Bleek, F (1994) *Wieviel Umwelt braucht der Mensch? MIPS – das Maß für ökologisches Wirtschaften*, Birkhäuser, Berlin/Basel

Tjallingii, S P (1995) *Ecopolis. Strategies for Ecologically Sound Urban Development*, Backhuys, Leiden

Umweltbundesamt (1998) *Nachhaltiges Deutschland. Wege zu einer dauerhaft umweltgerechten Entwicklung*, Erich Schmidt Verlag, Berlin

van der Voet, E, Kleijn, R, van Oers, L, Heijungs, R, Huele, R and Mulder, P (1995) 'Substance Flows Through the Economy and Environment of a Region', *Environmental Science and Pollution Research*, vol 2, no 2, pp90–96

von Weizsäcker, E, Lovins, A B and Lovins, L H (1998) *Factor Four. Doubling Wealth, Halving Resource Use*, Earthscan, London

2 URBAN ENVIRONMENTAL FLOWS: TOWARDS A NEW WAY OF SEEING

Simon Guy and Simon Marvin

INTRODUCTION

The challenge of infrastructure, or flow, management is now receiving wide attention from academics and policy makers alike. There is a wide consensus that a major shift is required, away from the conventional approach of merely delivering more supply capacity, to a new demand-oriented paradigm of more efficiently managing and conserving essential resources such as water, waste and energy (Guy and Marvin, 1996). The ensuing, often frantic, debate about the shape and form of policy strategies necessary to bring about this ecological turn and ameliorate the environmental crisis is underpinned by a shared, almost orthodox vision of what shapes material flows through cities.

On the one hand we have an understanding of the physical construction of urban form as a process of ceaseless *technological innovation in the production sphere*. Here the pathway to a sustainable future is through the development and implementation of new technologies designed to reduce resource use, abate pollution and generally minimize the impact of urban economic development on the environment. To this end policy makers have addressed themselves to likely scenarios of demand and associated emissions, the development of proven resource-saving technologies and the implementation of urban planning and policy strategies designed to ameliorate the intensity of resource use by strategies of physical intervention. The planning of infrastructure networks tends to be conceived as the rational management of resource flows through cities, regions and nation states with little regard to the dynamic, contextually contingent strategies of infrastructure suppliers and users. Alternatively, issues around the *social consumption of resources* tend to be treated separately. Here the focus is on the scope for community mobilization and the non-technical 'barriers' to sustainable development that privileges behavioural change as the primary source of environmental innovation. The emphasis is on the power of information, regulation and 'best practice' guidance to mobilize 'local' community action around environmental issues, thereby promoting more 'rational' or 'sustainable' consumption patterns.

We are left with a dual vision of the need for a transformation in the management of resources at the production level and a reconfiguration of our consumption of resources. At each level the shift required to create more sustainable cities is tied to a very particular vision of urban environmental change in which the technical and the social are kept firmly apart. This chapter argues that we urgently require a transformation in the orthodox view of urban environmental flows. Rather than viewing the realms of production and consumption as somehow autonomous we must become sensitive to their interconnections. We need to develop an alternative analytical framework which recognizes infrastructure systems as socio-technical networks and offers a new understanding of the interrelationships between physical production processes shaping the construction of cities and the changing social dynamics of urban consumption. We examine how dramatic shifts in the linkages between the physical (delivery of networked services) and the socio-cultural (patterns of consumption) dimensions of cities are powerfully reconfiguring contexts of socio-environmental action. Our analytical approach facilitates the identification of shifts in patterns of resource provision and contributes to the development of alternative policy strategies aimed at promoting patterns of sustainable resource use.

CONVENTIONAL APPROACHES TO MATERIAL FLOWS

An orthodoxy has been established in how urban environmental researchers and policy makers understand the flow of material resources through cities, which revolves around two related views of urban environmental processes. The first is a production-focused image that concentrates on physical places as its object of analysis and intervention, while the second is a consumption-focused image that concentrates on the social shaping of environmental choice. The aim here is to delineate the defining features of each view of resource flows and what they mean for the shift towards a more sustainable approach to infrastructure management.

A physicalist construction of flows

The conventional way of seeing the problem of urban sustainability has been as a set of technical problems amenable to technological solutions. In this image the city is viewed as a physical zone made up of material components with specific performance characteristics which are subject to improvement or replacement. In terms of energy, the city has been seen as a physical 'container' through which electricity flows can be measured and policies developed to ameliorate any resulting environmental impact (Owens, 1986). The physical bent of this view tends also to assume that the linkages between energy use, their environmental impacts and policy options can be accurately mapped through modelling and monitoring and that the most powerful tools for the implementation of local strategies are physical land use planning policies and initiatives (Nijkamp and Perrels, 1994). In this way environmental indicators allow the city to be 'read' by policy strategists and their technical advisers,

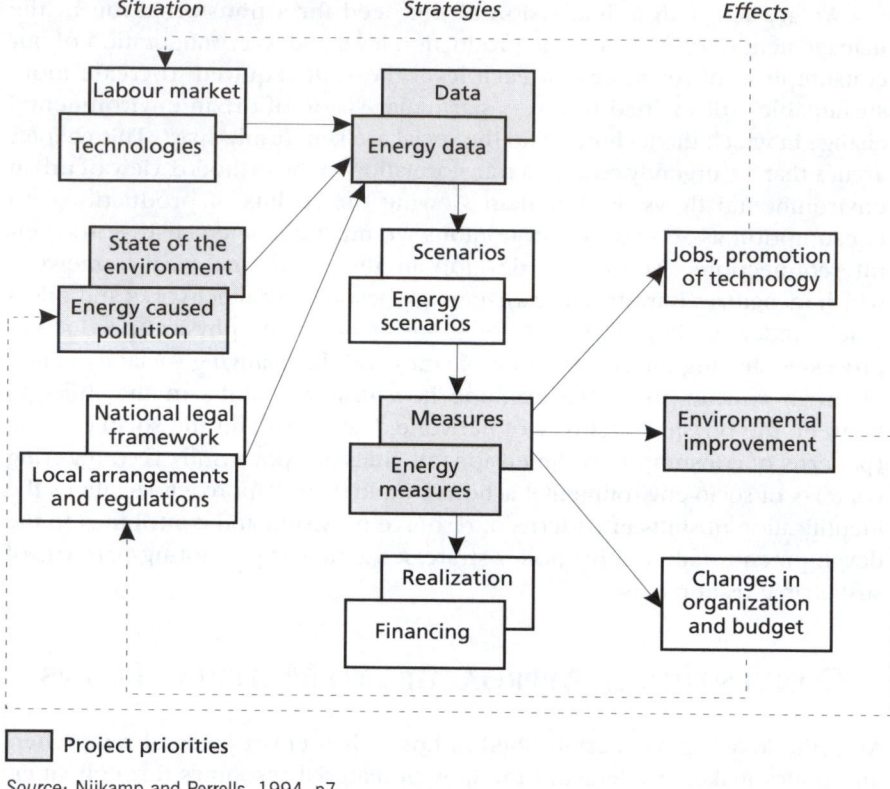

Project priorities

Source: Nijkamp and Perrells, 1994, p7

Figure 2.1 *Example of a 'Productivist' Urban Environmental Model*

enabling strategies to be prepared with the implicit assumption that particular effects will necessarily follow. Figure 2.1 is a good example of such a productivist urban environmental model.

Here the city is configured in terms of static categories such as 'the labour market' or 'local arrangements and regulations' in order to provide 'energy data' to feed into the urban energy model. From this model 'energy scenarios' are imagined, 'measures' developed, which (according to the model) will result in 'jobs, promotion of technology' and 'environmental improvements'. Although advocates of the modelling approach are aware of the difficulties in capturing the complexity of urban processes, their main objective is to find a method, strategy or analytical approach which will simplify urban dynamics into a physical measure. In order to fold the complexities of the 'social world' into a physical dimension, the 'behaviour of cities has to be seen as a rational decision-making process' (Nijkamp and Perrels, 1994, p9). Any social phenomenon which does not obey the laws of technical rationality is treated as 'observed noise signals representing under- and over-utilisation of existing amenities in the urban system, thus causing unbalanced in- and outflows to and from the city' (Nijkamp and Perrels, 1994, p10). In this view of urban sustainability the emergence of a more sustainable urban ecology depends upon overcoming 'fierce resistance' from an unregulated urban world (Nijkamp and Perrels, 1994, p14). Consequently, those who inhabit cities, including 'the business sector, the public sector, the public at large, and so on' (Nijkamp and Perrels, 1994, p10) must be directed through information campaigns or even disciplined through regulation into obeying the technical mandates of the modelling strategy. The belief is clearly that local actors involved in the energy sector such as utilities and energy users all have a shared interest in reducing energy consumption and that the environmental performance of cities could be improved if only consumers developed a more rational approach to energy efficiency.

The problem with this approach is that it divorces energy flows from the agencies responsible for their management. Utilities tend to have very different boundaries from those adopted by energy and environmental strategists, while territorial links between the companies supplying energy and local customers, who are now able to choose their energy supplier, are fast being eroded. Moreover, the simple model of overcoming the barriers to rational energy use fails to focus on the complex and often contradictory processes shaping the use of energy in cities. While modelling exercises have undoubtedly improved our technical and scientific understanding of energy flows and environmental emissions, they do not appear to provide much insight into the forces driving energy flows through cities, in particular the changing strategies of liberalized, private energy companies.

Promoting ecological action

There is great consensus in the debate over urban environmental management about the need for 'citizens' at all levels to become more environmentally aware and, in terms of the energy debate, take a more 'rational' attitude to energy efficiency in their decision making. As urban environmental policy strategists are fond of putting it: 'there are lots of people who have to be influenced, right from government to local authorities, developers, designers, material producers, professional and trade bodies. They all have a role to play. And what we have to do is try and influence all of them' (Newby, 1994, p3). Here we have an image of the sustainable city populated by 'thousands of decision makers' who are assumed to hold positive or negative views on the importance of green issues which direct the pattern of urban activity in a sustainable or, more typically, unsustainable direction (Olsson, 1988). Motivating energy-saving action is considered a relatively straightforward affair: to provide information that proves and praises the efficacy of energy-saving techniques, while applying regulatory pressure to promote 'sustainability'. For example, defining the 'barriers' to energy efficiency as revolving around 'lack of information' and 'low investment', the UK Energy Efficiency Office (EEO) strives to promote awareness and financial commitment to energy efficiency through various informational and publicity campaigns (National Audit Office, 1994). By promoting 'best practice' techniques and encouraging businesses to 'go green' the EEO hopes to stimulate widespread energy-saving action. The aim of non-governmental organizations (NGOs) is identical: to make energy and environmental issues a priority within the design of buildings and provision of

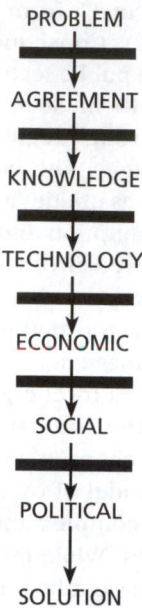

PROBLEM

AGREEMENT

KNOWLEDGE

TECHNOLOGY

ECONOMIC

SOCIAL

POLITICAL

SOLUTION

Source: Trudgill, 1990

Figure 2.2 *The AKTESP Barriers to the Resolution of Environmental Problems*

energy through an equivalent process of persuasive education. In this way, NGOs and government share a common view of the dynamics of technical change. Assuming a common goal – who could oppose energy efficiency? – a series of 'barriers' to finding and implementing solutions to the problem of thermal inefficiency are regularly cited. Stephen Trudgill has formalized this 'way of seeing' innovation in his formulation of the AKTESP barriers to the resolution of environmental problems (see Figure 2.2).

Trudgill cites awareness of 'environmental problems' as of paramount importance. Creating consensus around the importance of energy efficiency – 'gaining agreement' – is the first barrier to sustainability. Hence consumers must be persuaded of the urgency of raising energy standards. To this end public agencies desperately attempt to convince public and private organizations to make a corporate commitment to energy efficiency (National Audit Office, 1994). Once prioritized, the relevant scientific knowledge must be supplied to enable energy performance to be enhanced. This prompts energy advisers to endlessly repeat 'best practice' demonstration schemes, while environmental groups reproduce yet more 'guides' to policy and action in the fight against carbon dioxide pollution (FoE, 1994). With agreement and knowledge assured, there merely remain technological, economic, social and political barriers to be overcome. We are left with an image of technological innovation as a path from ignorance to enlightenment, with the 'evils' of social, political and economic reality cast as unpredictable obstacles to a paradigm shift in urban environmental performance.

Critically, the key to overcoming AKTESP barriers is almost always located within individual motivations. As Trudgill puts it: 'Motivation for tackling a problem comes from our moral obligation and our self-interest in enhancing the resource base and its life – thus enhancing, rather than destroying, planetary ecosystems and plant and animal species, including ourselves'. When such motivation arises we are in a position to solve the remaining barriers to the solution and implementation of environmental problems. The vocabulary of solution and implementation is similarly individualized: 'inadequacy of knowledge', 'technological complacency', 'economic denial or complacency', 'social morality/resistance/leadership', 'political cynicism/ideology'.

The problem with this paradigmatic view of what represents a sustainable urban lifestyle, with its emphasis on a 'paradigm shift' in consumption practices, is that attitudes, decisions and lifestyle patterns are always shaped and framed within wider social processes. Abstraction of the opinions and outlook of social actors from their particular contexts of action tends to isolate and freeze what are contingent practices. Moreover, it reinforces the link that exists popularly between the proliferation of choice over goods and services and deepening environmental degradation (Bocock, 1993).

THE SOCIO-TECHNICAL SHAPING OF MATERIAL FLOWS

We have so far criticized many features of the urban environmental debate for either focusing too closely on the production sphere and thereby falling into the trap of technological determinism, or focusing too narrowly on the consumption sphere thereby promoting an individualistic or socially deterministic view of an environmental paradigm shift. This section presents an alternative view of the sustainable city in which production and consumption interests are seen as mutually shaping, and individual choice always takes place within specific social contexts. It projects a network-focused image that is sensitive to political, cultural, economic and physical interconnections between supply and demand of essential resources. In this image of the city, physical networks are intimately tied to everyday life.

Technical systems are integral to our daily lives; they heat and light our homes and offices, fly us to conferences and vacation islands and allow us to call grandmother on Sundays. In other words, we as consumers are undeniably parts of these systems. When they are reshaped, parts of our lives are reshaped (Summerton, 1995, p2).

Tracing the networks of power that run through different energy sectors, we find ourselves caught up in an apparently seamless web of social and technical interconnections. For example, following daily routines of housing consumption (with Per Otnes, 1988) illustrates the fuzzy borderlines between private (individual) and public (mass) energy consumption by following the intermingling of technical networks and routines of daily life in a typical day. Starting with 'the rise' and connection to the telecommunication system (socio-material system No. 1) through a radio-alarm clock, then through the washing ritual with its mediation through water and sewerage systems (socio-material systems Nos. 2 and 3) and then to breakfast:

> *'I head for the kitchen – with system No. 4 waiting: its terminal, the kitchen stove, attached to the public electric power plant and its cable and wire network... On my way back to the kitchen check the heating, or system No.5, going through the rooms turning on electric radiators, or fan ventilators... I return with the paper, brew my tea and toast two bread loaves. In five minutes breakfast is ready – tea with milk (from the fridge, another privately owned terminal of system No. 4, electricity).'*

Here Otnes powerfully highlights the intertwining of the physical and the cultural in what he terms 'collective socio-material systems' (Otnes, 1988, p120). His biography of daily routines clearly shows how the nature of everyday life critically depends upon the availability of essential services such as power, water and telecommunications. In this way we can see how utility networks structure patterns of resource use, while at the same time changing lifestyles may crucially reshape systems of infrastructure provision, as any history of the home or the office will illustrate. As Ruth Cowan puts it:

> *'The industrialization of the home was determined partly by the decisions of individual households but also partly by social processes over which the households can be said to have had no control at all, or certainly very little control. Householders did their share in determining that their homes would be transformed ... but so did politicians, landlords, industrialists and managers of utilities'* (Cowan, 1983, pp13–14).

From a network standpoint, therefore, any understanding of urban dynamics of environmental 'paradigm shifts' requires an understanding of the changing strategies of the suppliers of networked services and a coherent understanding of how these strategies may reshape contexts of consumption. Such studies of socio-technical change are now finding a collective home in the sociology of science and technology (see Bijker et al, 1987; Bijker and Law, 1992). Common features of socio-technical studies include avoidance of individualist explanations of technological innovation (the rational energy consumer), moving away from any form of technological determinism (technical innovation as handmaiden to an energy efficient economy) and, critically, a refusal to prematurely distinguish between technical, social, economic and political aspects of energy use. As Thomas Hughes (1983) has graphically illustrated, in understanding the development of the electricity networks 'sociological, techno-scientific and economic analyses are permanently woven together in a seamless web'. In this world without seams, social groups and institutions can be considered, alongside technological artefacts, as 'actors' who actively fashion their world, constantly reshaping contexts of socio-technical interaction. Sociological analysis of energy use could then replace conventional descriptions of universal barriers to energy efficient innovation based on apathy, ignorance or lack of financial interest, with an analysis of how the changing social organization of energy production and consumption creates new opportunities for more efficient energy use.

NEW PARADIGMS OF NETWORK MANAGEMENT

Having replaced a conceptual approach that separates the technical and the social with a view of cities as assemblies of physical and cultural networks we will briefly examine the emergence of a new socio-material paradigm of network management. Here we will contrast technical strategies of network management in the process of modernization with a new logic of infrastructure provision that emphasizes consumer service and choice. The new analytical framework enables policy makers to identify new opportunities for sustainable resource use and how privatization and liberalization mutually reshape production and consumption cycles.

Consuming power in the Modern era

Efforts to create national, publicly funded infrastructure networks to provide energy, water, waste, telecommunication and transportation services have to be read as much as a cultural project as a technological exercise. For Peter Wagner 'the stabilization of a technology can be identified as the social sedimentation of a technical project' (Wagner, 1994, p78). In this way conventional processes of infrastructure planning, generation and supply have been inescapably caught up with the dynamics of modernism. Economies of scale encouraged the formation of large organizations that tended to be centralized public monopolies due to the need for long-term planning and technical standardization. The modern period was one in which 'social space (literally) was "perforated" by technical networks, from the railroad to the telephone and electricity networks to car-usable road networks to radio and television broadcasting systems' (Wagner, 1994, p80). A whole new set of technical innovations emerged and were incorporated into daily life as part of the rolling out of infrastructure networks. The success of particular artefacts was often linked to their compatibility with the new networks, or as Wagner puts it, 'the social sedimentation of some of these innovations occurred with, and as part of, the stabilization of an entire socio-economic paradigm' (Wagner, 1994, pp78–79). In this vision the creation of nationwide infrastructural systems was an integral part of the creation of modern citizenship with its associated rights to cheap, good-quality and accessible infrastructure services and its associated obligations of prompt payment and respect of technical boundaries.

Moreover, the creation of new standards of quality of life which again symbolized vibrant modernity were integrally wrapped up with the rolling out of technical networks. For example, Carolyn Marvin has written about how much of the literature on electricity in the late 19th century can be read as a 'wishful template of the world that electrical professionals believed they would create' (Marvin, 1988, p63). Engineers believe they were contributing to the creation of a more open, democratic society and one in which family life would be strengthened through the 'electrical decentralisation of industry and the electrical mechanisation of domestic chores' (Marvin, 1988, p69). Electricity would provide cleaner, safer, enabling environments in which the family unit could be nurtured and protected. In this way Marvin argues that the development of infrastructural services would promote 'the stability of familiar social and class structures' (Marvin, 1988, p63). The development and promotion of other, now familiar, services based on the availability of energy, water, telecommunications and transport services have similarly encouraged particular forms of consumption related to particular social constructions of the home, the factory and the office.

The whole rationale of infrastructure provision and use has, until recently, been one of predict and provide, a supply-oriented logic we have termed elsewhere as one of facilitating infrastructure provision (Guy and Marvin, 1996). The objective has been to maximize supply capacity through network expansion justified through extrapolated models of demand. The high capital costs of network expansion and the need for maximum access has meant that economies of scale have been pursued, encouraging a move towards 'standardization of products and homogenization of patterns of behaviour' (Wagner, 1994, p80). Engineers have accordingly controlled the process, standardizing practices of provision and use and rendering consumers passive. Cities and regions have been treated as homogeneous space to be colonized by networks. The result was prescribed patterns of consumption and notions of social identity which highlighted how 'structures of production and of use emerge that are linked to features of the technical artefact but reach into realms of other social practices' (Wagner, 1994, p78). In infrastructural terms, connection to the network(s) effectively nationalized social practices of resource consumption thereby providing a means for users to 'locate' themselves 'socially in the world' (Wagner, 1994, p88). In this way the stabilization of national infrastructure networks framed and even actively shaped social patterns of consumption, thereby limiting environmental innovation to engineering interventions and/or the persuasion of consumers to conserve resources.

New logic of production and consumption

Critically, Wagner argues that 'no stable state' was ever achieved in the 'modern period'. Rather an 'interim configuration' was achieved that demonstrated a 'certain internal coherence' but which 'bore the seed of its own demise' (Wagner, 1994, p77). Replacing vertically integrated industries dedicated to Fordist mass production techniques with a new paradigm centred on high technology based on advances in microelectronics, has diminished the centrality of mass production, standardization and homogenization. This changed allocative practice allows 'a greater variety of products to be produced according to more specific demand' (Wagner, 1994, p130).

This paradigm shift can be seen emerging in the British energy sector where privatization and liberalization of utility networks has revolutionized the provision and use of essential resources. The established logic of infrastructure management, in which fixed units of power and water were delivered at standardized cost as part of a wider universal service obligation, is being radically challenged. We are currently witnessing the dramatic emergence of a new logic of utility provision in which essential infrastructure resources are becoming commodified, gradually differentiated in terms of cost, availability and quality over space and time. These shifts have complex and contradictory implications for energy use. Escaping the spatially homogenized, technically standardized logic of nationalized infrastructure systems, private utility companies are, wherever profitable, developing infrastructure networks that more accurately match local market need. By balancing supply and demand, within and between local networks, utility companies can maximize profits while minimizing and/or postponing additional investment in supply capacity. At the same time, the process of liberalization, together with technological developments in advanced metering technologies, is selectively expanding consumer choice over utility services. This process is gradually enhancing the power of utility customers to influence utility strategies. Regional electricity companies are beginning to venture 'beyond the meter' into the homes, factories and offices of utility customers in order to tailor local demand profiles while catering more closely to the users' own energy requirements. These measures include offering new energy services, including energy audits, advice and conservation technologies, to spread the consumer base; the development of flexible pricing formulas/contracts to balance load, so maximizing network potential; and exploiting new communications technologies to extend remote load management techniques. By commodifying electricity as a form of 'service', warming rooms, heating water and powering machines, electricity companies have begun to build in a novel adaptability to the management of electricity systems. The emergence of 'choice' over these services is gradually reconstructing electricity users into energy consumers, creating new contexts of action within which energy efficiency and conservation activities may flourish (Guy and Marvin, 1996). Critically, we are not suggesting that this means energy consumers are or even will begin to act more sustainably, whatever that might mean. Rather, we argue that their 'universe of choice' (Cowan, 1983) is being expanded by the providers of infrastructure services which presents greater scope for the adoption of environmentally beneficial consumption patterns (Guy and Marvin, 1998).

Socio-technical systems: a new way of seeing

The conventional view of cities is of homogeneous physical spaces made up of buildings, pipes and wires which can be 'fine tuned' to maximize efficiency or reduce environmental impacts. Mirroring this technical view is a social vision which see cities as populated by isolated decision makers who need to be persuaded to adopt sustainable lifestyles. Orthodox analyses of infrastructure systems are then neatly divided between the technical and the social – production and consumption – and tend to be homogeneous in scope and scale across sectors and across space. By contrast, we argue that it is critical to locate the opportunities for, and limits to, environmental innovation created by processes of commodification within particular 'systems of provision', according to the 'distinct relationships between the various material and cultural practices comprising the production, distribution, circulation and consumption of the goods concerned' (Fine and Leopold, 1993, p5). Such an approach allows us to consider the wider political, institutional, social, technological and economic context within which relations between production and consumption interests are configured. Recognizing the limits and possibilities of environmental innovation in the development and management of infrastructure services necessitates moving away from any stress on individual decision makers and their environmental attitudes. Focusing instead on the twists and turns of active social and technical processes allows greater sensitivity to the dynamic contexts of infrastructure provision and use in different socio-political contexts.

Policy strategists taking this network view, and who aimed at encouraging a paradigm shift in energy management, would avoid focusing exclusively either on production or consumption processes. Instead these policy strategists would seek to identify how patterns of resource provision and use varied across the spaces of the city and between different classes of customer. In this way we would identify the ways in which the changing context of utility provision can 'provide the opportunity for utilities to operate in a more environmentally sensitive manner without compromising their commercial viability' (Brown, 1991, p198). This network view would reshape our vision of the city as a homogeneous space. Pockets of high and low – or hot and cold – demand would become visible, leading to very different strategies of infrastructure provision and different capacities for environmental action. For instance, areas of the city in which demand was low might be targeted by utilities and local planners for economic development initiatives, while areas of over-demand might be targeted separately for demand-side management initiatives designed to cool demand. Policy strategies would not homogenize all urban decision makers. Instead they would strive to understand the specific contexts of action which diverse groups of domestic, commercial and industrial consumers inhabited. Policy initiatives would then be targeted accordingly.

A spreading logic?

The emergence of a new logic of infrastructure provision problematizes the central assumptions underpinning the conventional perspective. In particular, the supply logic has been challenged by an emerging public and political movement around the social, environmental and economic limits to the physical expansion of the capacities of infrastructure networks. Infrastructure providers more broadly are no longer simply able to extend infrastructure in response to demand for expansion. New limits are emerging that are creating a shift to a more demand-oriented style of infrastructure provision. Awareness of the economic and social costs of supply-oriented infrastructure investment has prompted social resistance to the physical expansion of networks. This climate of social and political concern has also been mirrored by a transformation in the regulatory and financial frameworks governing infrastructure decision making. An increasingly competitive, international marketplace together with growing concern over environmental issues and a new focus on network efficiency are leading infrastructure providers to reinvent themselves around a new logic of network management. Water companies are increasingly operating within a broader commercial and policy context that shifts attention to the maximization of network efficiency rather than simply focusing on network expansion. At the same time much of the transport debate has shifted around a new logic of network integration and management rather than the old logic of network expansion.

Operationally, this means that utilities are looking much more closely at the technical and economic performance of each part of their distribution networks and planning improvements rather than simply expanding networks irrespective of cost. For example, 'hot' parts of electricity networks that have insufficient capacity to meet peak demands could be subjected to intense energy efficiency measures to reduce the level, or shift the timing, of peak consumption (Guy and Marvin, 1996). Similarly the water sector is more likely to adopt demand-side measures in areas suffering from water stress. Supply-led options are no longer the preferred mode of management as water companies are forced to examine the efficiency of the network, reduce its leakiness and examine ways for customers to save water before considering expanding supply through new resource extraction (Guy and Marvin, 1996).

There are also new forms of differentiation between users on stressed networks. As infrastructure providers attempt to alleviate stress on congested networks they are likely to engage with commercial and industrial users who create high levels of demand. These users are likely to benefit most from network-sponsored demand side management (DSM) programmes. On 'hot' parts of the network, providers may seek to calm demand by sponsoring energy and water efficiency and conservation measures, or finding alternatives to the private car. In contrast, where the network is running 'cold', with spare capacity, initiatives may well be developed to encourage demand, and utility companies may stimulate local economic activity by promoting inward investment.

While the conventional supply logic viewed new development as a largely passive form of demand whose growth was met with supply-oriented options, the demand logic seeks a closer form of engagement with users. Regional electricity companies are now marketing targeted energy services to industrial and commercial users rather than indiscriminately selling units of electricity. Privatized water companies are similarly keen to discriminate between customers based on their level of consumption and service needs. Infrastructure providers are seeking to develop new ways of engaging with large users in order to reshape patterns of demand to reduce stress on the networks. Electricity utilities are beginning to venture 'beyond the meter' to deepen relationships with electricity users by offering free energy audits and other energy services. Such initiatives signal a major re-fashioning of relationships between users and utilities within which energy-saving activities can flourish. Large users of water services in areas of water stress are developing new ways of modifying water demands in partnership with the Environment Agency and water companies. In sum, the privatization period appears to be characterized by the variety and range of approaches to infrastructure management (Guy and Marvin, 1998).

RESEARCHING CITIES AND INFRASTRUCTURE NETWORKS

Towards a socio-technical approach

This chapter has problematized orthodox conceptions of flow management that make a simple distinction between the technical and social components of cities. Instead, we have argued that analytical attention must focus on the reshaping of contexts of environmental action through dynamic production–consumption cycles. In this way, the chapter has highlighted the need for a new methodological framework to assess urban infrastructure processes in general and the possibility of an environmental 'paradigm shift' in particular. This methodological approach would acknowledge the socio-technical complexity of infrastructure systems. It would recognize the changing organizational interrelationships between public and private actors as new coalitions are forged between government departments, utility regulators, local planners and commercial infrastructure suppliers. It would identify how production interests strive to direct resource management along a techno-commercial pathway likely to proliferate opportunities for end users to play their part as co-producers of environmental value. In sum, by analysing how patterns of consumption connect with material processes of infrastructure provision the research will recognize the reciprocal and synchronous nature of production and consumption interests in contingent and dynamic local contexts.

Underpinning this new way of seeing urban environmental flows is a novel vocabulary and methodology designed to highlight the social structuring of technical network development and management and to identify the emergence of a novel logic of infrastructure provision that may deliver environmental benefits. Critical to this approach is our treatment of *sustainable flow management* as an empty category. That is, rather than view environmental innovation as a taken-for-granted technical achievement, we have tended to treat sustainable flow management as an 'empty conceptual space' to be tested and defined through our comparative analysis of infrastructure management across cities, countries and infrastructure sectors. While noting the potential of similar forms of technological innovation across case-study areas, we will analyse the ways in which the social organization and institutional contexts of service delivery differ in each country and across infrastructure sectors, and then question how these differing contexts of action structure processes of technological innovation, thereby encouraging or hindering the emergence of a new logic of environmental innovation.

Methodological innovation

In order to operationalize this analytical approach we developed a common investigative framework that, respecting the specific methodological challenges presented by each national case study, sought to comparatively map the social processes fashioning technical and environmental innovation. While each case study focused on different elements of the infrastructure delivery process, a common analytical process was followed. In particular, each case study sought to identify the *social organization* of technical services and the *actor networks* that underpinned the operational strategies of infrastructure providers. Again, in each case, an analysis was carried out on the changing institutional structure or *contexts of action* framing service delivery. Here, the various regulatory, commercial, political, technological and social signals designed to shape practices of infrastructure provision were identified and their relative influence mapped. The overall analytical aim of all case studies was to unpack the conflicting logic of infrastructure management by relating the structures of infrastructure provision to local contexts of resource consumption. In this way the research avoided over-emphasizing the realm of either production or consumption, instead emphasizing the interrelationships between the technical or the social.

A further methodological innovation lay in our structuring of the case studies. Rather than simply examining sectors one by one we developed a more socially and spatially differentiated approach designed to reveal the interconnections between technologies, actors, institutions and space.

Firstly, we took water networks as a cross-country exemplar of network management. In particular, this allowed us to compare and contrast how actors and signals shape resource management. All three urban regions face a pressing water resource problem, whether in terms of pollution, declining water resources, low water availability or major intra-regional disparities in the distribution of water resources. These issues illustrate the interdependency between cities and their wider regional context. For example, long distance supply networks or downstream pollution raise important questions of regional equity in the distribution of environmental, economic and social costs within and between regions. The focus of the water case studies is, therefore, at a regional level, examining how different social interests view a water resource issue and how their assessment of the problem shapes the type of solutions they propose. The case studies graphically illustrate the diversity of pathways along which network managers attempt to destabilize their water networks in response to water resource issues.

Secondly, we analysed the interrelationships between supply and demand in case studies of ecological building. The case studies focus closer attention on the relations between users and the providers of infrastructure services mediated through the design and development of buildings. This methodological window readily facilitates the cross-sectoral analysis of how water, waste and energy networks are provided and used. More broadly it enables the book to relate to wider debates about how sustainability issues are expressed through the development of 'green buildings'. Conventional approaches to analysing green buildings tend to focus on the management of building services and evaluations of the building's environmental performance. Such approaches tend to be blind to the complex social processes through which environmental technologies and practices are introduced into the specification, design and development processes. The case studies seek to redress this imbalance by examining the different social contexts that assist or hinder the application of particular measures rather than assessing their environmental impact. Here the emphasis shifts towards a focus on the complex social interests responsible for planning, designing, investing, installing and using infrastructure facilities in buildings and their motives for selecting or resisting particular technologies and practices. The case studies develop a conceptual framework for understanding the different social interests and the specific contexts within which they operate. This approach allows an escape from the orthodox problem of treating networks as free-floating technical objects unrelated to the social dynamics of the development process.

Finally, we focused on the treatment of infrastructure in local planning through a cross-national examination of local planning strategies. The case studies examine the complex relations between the planning process and the management of urban infrastructure networks. This methodological window provides us with an understanding of how a localist initiative based on a more open, bottom-up style of planning process resonates and conflicts with the social interest and logic of the conventional infrastructure managers. Plans can represent quite different visions of the development of infrastructure networks. These differing viewpoints can facilitate a greater understanding of the connections and disconnections between public and private agencies and between commercial and environmental objectives.

CONCLUSION

This chapter has problematized the 'orthodox' way of seeing infrastructure networks that makes a simple distinction between the technical and social components of resource flows. Instead, we have argued that analysis must focus on the reshaping of contexts of environmental action through dynamic production–consumption cycles. In this way a new conceptual framework to assess urban environmental processes in general, and the possibility of an environmental paradigm shift in network management in particular, has been identified. Taking the electricity sector in the UK as an exemplar, the chapter has highlighted the reciprocal and synchronous nature of production and consumption interests in changing strategies of infrastructure provision and acknowledged the socio-technical complexity of technical networks. This perspective has enabled us to begin to reconnect urban environmental policy to local contexts of infrastructure provision and use. Finally, we have shown how the shifts in the UK electricity sector are being paralleled by new styles of network management in the water infrastructure sector both in the UK and – as outlined in Chapter 1 – across infrastructure networks in Europe.

REFERENCES

Bijker, W, Hughes, T and Pinch, T (eds) (1987) *The Social Construction of Technological Systems*, MIT Press, London
Bijker, W and Law, J (eds) (1992) *Shaping Technology/Building Society*, MIT Press, London
Bocock, R (1993) *Consumption*, Routledge, London

Brown, I (1991) 'Energy Efficiency in Electricity', *Energy Policy*, vol 19, no 3, pp195–198

Cowan, R S (1983) *More Work for Mother: The Ironies of Household Technology From the Open Hearth to the Microwave*, Basic Books, London

Fine, B and Leopold, E (1993) *The World of Consumption*, Routledge, London

FoE (1994) *The Climate Resolution*, L301, Friends of the Earth, London

Guy, S and Marvin, S (1996) 'Disconnected Policy, the shaping of local energy management', *Environment and Planning (C):Government and Policy*, vol 14, no 1, pp145–158

Guy, S and Marvin, S (1998) 'Electricity in the Marketplace', *Local Environment*, vol 3, no 3, pp313–332

Hughes, T P (1983) *Networks of Power: Electrification in Western Society, 1880 – 1930*, Johns Hopkins Press, Baltimore

Marvin, C (1988) *When old technologies were new*, Oxford University Press, Oxford

National Audit Office (1994) *Buildings and the Environment*, HMSO 365, London

Newby, H (1994) *Materials and Energy Flows, Cities, Sustainability, and the Construction Industry*, Engineering and Physical Science Research Council, Swindon

Nijkamp, P and Perrels, A (1994) *Sustainable Cities in Europe*, Earthscan, London

Olsson, R (1988) *Energy in the Built Environment*, Swedish Council of Building Research, Stockholm

Otnes, P (ed) (1988) *The Sociology of Consumption*, Solum Forlag, Humanities Press, Oslo/New Jersey

Owens, S (1986) *Energy, Planning and Urban Form*, Pion Ltd, London

Summerton, J (1995) *Changing Large Technical Systems*, Fairview, London

Trudgill, S (1990) *Barriers to a Better Environment*, Belhaven Press, London

Wagner, P (1994) *A Sociology of Modernity: Liberty and Discipline*, Routledge, London

PART 2

RECONFIGURING NETWORKS

Credit: Susanne Balsev Nielsen

INTRODUCTION

Susanne Balslev Nielsen and Simon Marvin

In this part of the book we examine how three approaches to the analysis of socio-technical networks give us different insights into the complex process of network reconfiguration in each of our city regions. Each of our examples is drawn from the water sector and addresses a critical dimension of network transformation.

In Berlin, the crucial issue is the deteriorating quality of groundwater resources and competing socio-technical options for dealing with the problem. The momentum that has underpinned the development of the water system has been disrupted by these new environmental concerns together with the institutional complexities of Berlin's reunification and economic constraints on public expenditure. Network managers are attempting to deal with increasing social and technical complexity as different styles of water recycling appear to compete for ascendancy.

Water quality is also a central issue in our Copenhagen case study. The conventional approach to storm-water disposal has been the development of common systems where both sewage and rainwater are collected in a combined network. At peak rainfall the combined network could not cope with the flows and discharges of sewage and rainwater, causing serious environmental problems. The case study examines the complex relations between a well-established and decentralized technology called rainwater percolation and the conventional logic of centralized collection and treatment.

The Newcastle case study shifts our attention back to water resource issues and examines the response of Yorkshire Water to the drought crisis in 1996. An apparently stable network was disrupted by the drought, and the water company searched for ways of restabilizing the network under intense social and political pressure. A multiple approach to network stabilization was developed, each involving the enrolment of different types of social and technical actors with varying degrees of complexity and success.

The complexities and contradictions involved in our examples of network reconfiguration will probably be familiar to many network managers, urban governments and the academic communities with an interest in infrastructure networks. In Chapter 2 we outlined a broader shift in the logic underpinning the management and development of technical networks. The messiness of technical network development reflects a broader transition as network managers cope with new environmental concerns, demands for more user involvement in shaping networks, the increased range of technological choices, resource constraints on new investment and the need for cities to provide high-quality infrastructure that allows them to compete globally.

In this context how do we begin to understand network reconfiguration as a process? More specifically we need to ask:

- How does the new logic of network management emerge?
- What possibilities are there for more environmentally sensitive forms of network management?
- How can new decentralized technologies be incorporated into large technological systems?
- What are the opportunities for user involvement in the management of networks?

We address these issues and questions by adopting three related theoretical approaches to the study of socio-technical networks. Drawing from science, technology and society studies, each of our case studies uses a particular set of theoretical and methodological lenses that focus our attention towards different agents, dimensions and types of change in the networks.

3 BATTLE OF THE SYSTEMS? CHANGING STYLES OF WATER RECYCLING IN BERLIN

Timothy Moss

INTRODUCTION

Until recently, it was widely assumed that the technological systems which developed around the physical artefacts of pipes and cables, water works and power stations were inherently stable structures, developing along a predictable trajectory set by technical modernization. However, recent changes in the way technical networks are managed are revealing a dynamic interplay of forces that are capable of reshaping technical networks in new directions. Adapting technical networks to a changing context is a particularly poignant theme in the Berlin region, where, post-unification, a variety of new economic, social, commercial and environmental pressures are prompting utility managers to revise their strategies for network expansion and explore alternative ways of operating their electricity, water, sewage and waste systems. This chapter draws for its empirical evidence on a case study of diverse schemes to relieve water stress in the Berlin metropolitan area. The process of change in the water supply and sewage disposal system is explored through the concept of large technological systems (LTS) (Hughes, 1983). The LTS approach presents a model of how technological systems develop and change in response to shifting socio-technical forces. This chapter applies this approach as an analytical tool to uncover the forces for change in the water and sewage networks of our case study and suggests ways of developing our conceptual understanding of technical networks. The conclusion highlights the implications of this approach for policy makers, regulators, infrastructure planners and utility managers.

UNDERSTANDING LARGE TECHNOLOGICAL SYSTEMS

The LTS concept is based on the premise that large technological systems, such as electricity or telecommunications networks, cannot be understood solely in terms of their technological components but as complex systems which link material technologies with organizations, institutional rules and cultural values (Hughes, 1987; Summerton, 1994, pp3ff; Bijker et al, 1989; Bijker et al, 1992). The development of LTS is determined not by technological advancement alone but also by the interplay between these components. As Thomas Hughes demonstrated, in his pioneering study of the historical development of electricity networks in the USA, the UK and Germany, the technology of the electric light bulb and the organizational structure of utility companies shaped each other to set the framework for electricity provision in the 20th century (Hughes, 1983).

Water supply and sewage disposal networks have received little attention within the LTS debate but they bear most, if not all, of the principal characteristics of large technological systems. Like electricity networks, they are complex systems consisting of physical artefacts (pipes, processing plant), organizations (utility companies, planning bodies) and regulatory structures (legislative framework, contractual obligations). They evolved in response to the increasing complexity and problems of control relating to drinking water and sanitation needs in the late 19th century. Since then, under the direction of their system-builders, they have generally followed the familiar pattern of development of LTS into large-scale, centralized and hierarchical systems built around a dominant technology (such as mains sewers) and comprising several sub-systems (such as storm-water collection). Typical of many LTS, water supply and sewage disposal networks are engaged in regulating the input and output of resources on a large scale: in this case, the natural resource water and water pollutants as well as – less visibly – energy, building materials and money. Given their importance to human well-being, high capital needs and long-run cost curves, they have traditionally – like other LTS – been treated as natural monopolies, either publicly operated or at least publicly regulated (Galambos, 1991, p177).

The purpose of LTS theory is to explain how actors, technologies, markets and regulations interact to shape the initiation, evolution and expansion of large technological systems (Guy et al, 1997, p193). Central to the argument are three concepts introduced by Hughes: *system-builders, momentum* and *reverse salients* (Hughes, 1987). The system-builders are defined as the inventors, engineers, managers, financiers and other key actors with a vested interest in LTS. Each actor group influences a large technological system in different phases of its development: the inventors creating the initial techniques, the engineers applying the techniques to solving a problem, the managers devising a suitable organizational structure and so on. The important characteristic of system-builders is their interest in promoting and protecting their own technological system against competition from other systems. In Hughes's words, they try to create 'closed' systems to the exclusion of competing components, constructing 'unity from diversity, centralization in the face of pluralism, and coherence from chaos' (Hughes, 1987, p52).

As a result of these efforts by the system-builders, large technological systems develop a momentum of their own. Early decisions on the type of technology chosen or the way utilities are regulated limit the options for future development, guiding LTS in a particular direction. Once established, the homogeneous, standardized networks become stable forces which continue to reinforce themselves internally and sustain other systems, such as urban development, externally (Guy et al, 1997, pp193-194). According to LTS theory the momentum of a large technological system increases over time; in other words, LTS grow inflexible and resistant to radical change as they stabilize, with the system-builders seeking continuously to protect their system from outside competition.

The way in which major change does occur in and between LTS is explained in terms of reverse salients (Hughes, 1987, pp73-76). Reverse salients are retarded components that hinder the further development of a system. These blockages might be technical but, equally, might be social, organizational, economic or cultural. As LTS expand, reverse salients develop. In minor cases – such as inadequate electricity-generating capacity – the reverse salient can be corrected within the context of the existing system: in this case with the construction of a power station. When this is not possible – say, in the event of a binding commitment to reduce CO_2 emissions in industrialized countries – the solution to the problem may be to introduce or strengthen competing systems: in our example, new forms of energy efficiency. Under such circumstances a 'battle of systems' is engaged (Hughes, 1987, p77) – a military metaphor which captures the conflictual nature of radical change according to LTS theory.

The combined impact of these three characteristics of LTS – system-builders, momentum and reverse salients – is visible in the various phases of development which each large technological system experiences. Hughes identifies two broad phases of historical development: an initial phase of invention, development, innovation and transfer followed by a secondary phase of growth, competition and consolidation (Hughes, 1987, pp57ff). Gökalp has added to the list of initial phase, accelerated development phase and stabilization phase a fourth phase of decline, characterized by the diminishing importance of network extension, involvement in new activities and gradual replacement by a new large technological system (Gökalp, 1992, p58). Although the boundaries between the different phases are fluid, each phase is regarded as distinctive in terms of the principal actors involved and the openness of the structures to change.

WATER STRESS IN THE BERLIN REGION: CHANGING TECHNICAL STYLES OF WATER MANAGEMENT

The water supply and sewage disposal systems of the Berlin region have been selected to illustrate how the LTS approach can contribute to our understanding of the dynamics of change from a socio-technical perspective. The technical problem at the heart of the case study is the search for ways of combating water stress in the Berlin metropolitan area where concern has shifted from the quantity to the quality of drinking-water resources. Fears of a water supply crisis, voiced in 1991 in anticipation of a dramatic increase in water use following rapid urban development in the city, have since subsided. Water consumption in Berlin in fact fell by 35 per cent between 1989 and 1996, from 375 million m^3 to 246 million m^3, owing to a decline in industrial production, a sharp rise in prices and the more widespread use of water-saving appliances (BWB, 1997, p24). The principal problem in the system today is the pollution of surface water and contamination of groundwater resources. It is estimated that some 7 per cent of the groundwater reserves theoretically available for water supply is so contaminated that it is unsuitable for drinking even if treated. A further 27 per cent is potentially threatened; that is, it will be contaminated by existing ground pollution in time if remedial measures are not taken (MUNR/SenStadtUm, 1994, pp91-92; Schulze, 1997). Meanwhile, surface water in the city is polluted by nutrients, in particular, as a result of inadequate sewage treatment in the region, discharges from industry and run-off from agricultural land. What has turned this long-standing problem into a true reverse salient of late is the recent political objective of the Berlin environmental regulator to raise the quality of surface water in the city to bathing-water standards according to EU specifications. The sharp decline in water consumption and the resulting problem of overcapacity in the water and sewage networks offer a classic example of a large technological system moving from a phase of growth and expansion to one of stagnation and reorientation.

The water managers in Berlin – the water utility (Berliner Wasser Betriebe, BWB) and the water regulator (Senate Department for Urban Development, Environmental Protection and Technology, SenSUT) – are pursuing technical solutions to what they see as a technical problem. Among the schemes they are operating or proposing in order to maintain drinking-water resources of adequate quality, several aim at closing – or, at least, slowing down – the cycle of water passing through the city. The solutions differ greatly in their spatial and technological focus; three are selected for closer study here (see Figure 3.1).

Groundwater replenishment with surface water

Since the 1950s a scheme has been in operation in West Berlin to pump surface water onto infiltration beds serving groundwater aquifers, allowing the water to be purified in passage through the soil and, in some cases, via prior treatment. In this way groundwater levels are partially replenished with purified water and the through-flow of surface water is reduced – the two cyclical features of the design. Currently, groundwater replenishment – serving the waterworks of Tegel, Spandau and Jungfernheide – contributes 57 million m^3/year to groundwater reserves, or one-fifth of the city's total groundwater extraction. This technology was designed to secure West Berlin's water supply and minimize its dependence on the surrounding GDR by creating an artificial, urban water cycle (Schulze, 1993). With the reunification of the city in 1990 and expectations of rapid development in the Berlin region, plans were made to extend the technology – the technological flagship of the water utility – to the eastern half of the city.

Schemes	Groundwater replenishment with surface water 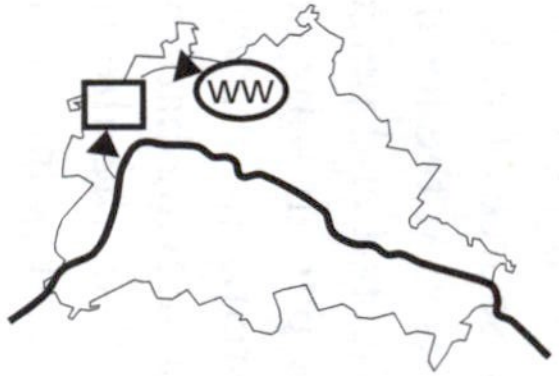	Treated effluent redirected upstream 	Localized storm water retention and percolation 
Key			
Function	Artificially replenishing depleted groundwater stocks with surface water to secure water supply and maintain groundwater levels	Redirecting treated effluent upstream of waterworks to secure constant flow of bank infiltration to drinking water wells	Retaining urban run-off locally in order to minimize pollution from storm water, reduce pressure on sewer networks and replenish local groundwater resources
Technology	Surface water pumped onto infiltration beds serving groundwater aquifers, water purified via soil passage	High standard of sewage treatment; treated effluent pumped into receiving water course upstream of drinking-water wells	'Soakaways' (eg trough-trench system)
Spatial dimension	Strictly urban	Urban region	Property / housing block / street
Projects: – in operation	Since 1950s: surface water from Havel river replenishing groundwater serving the waterworks Tegel, Spandau and Jungfernheide	Treated effluent from Ruhleben sewage treatment plant fed upstream into Spree river (winter only)	Several large-scale trough-trench systems in recent development areas (eg Rummelsburger Bucht, Adlershof)
– under construction	1990 until recently: plans to apply technology in eastern Berlin	All-year operation of Ruhleben project; Treated effluent from Waflmannsdorf sewage treatment plant fed upstream into Dahme/Notte rivers	Storm water percolation systems in development projects across the city

Key: WW Water works; STP Sewage treatment plant

Source: IRS

Figure 3.1 *Three Schemes for Water Recycling in the Berlin Region*

Treated effluent redirected upstream

The scheme to redirect treated effluent upstream is simple; instead of discharging treated effluent downstream of the city's water wells, it is reintroduced into waterways upstream, passing through the city again and feeding its wells via bank infiltration. The principal attraction for water managers lies in securing a constant flow of water serving the urban water wells even in dry periods or when the through-flow of surface water is low, since effluent levels are very steady all year round. Effectively, treated effluent is recycled as drinking water subsequent to bank infiltration – the second cyclical dimension to the scheme. This necessitates, of course, a very high standard of sewage treatment prior to discharge in order to ensure adequate drinking-water quality. Indeed, under this scheme we see sewage treatment, removing bacteria and nutrients to a high degree, increasingly resembling drinking-water purification (Dorau, 1990).

In practice, there are currently two projects applying the technology in the Berlin region. The first involves discharging treated effluent from the Ruhleben sewage treatment plant upstream of the drinking-water extraction wells along the Havel river rather than pumping it to an outlet downstream. This project has been in operation for the winters since 1997 without a deterioration of drinking-water quality. The second scheme is more ambitious but less advanced. On the basis of experience with the Ruhleben plant, the idea is not to discharge effluent from the treatment plant at Waßmannsdorf into the Teltow canal as at present but to pump it into one of several waterways to the south of the city. This water would then re-enter Berlin via the Dahme river, passing the drinking-water wells on its way through the city. The project is currently at an experimental phase and there are several variations for the route the treated effluent should take.

Local percolation of storm water

The retention and percolation of rainwater at or near the place it falls has the dual purpose of reducing storm-water run-off – a major source of surface water pollution – and replenishing local groundwater resources. At the local level of the property, housing block or street, rainwater is collected and percolated – so far as hydrological and geological circumstances permit – by means of simple troughs or more complex trough-trench systems (soakaways). The technology is seen as an important contribution to achieving bathing-water quality for Berlin's waterways and is less expensive than the alternative of collecting and purifying storm water centrally at the end points of separate sewer systems. For these reasons, the Berlin water utility has been introducing local storm-water percolation in many new urban development areas in the city, such as Adlershof, Karow-Nord and Rummelsburger Bucht. In these three development areas storm water is percolated locally over an area of some 270 hectares, or 46 per cent of the total surface area (Moss, 2000). The environmental regulator SenSUT is keen to promote further on-site storm-water percolation via the approval of rainwater discharges, local building regulations, urban development plans and a tax on sealed land.

CHANGING SOCIO-ECONOMIC RATIONALES

The application of these three very different technologies, however, does not only depend on their technical virtues. As the water managers are learning through their experience in introducing or extending these technological sub-systems, wider socio-economic issues are also having a determining influence on whether and how each scheme is adopted. Presenting and debating the schemes in terms of their technical logic, that is, how a specific technology is suited to meet a specific problem of water use, overlooks a variety of political, financial, social and spatial factors that can underpin or undermine each scheme. In the following section we explore the socio-economic implications surrounding each of the three schemes.

Weakening attachment to groundwater replenishment

The case of groundwater replenishment with surface water is a good example of how changing circumstances can undermine the rationale behind an established and successful technology. The rapid decline in water consumption – itself a socio-economic phenomenon – has caused the plans to extend the technology of groundwater replenishment to eastern Berlin to be shelved. Furthermore, even in the western half of the city, where water use has not declined so rapidly, the continued operation of the existing schemes is being questioned. The new factor here is a possible cut in public subsidies for the technology. Currently BWB receives DM 0.60 from the Senate for each cubic metre of replenished groundwater, in the form of an exemption from the groundwater extraction charge. Should this subsidy fall victim to the Senate's rigorous cuts to reduce its huge budget deficit, then groundwater replenishment may no longer appear economically viable for the water utility. BWB hopes, however, that the technology can be pursued, since it represents not only an integral part of the utility's drinking-water purification but also an element of its technological know-how of importance to the company's commercial activities in central and eastern Europe. We see here, therefore, how changing consumption patterns are undermining the original environmental argument for groundwater replenishment and how budgetary pressures and the new geo-political situation have weakened the city government's attachment to the technology.

Environmental constraints on treated effluent

Both projects to redirect treated effluent upstream are confronting obstacles of an environmental nature, beyond which lie questions of cost and regional cooperation. The environmental concerns surrounding recycling treated effluent are that, despite a three-stage treatment, discharges would contain significant residual amounts of bacteria and phosphate. On this understanding the city health authorities currently prohibit the operation of the Ruhleben project during the summer months as a precautionary measure to maintain bathing-water standards on the Havel. It is precisely in the summer months, when surface through-flow is low, though, that the project is needed most by

BWB. The alternative solution – for BWB to introduce a fourth stage of sewage treatment prior to discharge – would cost an additional DM $0.50/m^3$, which the company finds unacceptable. While the utility argues that more thorough tests would reveal treated effluent to be safe enough for the Havel even in the summer, it is currently having to bear the financial burden of operating two sub-systems, one for the summer and one for the winter.

Similar reservations have been voiced by the environmental regulator over the second project. In this case BWB is exploring the possibility of percolating the treated effluent prior to discharge into the waterways as a means of avoiding the need for a costly fourth stage of sewage treatment. Soil infiltration would raise the quality of the discharge such that it could actually improve the water quality of the Rangsdorfer lake or the Notte canal. This variation on the project has, interestingly, awakened the interest of the local authorities in the areas feasible for such percolation. They see in it the possibility to offset the major loss of local water resources following the termination of sewage irrigation after 1990. They are concerned that a strict adherence to water-quality standards is ignoring a local water quantity problem of far-reaching implications for the local ecosystem. We thus detect here, as a result of financial and environmental considerations, the emergence of a community of interest between BWB and local authorities outside Berlin, which is at odds with another actor alliance between the environmental regulators in Berlin and Brandenburg.

Social complexity of local storm-water percolation

The introduction of this small-scale technology to an existing centralized system not only reorders the technical structures but also social responsibilities, challenging the conventional structures and processes of water management (Moss, 2000). On-site rainwater management is no longer the realm of a sole utility and treated as a branch of sewage disposal. A far larger number of actors are now involved, including house-owners, developers, architects and borough parks departments. Each is acquiring a new set of responsibilities. Property owners, for instance, are not only building their own storm-water retention systems but having to maintain them in good working order as well. Architects are having to incorporate retention troughs and trenches in their designs for green spaces. Parks departments are required to mow the grass of the troughs in public spaces. Bringing technology above ground has thus shifted responsibility from the utility – traditionally responsible for underground infrastructure – onto other actor groups. With this, liabilities and costs are also rearranged. Thus house-owners pay for installing percolation systems and are liable for damages resulting from their malfunctioning. Investment costs for percolation systems in the public spaces of urban development areas (for example side streets) are borne by the developers rather than the city government.

As a result, opinion on local storm-water percolation in Berlin is divided less over the technical system itself than over how it should be managed. It is here that incompatibilities are perceived; for instance by architects, who resent restrictions on their use of open space (estimated at 10–15 per cent of the sealed area served) or by parks departments, who object to maintaining a technology whose financial benefits they do not reap. Of pressing concern are the implications of the technology for the pricing system for water and sewage services. Under the current system, in which a combined water and sewage charge is calculated according to water consumption, there is no financial incentive for house-owners to disconnect and percolate rainwater on site. Plans of the water utility and environmental regulator to remedy this by introducing a separate rainwater disposal charge, however, raise the social problem of creating an additional financial burden on those living in inner-city areas where local rainwater percolation is often not viable. In other words, we can observe here how the adoption of a local technology within an existing centralized system requires a redistribution of costs and responsibilities. The search for an optimal solution is being complicated by different perceptions of who is actually responsible for which parts of water management.

NETWORK RECONFIGURATION?

The development of water supply and sewage disposal networks is not determined purely by technological progress but also by the interplay between technologies, institutions and – above all – actors. The progress of the three schemes of water recycling in the Berlin region would appear to confirm that, besides the availability of a particular technology, other financial, organizational, regulatory and political forces shape the direction and speed of development. The future of the technology of groundwater replenishment in Berlin, for example, will depend on a combination of economic, environmental and even commercial factors. The case study demonstrates the need to consider the interaction of local factors, historical precedents, actors' motives and natural features that shape the fate of a scheme. Yet there are three aspects of LTS that are worth revisiting in further detail.

The system-builders

The concept of system-builders needs to be extended to encompass the full range of actors who shape today's technical networks. The system-builders defined by Hughes – inventors, engineers, managers, financiers and so on (Hughes, 1987, p52) – clearly continue to represent a driving force of technical networks. All three schemes of the case study have been devised, designed and implemented by managers and engineers of the water utility, the principal system-builders of today. Nevertheless, the circle of influential actors now needs to be enlarged. As Hughes argues, each phase of development is characterized by different dominant actor groups, and today there are other actors besides those engaged on the supply side of utility services who have a say in how they develop.

A major actor group, which is largely absent from LTS studies, is the users, who are treated as passive recipients of system-builders' products. The importance of user groups may still be marginal in some aspects of network management, but their degree of involvement is growing rapidly in selected parts of the networks. This development has been precipitated by measures of demand side management (DSM), by resistance to price increases and perceived mismanagement and by the impact of new techniques. This third factor is particularly visible in the case of local storm water percolation, where the introduction of a new technology has drawn several new actor groups – house-owners, architects, property developers and parks departments – into the process of designing and operating part of a technical network. Here, we can speak of new techniques themselves reordering the social organization of a technological system (Mayntz, 1993).

By involving user groups, the LTS approach can be significantly strengthened. Our study of local storm-water management offers clear evidence of the growing number of involved actors, the redistribution of roles in some subsystems of the networks and new forms of interaction between actor groups. We have observed here how house-owners and, to a lesser extent, parks departments have effectively become operators of a small part of the waste water disposal network, taking over responsibilities previously borne by the utility. Through their operation of local percolation systems, certain user communities have gained empowerment over the way they use rainwater and – in the probable future – over the size of their water bill (cf Galambos, 1991, p181). Conversely, occupiers of densely built housing in inner city areas stand to be excluded from this empowerment, since they often have no option to percolate rainwater. The problem of managing the transition to local percolation in Berlin's urban development sites has also revealed the importance of closer interaction between the utility and the other key actor groups to reach agreement on the redistribution of responsibilities under the new technology. To take another example of interaction: in the case of redirecting treated effluent upstream, we have noted how shared interests – as over effluent percolation outside the city – create the potential for new and sometimes unexpected alliances between actor groups with very different functions of water management.

Obstacles to change?

Explaining forces for change to technical networks in terms of reverse salients is helpful in pinpointing the obstacles that block the development of a large technological system in a certain direction. LTS theory is right in emphasizing that these reverse salients can be technological (such as technical deficiencies or network stress) or socio-economic in nature (such as consumer pressures or changing competitive conditions) (Summerton, 1994, pp12–13). In our case study of water stress in the Berlin region, for instance, the principal reverse salients can be defined as pollution and political pressure for improved water quality.

Where the concept of reverse salients is less helpful is in explaining how technical systems adapt to shifts in their context of operation. In a situation where several key factors are changing simultaneously and in interaction with one another, it is misleading to speak of individual factors 'holding back' or disrupting the development trajectory of a technological system. This is the case in Berlin, where the new contextual forces include, primarily, stricter environmental standards, declining water consumption, greater commercialization of the Berlin water utility, cuts in public subsidies and the improved viability of new technologies.

These new 'signals' are altering the logic underpinning each water-recycling scheme, causing some projects to be shelved and others to be pursued with greater vigour, often under a rather different rationale. We can see, for example, how the fall in water consumption and the possible removal of subsidies have, first, caused groundwater replenishment not to be extended to eastern Berlin and, second, to be jeopardized even in western Berlin. In the cases of redirecting treated effluent we can observe how the rationales underpinning each project are shifting from securing Berlin's water supply to saving costs (for example on additional sewage treatment) and protecting local, water-based ecosystems.

What these examples illustrate further is that it is not just the shifting context that creates the need for change, but the way it alters actors' perceptions of infrastructure problems. A combination of new factors can cause a key actor group to define a problem differently, to focus on another problem or to reprioritize problems. The new positions thus reached become themselves a force for reordering a technological system. Put in terms of LTS theory, if we do talk of reverse salients, it is important to include not only real, 'objective' barriers, as Hughes has argued, but also actors' perceptions of where problems lie (Summerton, 1994, pp12-13).

Network flexibility

The final section of the analysis relates to the concept of momentum and its consequences for the flexibility of a technological system. A large technological system acquires 'momentum' as it develops; a term selected because it encapsulates the growing 'mass' of components and 'velocity' of growth. Further, the concept of momentum avoids the notion of autonomous technological development, permitting consideration of the social construction of technology. This approach to the persistency of technological systems, including socio-economic forces, is helpful in widening the range of explanations for sudden breaks in the advancement of a specific technology. The reasons may well not be technical at all. The LTS approach is also right to point to system-builders as major contributors to the momentum of a technological system, seeking to defend their vested interests by preserving the stability of the dominant system.

While the basic concept of momentum relates well to the persistency of dominant technological systems, it tells us little about how these systems adapt to changing pressures. The general argument is that LTS grow increasingly inflexible to change as they develop and that where a reverse salient cannot be solved within a system, a 'battle of systems' ensues, resulting perhaps in the replacement of one large technological system by another. This image is highly conflictual, suggesting not only a high degree of competition, but also of incompatibility between different systems or their components. A classic example of (assumed) incompatibility is between 'hard', high-tech solutions (for example centralized sewage treatment plant) and 'soft', low-tech solutions (for example reed-bed sewage treatment). Our case study supports a contrary view, voiced by Jane Summerton and others, that many new 'soft' technologies are neither technically nor economically incompatible with existing systems, but that they may appear incompatible in the minds of many system-builders (Summerton, 1994, p10).

Local storm-water percolation is a good example of this. The technology, promoted by environmentalists, was long dismissed by water managers as unsuitable for urban settlements for technical reasons. As the technology matured, unit costs of production fell and the problem of storm-water run-off rose on the political agenda, both the water utility and the environmental regulator in Berlin changed their tune and now actively support the technology. Some of the technical concerns still remain (for example, relating to the reduced water flow in combined sewer systems), but they are considered less important than the potential benefits of the scheme. Furthermore, the new technology has not replaced the existing system, nor is it seen as competing with the centralized sewer network. Instead, local storm-water percolation can improve the existing system by relieving the sewer network and saving investment costs on retention basins.

This case study suggests that the process of transition in technological systems can be less conflictual than is widely assumed. Certainly, competition between technologies and between other components of technological systems does exist and can, indeed, be exacerbated by new commercial pressures. However, initial rivalry between two or more technologies may rest on perceptions of incompatibility and these perceptions may alter in time, as contextual factors change. There is evidence of a surprising degree of flexibility in technical networks, even those which are well established and have – in LTS rhetoric – a strong momentum. The fact that infrastructure management in the Berlin region, as elsewhere in Germany, is currently in a phase of post-expansion, readjusting to saturated networks, suggests that this phase of LTS development is even less 'closed' to change than earlier stages of growth and consolidation.

CONCLUSIONS

The development of large technological systems like urban utility networks needs to be viewed against the backdrop of societal changes, which are constantly, if subtly, altering the context within which decisions on infrastructure are made. This appears particularly important today, as utility services across Europe are coming under pressure to adapt in the face of such forces as liberalization, public sector cutbacks and new environmental regulation. Even the choice of technology will in future need to respect the shifting conditions. It is, however, difficult to grasp how these various forces for change operate in an abstract setting. As the cases of this chapter indicate, it is essential to appreciate the local or urban context in order to understand the importance attached to each signal and how they combine to shape developments in a particular direction. Above all, it will be important in future to respond to the growing role of user groups, not just as passive recipients of utility services, but as actors with considerable potential to influence the way technical networks are used, either by reducing consumption or by 'operating' small parts of a network themselves.

At the same time we need to recognize that radical technological change does not necessarily lead to conflict between competing styles of management. While the existence of competition between technologies and the systems they represent is undeniable, evidence suggests that a change of circumstances can increase the compatibility of competing technologies and the openness of existing technological systems to adaptation. Thus, rather than assuming incompatibilities between, say, high-tech and low-tech solutions, which could overlook possible synergies for environmental protection, we should be looking at new openings for technological linkage created by the recent transformation of infrastructure management. Incompatibilities between technologies or other components of a large technological system may not be real or even rational but may rest on the perceptions of actors. Since the consequences of actor viewpoints can, however, be very real, it is necessary to reflect on the values attached to a particular aspect of network management by the relevant actor groups. By developing an awareness for the sensitivities of specific groups, it will be easier to avoid friction and dispel misunderstandings over network change. Moreover, by exploring and comparing actors' motives, it may be possible to detect common interests not immediately visible.

ACKNOWLEDGEMENTS

I would like to thank Dr Ursula Krause and Corinna Kennel for their help in researching this chapter.

REFERENCES

Bijker, W E, Hughes, T P and Pinch, T J (1989) *The Social Construction of Technological Systems. New Directions in the Sociology and History of Technology*, MIT Press, Cambridge, Massachusetts

Bijker, W E and Law J (1992) *Shaping Technology/Building Society. Studies in Sociotechnical Change*, MIT Press, Cambridge, Massachusetts

BWB (Berliner Wasser Betriebe) (1997) *Geschäftsbericht 1996*, BWB, Berlin

Dorau, W (1990) 'Mit technischen Maßnahmen der Wasseraufbereitung den ökologischen Wasserkreislauf im Kleinen nachahmen', in Senatsverwaltung für Stadtentwicklung und Umweltschutz (ed) *Umwelt- und Naturschutz für Berliner Gewässer*, vol 8, Senatsverwaltung für Stadtentwicklung und Umweltschutz, Berlin, pp181–199

Galambos, L (1991) 'A View from Economic History', in T R La Porte (ed) *Social Responses to Large Technical Systems. Control or Anticipation*, Kluwer Academic Publishers, Dortrecht, pp177–181

Gökalp, I (1992) 'On the Analysis of Large Technical Systems', *Science, Technology and Human Values*, vol 17, no 1, pp57–78

Guy, S, Graham, S and Marvin, S (1997) 'Splintering Networks: Cities and Technical Networks in 1990s Britain', *Urban Studies*, vol 34, no 2, pp191–216

Hughes, T (1983) *Networks of Power: Electrification in Western Society 1880–1930*, Johns Hopkins University Press, Baltimore

Hughes, T (1987) 'The Evolution of Large Technological Systems', in W E Bijker, T P Hughes and T Pinch (eds) *The Social Construction of Technological Systems*, MIT Press, Cambridge, Massachusetts, pp51–82

Mayntz, R (1993) 'Grosse technische Systeme und ihre gesellschaftstheoretische Bedeutung', *Kölner Zeitschrift für Soziologie und Sozialpsychologie*, vol 45, no 1, pp97–108

Moss, T (2000) 'Unearthing Water Flows, Uncovering Social Relations: Introducing New Waste Water Technologies in Berlin', *Journal of Urban Technology*, vol 7, no 1, pp63–84

MUNR/SenStadtUm (Ministerium für Umwelt, Naturschutz und Raumordnung des Landes Brandenburg and Senatsverwaltung für Stadtentwicklung und Umweltschutz Berlin) (1994) *Wasserwirtschaftlicher Rahmenplan Berlin und Umland. Entwurf,* Kulturbuch Verlag, Berlin

Schulze, D (1993) 'Naturnahe Grundwasseranreicherung – Ein Beitrag zur Sicherung der Wasserversorgung des Großraumes Berlin', *Wasser + Boden*, vol 4, pp220–224

Schulze, D (1997) 'Wassermengenwirtschaft im Ballungsraum Berlin. Probleme und Lösungsansätze', lecture at seminar 'Wasserkrise in der Region Berlin/Brandenburg?' April

Summerton, J (1994) 'Introductory Essay: The Systems Approach to Technological Change', in J Summerton (ed) *Changing Large Technical Systems*, Westview Press, Colorado, pp1–21

INTERVIEWS

Representative of Senate Department for Urban Development, Environmental Protection and Technology (SenSUT), Water Authority, General Planning Department, 1 August 1997

Representative of Berlin water utility (BWB), Corporate Planning Department, 6 August 1997

Representative of *Berliner Stadtgüter* (owners of several former irrigation beds), 8 October 1997

Representatives of District Council of Teltow-Fläming, Environment Department, 10 October 1997

Representative of Berlin water utility (BWB), Network Construction Department, 28 October 1997

4 DECENTRALIZED TECHNOLOGY IN CENTRALIZED NETWORKS: INTERPRETATIVE FLEXIBILITY OF RAINWATER PERCOLATION IN COPENHAGEN

Susanne Balslev Nielsen

INTRODUCTION

Within the last 10 years there has been an increasing interest in small-scale solutions to technical and environmental problems in Danish cities. The numbers of green buildings where many of these small-scale technologies are used have increased dramatically and the ideas of decentralized solutions have spread from the alternative environmental movement to the more formal arena of municipal utility service. Recent interest in environmental issues and new demands on sewage treatment have reopened the debate about the sustainability of current treatment systems. Until recently the sewage system has been taken for granted and the rationale of draining rainwater within the system has not been questioned. But the environmental problems within the existing systems and the interests in implementing small-scale technologies have created an opportunity for reordering the municipal sewage systems by implementing infiltration trenches. Yet there is very little understanding of the socio-technical implications of implementing decentralized technologies such as infiltration trenches in large technological systems like the sewer system. This chapter examines the technological and social incentives that, according to flow managers, support or hinder the process of implementing a small-scale technology in a large-scale system. Through a case study of two Danish municipalities this chapter analyses the different technological frames shaping the implementation process. It concludes by examining why infiltration trenches have been implemented in the case of Hillerød and not in the case of Roskilde.

Water Stress in Copenhagen: SCOT

Storm-water pollution in central sewerage systems

Storm water is a problem for central sewerage systems because of the variation in the flow of water. The first generation of sewerage systems in Denmark entailed combined networks with sewage and storm water mixed in a single pipe. These were constructed with overflows to local waterways to take the pressure off the system and avoid local floods in situations when the flow of sewage and storm water exceeded the capacity of the pipes. In practice this meant that a mixture of sewage and storm water was discharged directly into a stream, a lake or another kind of receiving body of water. In contrast, the second generation of sewerage systems are independent systems where sewage and storm water are drained in separate pipes. Although storm water is still discharged to water courses at peak times, the environmental and aesthetic problems are reduced because the discharge consists only of storm water. The national water plan (Minsitry of Environment and Energy, 1987) set new targets for sewage treatment to improve the quality of water discharged to recipient bodies of water. Municipalities were obliged to revise their sewage treatment plans and to upgrade the technical network to meet the new demands. Today the municipalities have upgraded the most critical aspects of their sewerage systems, but they still need to reduce the overflow from some parts of the sewer network. Avoiding the entry of rainwater into the treatment system is top on the list of problems facing Danish sewage treatment plants. Most municipalities have a sewerage system where some parts are combined systems and other parts are separate systems. The problem of overflow is generally connected to the areas with combined systems, which, on a national basis, are about 50 per cent of all sewerage systems in urban areas. To reduce the level of overflow of diluted sewage, the conventional solution is to build a retention basin for storing storm water until spare capacity is released at the treatment plant. An alternative solution is to percolate the storm water into the ground, avoiding the storm water entering the sewerage system.

There is now renewed interest in infiltration trenches for percolating storm water from roofs. Until recently it was illegal to use infiltration trenches in areas with central sewerage systems but the Ministry of Environment and Energy now recommend storm-water percolation (Miljøstyrelsen, 1995). There seems to be a general consensus that storm water should be percolated when it is possible. But beneath this consensus there are very different arguments for implementing infiltration trenches. The present status is that many municipalities are positive towards the use of infiltration trenches for percolating roof run-off but very few have yet taken action to actually implement infiltration trenches systematically in their sewage management. There appear to be very few structural barriers to the implementation of infiltration trenches because storm water is regarded as a general problem within the existing sewerage systems, the technology is available, legislation has been changed in favour of storm-water percolation and the municipalities have to make exceptionally large investments in the upgrading of their sewerage system. Few municipalities have used infiltration trenches to meet new demands on sewage treatment, indicating that the critical factor of the implementation process is the local context rather than structural conditions.

Social construction of technology

The theory of social construction of technology (SCOT) explains technological development by emphasizing the role of social actors and local context. SCOT offers an analytical frame to identify the technological and social incentives that support or hinder the implementation process, which emphasizes that actors have different perceptions of whether infiltration trenches can be implemented in a conventional sewerage system. SCOT views technology as a social construction and technological development as the result of conflicting interests between different actors, individuals or groups. The researcher's task is, therefore, to uncover the actors' interests and strategies. The theory of SCOT was originally developed to describe the historical development of one single technology (Pinch and Bijker, 1987). However the theory offers a basic understanding of technological development from which an analysis of more complex technological systems like technical networks can benefit (eg Hansen, 1997; Hoffmann, 1997; Nielsen, 1998).

A SCOT analysis consists of three steps. The first step is a deconstruction of the relevant actor groups' different perceptions of the artefact. The second step is an analysis of the negotiation processes among the actors involved. The aim is to describe the competing understandings of the artefacts and reveal the openings and closures of the negotiations. An opening is a phase where the negotiation opens for new interpretations and closure is a phase where some interpretations are excluded from the negotiations. The final step is a generalization of the competing perceptions of the artefact influencing the development process. The Municipality of Roskilde and the Municipality of Hillerød are the cases considered for this analysis of the implementation process. Both municipalities are located in the Copenhagen area. Roskilde is still in the preliminary phase of implementing infiltration trenches whereas Hillerød is more advanced in the implementation process than most Danish municipalities and has already incorporated the systematic use of infiltration trenches in a municipal sewage plan.

ROSKILDE: INFILTRATION TRENCHES AND AGENDA 21

The municipality of Roskilde has nearly finished a massive upgrading of the sewer system that includes construction of retention basins, pipe renovation and improvements to the sewage treatment plant, and is now close to fulfilling its goals for the reduction of overflow. Although infiltration trenches have not been included in the strategy there is now a significant debate about their future role, particularly in the context of Local Agenda 21 activities. The negotiations about infiltration trenches are mainly between two groups of technicians and a group of urban planners, all within the municipality.

The system designers

The system designers are situated in the construction department where they have been responsible for designing the upgrading of the sewerage system. This has been a very challenging task, which has brought vitality into the department, and the system designers are very proud of the present system. They accept that the use of infiltration trenches is beneficial when the option of central solutions is non-existent. But in the particular local context they argue that the trenches are too expensive, too complicated and the effect of an infiltration trench too small compared with the conventional solutions.

The environmental planners

The environmental planners, based in the environment department, are responsible for operating the system once it is established and working. Within the last 5–10 years there has been an increasing interest in preventing environmental problems and trying alternative solutions to the conventional sewerage systems. According to the environmental planners this is a very positive development which means that the municipality must adopt new technologies and new management practices. Even though the sewerage system is upgraded to current standards and demands, the environmental planners support the implementation of infiltration trenches. The reasons are, firstly, it improves the local environment because it reduces the number of overflows to Roskilde Fjord and contributes to local groundwater regeneration. Secondly, it improves the functioning of the existing system because it reduces the risk of flooded basements caused by local capacity problems in the drains and reduces the strain on the sewage treatment plant. Thirdly, it provides an alternative to economic investment in the enlargement of the only treatment plant that is close to its maximum capacity. Finally, infiltration trenches are a more visible solution than the large central systems, creating local awareness of environmental issues. The environmental planners are keen to develop demonstration projects of infiltration trenches.

The urban planners

The Agenda 21 Plan (1997) is the latest document in a number of plans to improve the environmental perspective of the municipality of Roskilde. The first environmental plan in 1990 focused on municipal utilities but since then new aspects have been added to the environmental plans and recently also the aim of participation of users and citizens. The urban planners are supportive of infiltration trenches because they are a decentralized technology, highly visible in the urban environment and they are simple to construct and explain. Even though the urban planners and the politicians are positive towards infiltration trenches it should be noted that the idea of infiltration trenches is only one of many ideas listed in the Agenda 21 Plan. It is proposed that a demonstration initiative is developed to test the feasibility of infiltration trenches.

The choice between infiltration trenches and retention basins

According to the sewage planners in Roskilde, they had no choice between infiltration trenches or retention basins, due to limitations set by the existing sewerage system. The amount of storm water from the urban areas with combined systems was too large to be handled by percolation. Due to the physical structure of the urban area it is impossible to establish the necessary volume of infiltration trenches. Such a strategy would need acceptance from the landowners and this was impossible to get within the given time limit. Even though infiltration trenches were not implemented in the upgrading strategy the environmental planners argued that they should be constructed in new settlements to aid ground-water regeneration and reduce the risk of local floods. But the system designers rejected the use of infiltration trenches in new settlements because they argue it is still necessary to establish a pipe system to handle storm water from other surfaces like roads. The cost of constructing infiltration trenches is still more expensive than the savings from constructing a storm-water pipe with reduced dimensions. Within existing settlements with sewer systems the use of infiltration trenches is far more problematic according to the system designers. If the existing system is a combined system, there is a risk of pipes blocking due to insufficient amounts of water to flush away the solid waste and there is a risk of damp basements due to local percolation. The system designers also question the rationale of making new investments in alternative systems when the investments in the present system have still not been paid back.

HILLERØD: INFILTRATION TRENCHES AS JOB TRAINING

The case of Hillerød differs from the case of Roskilde because the implementation process is more advanced and because the construction of infiltration trenches has been organized as a job-training project. When the municipality of Hillerød was revising its sewage plan in 1992 to meet new standards for the water quality of the aquatic environment, Tue Tortzen, a local politician, saw an opportunity to realize his idea of creating job-training and environmental improvements with the construction of infiltration trenches. At first there was general resistance to the idea. Construction was stopped by the state administration for two years because the project was claimed to be illegal. The obstacle was a restriction on the sewage fund, which prevented the use of funds for projects on private property. The legislation has since been revised so the municipality can repay a part of the connection fee if the house owners agree to percolate their roof run-off and cut off the connection to the public sewer system. The job-training project is now a permanent scheme in Hillerød. There have been more actors involved in the implementation process in Hillerød because the process is much more advanced than in Roskilde. The focus in this case study is primarily on the municipal sewage managers, although the viewpoints of house owners, the job-training team, the county and others are also mentioned.

The politicians

Tue Tortzen is the politician who introduced infiltration trenches into the debate on the upgrading of the sewage system. His priority was to combine job creation with environmental protection, and the upgrading of the sewerage system was an opportunity to realize this aim. At first the local politicians were divided in their attitude towards the proposal. One critical voice claimed it would be disrespectful to send unemployed people to construct infiltration trenches without the house owners' approval. Others were worried about the economic costs. Most were not interested in whether the new standards were met by the proposed small-scale solution or by the conventional large-scale solution. When the economic assessment showed that infiltration trenches in some cases were less expensive than retention basins, the majority of the Committee of Environment and Technology agreed on a strategy of retention basins in the most critical areas and a trial period to examine if construction of infiltration trenches could avoid new investments in retention basins in areas with less need of retention volume.

The job-training managers

The Social Committee and the job-training department reacted positively towards the idea of constructing infiltration trenches as a job-training project. The municipality is, by law, obliged to create job training and, with a high unemployment rate, any good ideas are welcomed. First, construction of infiltration trenches was a meaningful job that addressed a technical and environmental problem within the existing sewerage system. Second, the job-training team needed few qualifications to carry out the job, the construction was easy for the participants to relate to and it gave potential for personal interaction with the house owners. Finally, it was a relatively inexpensive way of offering job training. When the financial basis of the project became insecure owing to restrictions on the expenditure of the sewage fund, the Social Committee offered to pay not only the wages but also all materials and operation costs during the construction period.

The sewage planners

The sewage planners' first draft of the sewage plan included the construction of retention basins and excluded infiltration trenches. Yet the idea of infiltration trenches was positively received in the sewage department where the head of the department had personal experience of the percolation of storm water in earlier employment. The sewage planners view infiltration trenches as one of two means for meeting the demands on the reduction of overflow. Since the problems of overflow of diluted sewage relate to areas of combined sewers, the sewage planners were only interested in infiltration trenches in these areas. In areas of combined sewers there is possibly a technical and economic interest in reducing the need for retention basins.

The choice between infiltration trenches and retention basins

Tue Tortzen's vision was to provide all houses with infiltration trenches instead of retention basins to meet new demands on water quality in streams and to create jobs. But the sewage engineers argued that infiltration trenches could not replace retention basins in general due to technical conditions in the existing system. After negotiations the politicians agreed on a strategy whereby some of the smaller retention basins in the original plan proposed by the sewage department were postponed in order to construct infiltration trenches. The largest retention basins were still to be built. The construction of infiltration trenches was initiated as an experiment. Evaluation of the test period came out in favour of infiltration trenches and the municipality made construction of the trenches a permanent job-training scheme. The sewage department estimates that the job-training team will establish about 50 infiltration trenches a year. A major issue in the debate on infiltration trenches was the cost compared with retention basins. Detailed calculations showed that infiltration trenches were less expensive than closed retention basins of less than 300 m^3. Tue Tortzen argues that these economic benefits need to be seen in a wider perspective and include: environmental benefits, mobilization of environmental awareness; and savings on the job-training account.

Planning infiltration trenches is a new social process for the sewage department. Because the house owners' participation is voluntary, the sewage department runs campaigns to find volunteers. Information sheets, adverts and articles in newspapers were used to identify 150 volunteers. Despite the campaign and the positive responses from the first house owners to receive an infiltration trench, the sewage department has not had as many responses as it had hoped for. At the same time there is pressure from the county and a local environmental organization to finish the upgrading of the sewage system as quickly as possible. Another problem is that the established infiltration trenches are spread over the whole town so that the concentration of infiltration trenches is too low to replace retention basins. The second campaign was focused on one specific road where information sheets were handed out to all houses. However, this was not very successful either and the head of the sewage department has found it difficult to mobilize the necessary interest of house owners. New campaigns will still focus on a specific area but Tue Tortzen argues that the ideal is to spread information by word of mouth all over the town.

COMPARATIVE ANALYSIS

The case study of Roskilde and Hillerød shows that actors have very different approaches towards implementation of infiltration trenches, and the actors' perceptions of the conditions for implementing infiltration trenches depend on their local context. Three different technological frames appear in the negotiations in Roskilde and Hillerød with very different interests in the sewerage system and, in particular, in the implementation of infiltration trenches (see Table 4.1). Within the *technical frame* infiltration trenches is one means among others for optimizing the performance of existing large-scale systems. The introduction of infiltration trenches is only useful when it is a less expen-

Table 4.1 *Three Different Technological Frames of Storm-Water Management*

	Technical Frame	Ecological frame	Job-training frame
Aim of the sewerage system	An effective and robust drainage system	An environmentally friendly water cycle	Interesting and qualifying job training
Problems of the existing network	Capacity problems in drainage system and the sewage treatment plant and the need to meet environmental demands	Environmental problems: water quality of receiving water body; regional water cycle Lack of user involvement	Little potential for job training
Benefits of infiltration trenches	Reduces risk of overflow and need for retention basins	Local percolation of storm water and regeneration of groundwater Draws local attention to storm water	Job-training qualities: practical work, simple to construct, teamwork, contact with house owners
Disadvantages of infiltration trenches	Many small construction projects need house owners' approval Maintenance problem Uncertainties about the risk of groundwater pollution and the effect of concentrated sewage Time scale	Hinders collection of rainwater for substituting drinking water	Dependence on house owners' interest
Potential areas for infiltration trenches	New settlements or areas with critical capacity problems	All areas where the soil is suitable	All areas where house owners are interested, where the soil is suitable and the necessary space is available

Source: DTU

sive solution than retention basins. Within the *ecological frame* the use of infiltration trenches is an end in itself because it is a small-scale, environmentally friendly solution. Even though the effect of a few infiltration trenches is small when compared with the total water flow, the use of infiltration trenches is important as a symbol of a sustainable sewerage system based on new principles of local water cycles. In the *job-training frame* the interest in infiltration trenches is construction and solving technical problems in a way that creates jobs for people with low educational skills.

The technical and ecological frames are the dominant technological frames in Roskilde. The system designers are primarily oriented towards the technical frame, the urban planners work within the ecological frame in the LA21 plan and the environmental planners are oriented towards both the technical and the ecological frames. In the case of Hillerød, the job-training frame exists parallel to the technical and ecological frames. Even though some actors mainly belong to the technical frames, the consensus around job training means that all actors are involved in all three technological frames.

The process of implementing infiltration trenches has developed differently in the cases of Roskilde and Hillerød. First, we consider the origin of the initiative to implement infiltration trenches. The process of implementing infiltration trenches started in Hillerød in 1992 when Tue Tortzen managed to raise the issue on the local political agenda in the context of job training. Even though he was the initiating actor, other circumstances were decisive for his success. The most striking factor is that the city council was about to decide on major investments in upgrading the sewerage system, and the solution of infiltration trenches appeared to be economically beneficial. But it was probably just as important that the sewage planners who had to carry out the administrative work had a positive attitude towards the idea. In contrast, the new demands on sewage treatment did not open the negotiations on infiltration trenches in Roskilde. Instead, the relatively recent debate has been opened by an increasing interest in storm-water percolation in the context of a LA21 project.

Second, we can compare the actors involved. During the long process in Hillerød many different actors have been involved in different phases of the project. The job-training project is now a permanent scheme with a high degree of support. Because so many actors have been involved, the network in support of the project is relatively strong. One central factor in the process of reaching consensus in Hillerød was the local opposition to current legislation. When the job-training project was claimed to be illegal local politicians stood together to fight the cause of a project with economic, environmental and job-training benefits. In this phase local disagreements faded and former opponents of the project became supporters. At this point it is the lack of interest among house owners that is slowing down the process. In Roskilde the debate on infiltration trenches has, until now, included only a few actor groups, while the politicians and the house owners have only had a peripheral role. This means that the implementation process is still at a rather fragile phase in Roskilde.

Third, we look at the changing status of the sewerage network. The fact that infiltration trenches became a part of the solution in an upgrading problem in Hillerød made it much easier to proceed to implementation. The existing sewerage system was about to change and Tue Tortzen managed to exploit this pressure by making implementation of infiltration trenches a part of the negotiations on the budget. In Roskilde the same pressure did not exist, because the upgrading plan had already been developed. Even though they still need to build the last small retention basins, the technicians claim they have missed the opportunity of making infiltration trenches a part of upgrading. At this point it is too late to reopen the negotiations on the upgrading plan.

Finally, we compare the strategies for implementing infiltration trenches. The strategy in Hillerød developed a combination of retention basins and infiltration trenches. In Roskilde the sewage planners claim they do not have this possibility because they already have invested in retention basins. When they say it is not possible it is because the negotiations on the upgrading plans are at an advanced phase and they are not likely to reopen. In principle the negotiations could be reopened if the arguments for an alternative solution were strong enough, but the time scale, the high number of infiltration trenches and the house owners' voluntary participation are planning conditions which are not in favour of infiltration trenches. Although the Hillerød case has been the most successful in terms of implementing infiltration trenches, they have exceeded the time limit given by the county for compliance with the new water standards. In contrast, Roskilde has acted within the given time scale. The uncertain time scales of project implementation are an important constraint on the development of network management based on small-scale solutions with user involvement.

CONCLUSIONS

This case study has examined the technological and social incentives that, according to flow managers, support or hinder the process of implementing a small-scale technology in a large-scale system, using the infiltration trenches for percolation of roof run-off as an example of a small-scale technology. Flow managers have different perceptions of the need for small-scale technologies like infiltration trenches. In the negotiations in Roskilde and Hillerød we identified three different technological frames – a technical, an ecological and a job-training frame – with different perceptions of the problem, aims, means and criteria for success. In Hillerød it was the job-training frame which originally brought infiltration trenches onto the political agenda. Because infiltration trenches had a meaning within an ecological and technical frame as well, it was relatively easy to create a consensus around the project. In Roskilde, on the other hand, a job-training frame is non-existent and the technical frame dominated the upgrading plan. Because the present system already fulfils the new standards for sewage treatment the pressure for changing the sewerage network is reduced.

Small-scale technologies like infiltration trenches are often excluded from the management of large technological systems. In Hillerød as well as in Roskilde the original plan met new demands with a large-scale solution like large retention basins. Tue Tortzen managed to initiate a deviation from the conventional planning strategy in the context of job training. The cases show that technologies like infiltration trenches are more than a matter of technique and that decentralized technologies can be implemented for different purposes from only technical ones. A choice of deviating from the conventional planning strategy by implementing decentralized technologies in centralized systems is a process where the opportunities as well as the barriers are likely to exist in a specific local context. Because of the dependency on the local context it is not possible to generalize the level of compatibility between the large-scale system and a specific decentralized technology.

The case of rainwater percolation shows that even if the decentralized technology is technically simple and well known, at least in a historical perspective, the implementation process is still very complex and sensitive towards different kinds of emerging barriers. The case of Hillerød shows that house owners' participation appears to be a critical factor in the implementation process. One reason why house owners hesitate to volunteer could be a high degree of user resistance at the household level. Despite the different incentives presented to the house owner, this possible resistance is not overcome. Another reason could be that relations between individual households and the sewage managers were too weak to make the house owners commit themselves. To prove decentralized technologies to be reliable solutions it is important to change sewage management in order to overcome this kind of barrier by using other tools and planning methods to establish new relations and develop new social networks around a partially decentralized technical system.

REFERENCES

Hansen, K H (1997) *Den sociale konstruktion af miljørigtig projektering* (*Cleaner Technological Changes in the Danish Building and Construction Industry*, with English summary), Department of Planning, Technical University of Denmark, Lyngby

Hoffmann, B (1997) *Affald er jo ikke noget vi taler om* (*We don't talk about waste*, with English summary), Department of Planning, Technical University of Denmark, Lyngby

Miljøstyrelsen (1995) *Spildevandsredegørelse 1995*, Miljøstyrelsen, København

Ministry of Environment and Energy (1987) *Beretning om vandmiljøplanen*, Ministry of Environment and Energy, Copenhagen, Denmark

Nielsen, S B (1998) *Omstilling af teknisk infrastruktur: Ph.d.-afhandling* (*Changing technical infrastructure*, with English summary), Department of Planning, Technical University of Denmark, Lyngby

Pinch, L T J and Bijker, W E (1987) 'The Social Construction of Facts and Artifacts: Or How the Sociology of Science and the Sociology of Technology Might Benefit Each Other', in W E Bijker, Hughes, T P, Pinch, T J (eds) *The Social Construction of Technological Systems*, MIT Press, Cambridge, Massachusetts

INTERVIEWS

A representative from Hillerød Municipality, 21 October 1997

A representative from the environmental department, Hillerød Municipality, 14 October 1997

An engineer in the sewage department, Hillerød Municipality, 4 July 1997, September and 14 October 1997

A representative from Frederiksborg County, sewage department, 16 October 1997

A politician and member of the Committee of Environment and Technology (Tue Tortzen), Hillerød Municipality, 18 August 1997

An engineer in the construction department, Roskilde Municipality, 23 September 1997

An engineer in the department of water supply, Roskilde Municipality

An environmental planner in the department of sewage and environment, Roskilde Municipality, 10 July 1997 (and September)

An urban planner in the department of planning, Roskilde Municipality, 17 September 1997

5 RESTABILIZING A HETEROGENEOUS NETWORK: THE YORKSHIRE DROUGHT 1995–96

Suzie Osborn and Simon Marvin

INTRODUCTION

West Yorkshire had been experiencing below-average rainfall throughout the winter of 1994/1995 and by the beginning of the summer of 1995 reservoirs were not even half their usual depth and rivers were beginning to run dry. The Regional Water Company, Yorkshire Water, responsible for providing clean water to 1.5 million customers in the area, experienced great difficulty meeting demand. By October 1995 things were so bad that customers were implored to save water, trial standpipes were erected and unprecedented water rationing was threatened (Harrison, 1996). Local businesses and schools were even being asked to evacuate the most severely affected areas and relocate elsewhere! The health and livelihood of the people in the region were being threatened. So, too, was the local aquatic environment. The water industry's environmental regulator, the Environment Agency, along with local fishermen and naturalists, were highly concerned about the impact that low water levels and associated poor water quality were having on local wildlife, particularly on fish stocks.

But exhortations to customers to reduce their water consumption failed and the drought got worse. Rain continued to ignore Yorkshire's thirst and as the 'crisis' assumed national importance Yorkshire Water was forced to buy water from neighbouring regions and tanker it into the worst hit areas by road at the cost of some £50 million. In the aftermath of the crisis Yorkshire Water 'strengthened' its water supply network in the hope that this unfortunate situation would not occur again. The company made its network more robust by building a large-scale transfer pipe through which water from the more water-rich areas of the north east of England could be transported to the drought-prone neighbouring county of West Yorkshire in times of future water stress.

The vulnerability of water infrastructure only becomes apparent when something goes seriously wrong. The West Yorkshire drought in 1995/96 developed into a crisis that raised major technical, social and environmental issues about the future development of the water infrastructure in the region. This chapter uses insights from the actor network approach to analyse the breakdown and subsequent reordering of the water network in Yorkshire. First, we present an explanation of water networks as actor networks and the implications this has for our understanding of the concept of heterogeneity and the relations between animate and inanimate objects. Second, we review the breakdown of the water network in Yorkshire. Third, we examine the initial response of the water company to this destabilization and their unsuccessful attempts to enrol users in the temporary stabilization of the network. Fourth, we examine how new definitions of network robustness led to three forms of reordering, increasing network mobility, durability and calculability. Finally, the conclusions explain how actor network perspectives help us to understand the complexities involved in the restabilization of water infrastructure networks.

WATER NETWORK/ACTOR NETWORK

Modern water supply systems are extremely complex social and technological networks. Major engineering systems capture water, often over a large area involving entire regions, and treat the water for dispersal through immense distribution systems. A high degree of central control and coordination is required to manage and organize these engineering networks. These forms of social organization also embody and express power relations both within the organization and in terms of control over urban form and development. The nature of a settlement pattern and dynamics of urbanization have a central role in shaping water supply. The relative scarcity of water means that different social groups engage in competition for its use and these relations are often translated into specific managerial, technological and institutional systems. Consequently there are different 'ways of seeing' water networks. From an engineering perspective they are technical networks, from a shareholders' perceptive they are economic networks and a hydrologist would see them as natural networks. Each of these different views is usually based on a separation between the 'social', 'technical' and 'natural' dimensions of water networks. An actor network perspective would question the separation between these different dimensions.

Actor network approaches focus on how human actors 'enrol' pieces of technology and machines, as well as documents, texts and money, into 'actor networks', configured across space and time. The central message is that 'modern societies cannot be described without recognizing them as having a fibrous, thread-like, wiry, stringy, ropy, capillary character that is never captured by the notions of levels, layers, territories, spheres, categories, structures, systems' (Latour, 1997, p2). This approach abandons any *a priori* distinctions between the 'social' and the 'technological'. Rather, complex and heterogeneous assemblies of both 'social' and 'technological' actors make up contemporary life. Drawing on Thomas Hughes's (1983) idea that 'society' is a 'seamless' web of socio-technical constructions, the approach rejects firm boundaries between the social and technical in favour of an emphasis on connection, interdependence and mutuality. In this context networked infrastructures are only 'one possible final and stabilized state of an actor network' (Latour, 1997). Infrastructure networks are only able to produce contingent and diverse effects through the ways they link together technology and society to build order. This is a profoundly difficult process requiring continuing efforts to sustain relations that are *both* social and technical. But successfully linking together such arrays of actors over distance requires continuous effort, even within mature 'black-boxed' infrastructures. Connections are always perilous and fragile and never-ending efforts are required to sustain them.

Before the drought the water supply network in Yorkshire appeared and acted as a single and coherent network. The complexity of the network was largely concealed from view because there was sufficient water to meet demand. This apparently simple network was based on the durability of the connections between six sets of actors. The first two are relatively recent – they are regulators and shareholders. The former mobilizes governmental and quasi-governmental officials while the latter mobilizes thousands of shareholders and investors. Their characteristics are well defined: regulators attempt to ensure that various environmental, economic and social standards are met, shareholders to invest and buy shares in the company to ensure it can meet these standards.

The other four actors are: a customer base or consumption/demand that mobilizes millions of customers; rain, which mobilizes trillions of raindrops; a supply augmentation and large-scale transfer capacity; and a distribution system (all of which mobilize thousands of pipes). These actors have well-defined characteristics. The customer base is relied upon to use water in adequate quantities to ensure public health. Rain is to fall in the region in adequate quantities and any shortfalls are to occur in the drier east of the county where surplus water from elsewhere can be transferred. Supply augmentation and large-scale transfer capacity is to enable this transference of surplus water. Distribution capacity is depended upon to distribute water to customers' homes.

The stability of the water supply network relied on the durability of the bonds between these elements in the network. These bonds define the contribution of each element and conversely define the solidity of the construction of the whole; remove, add or alter one of these elements and the whole shifts and changes. In other words, each element is part of a chain that guarantees the proper functioning of the water supply network. The network could be compared to a 'black box' that contains a network of 'black boxes', each of which depends on one another both for their proper functioning as individuals and as a whole (Callon, 1987, p95).

This brings us to our central argument. Stabilization is precarious; it is a process or effect rather than something that can be achieved once and for all. It is never complete, autonomous and final. Social effects are generated in a relational and distributed manner or, to put it another way, any of the bits and pieces assembled into an order are constantly liable to break down or make off on their own disturbing the whole relational effect (Law, 1992, p385). An actor network perspective undermines the notion that we can simply and unproblematically generalize a single, material 'thing' called an infrastructure network, just as it challenges the idea that we can simply generalize a 'city'. Instead, the socio-technical world emerges as a complex picture of change, fragility and interdependencies. This perspective offers new insights into the complex socio-technical negotiations that have surrounded the development, maintenance and reconfiguration of infrastructure networks.

BREAKDOWN OF THE WATER NETWORK

The Yorkshire drought caused a breakdown in the water network that put industry, education and health services at risk. The breakdown revealed social and technical complexities that were previously hidden under the old relational circumstances of a stabilized network. Critically, there had been no need for this heterogeneity and complexity to be an issue and no need to look 'beyond' the network before the drought as long as the entities remained stable. The drought did, however, bring three new complexities into view.

Firstly, the drought revealed that rainfall, contrary to previous beliefs, could fall short in the typically wetter west but remain relatively abundant in the typically drier east. What then became starkly apparent was that intra-regional transfer capacities were inadequate to prevent water shortages in the county. Although there had been a plan to construct a regional transfer grid to transport water around the county in all directions, the system had never been completed due to the probability that this would be an unnecessary expense. The 'incompleteness' of the Yorkshire grid only became an issue during the 1995 drought.

Secondly, investigations into the drought now brought leakage rates under much closer scrutiny. Closer investigation revealed that previous knowledge was inaccurate and incomplete. Leakage rates were a lot higher than previously thought and therefore leakage was seen as a significant contribution to the wastage and shortage of water in the region.

The 1995 drought also 'revealed' a third, highly significant, 'new' actor: rising demand. Before the drought it was known that demand had been rising but this had not been an issue. There was a distinct lack of incentive or need to curb rising demand because there was sufficient supply to meet demand. But in the context of the drought Yorkshire Water effectively 'revealed' rising demand by pinpointing it as one of the most important factors in creating the crisis. During the subsequent inquiry demand was brought under closer scrutiny and became the subject of intense controversy.

By revealing these 'new' social, technical and natural actors and subjecting them to closer scrutiny the situation became one of growing instability. The stabilized socio-technical water network that existed before the drought was transformed into a system of ever-increasing heterogeneity. For example, the drought revealed thousands of leaky distribution pipes and 100,000 customers with increasing demand for water. Furthermore, the water-resource network was transformed into a system whose ever-increasing elements that were once easily mastered – or at least thought to be easily mastered – now turned out to be beyond control.

RESTABILIZING THE NETWORK

Yorkshire Water made several attempts to restabilize the network during the drought crisis, each of which required the reordering of different sets of social and technical relations. We focus on two of the most important and notorious: Yorkshire Water's failed attempt to implore customers to reduce their water consumption and the 'face saving' strategy of tankering water into the drought ridden area.

Appealing to the 'public good'

Initially Yorkshire Water appealed to customers to respect the 'public good' in order to lock customers into the roles that had been proposed for them in a water-saving programme. Appealing to the common good was thought to be a robust enrolment device for Yorkshire Water. The relationships envisaged by Yorkshire Water – 'users reducing demand for all' – had been tested before in previous droughts and had been successful. For example a concentrated publicity campaign in North Humberside during the 1992 drought (an area supplied by Yorkshire Water) helped bring home the 'save water' message (Varley, 1992, p12). Appealing to the public good was thought to confirm Yorkshire Water's problematization of the 1995/1996 drought. But the customers targeted by this problematization refused to be enrolled. Households defied calls to stop running baths and watering their gardens and businesses refused to relocate themselves to wetter areas of the county. Indeed some of these users took their own counter-action: they told the company they were letting their taps run continuously!

Customers' identities, motivations and interests were being defined in a strongly 'competitive' manner to the water-saving user being constructed by Yorkshire Water. Importantly the 'competitive' identities of the customers had been formed before the drought and attempts to persuade them to reduce water, under the privatization process. But these identities only became really prominent and were strengthened during the drought. The 'competitive' identity of customers was incubated six years earlier under the growing politi-cization of the management of natural resources in general and in particular the privatization of water supply from a publicly run service to a privately owned business.

Without a direct link to political accountability and indirect regulatory supervision only, disbelief in the market as a suitable mechanism for the management of water – a resource still viewed by consumers (now customers) as a public resource – escalated throughout the early 1990s. The public was simply unconvinced that the privatized water industry was acting in their best interests as opposed to the interests of company shareholders. Rising water prices, declining investment, and service and job shedding were being inevitably linked in the public mind to rising company profits and dividends for shareholders and increased salaries for directors and senior executives (Haughton, 1996, p7). This context defined the identities of customers in increasingly 'competitive' ways to those defined by Yorkshire Water in the problematization of the drought crisis.

During the water crisis in 1995/1996 the changing nature of customers became acutely prominent. Customers were being threatened with water rota cuts and standpipes. In the eyes of the customer the ultimate had happened; they were not only being denied a public right but they were also being denied a commodity that they had paid for. Water supply, after all, was now a market activity (Pearce, 1995). Appealing to the common good was no longer a 'strong' enough device to break this new identity. The strategy had failed; indeed it had the opposite effect to that which it was supposed to, as customers were no longer willing to reduce their consumption of water through involvement in Yorkshire Water's water-conservation strategy.

The failure was strengthened still further by a series of 'tricks' performed by Yorkshire Water which were supposed to create water-saving customers. Two of the most notorious of these counter-productive tricks are worth recalling. One was the Managing Director of Yorkshire Water, Trevor Newton, identifying himself as a water-saving customer by proclaiming that he had not had a bath or shower for three months, only for it to be 'uncovered' by the press that he had been travelling to the Lake District to take a bath at his mother's house (Hosking, 1996). The other was the launching of a campaign to attack the complacency of its own customers by blaming the drought situation on their cultural ignorance (Haughton, 1996, p16). Although not all of the enrolment tricks used by Yorkshire Water were as counter-productive, these two examples were a public-relations disaster and had a significant role in denying Yorkshire Water's attempts to construct water-saving users.

Water Tankering

The failure of Yorkshire Water's water conservation strategy and the worsening of the drought crisis during the summer of 1995 brought in a new actor: central government. Yorkshire Water was called in by the Secretary of State to see why it had failed to regain control of the situation (Haughton, 1996, p14). The government imposed its own construction of the drought crisis on Yorkshire Water; it said that they had to start tankering in water from outside. Tankering was a policy option that had been initially rejected by Yorkshire Water but now the option was reopened and thrust upon them (Field, 1996a).

The tankering story itself brought in an array of new entities into the story: reservoirs and engineers to provide surplus water, lorries and their associated lorry drivers and haulage companies to transport this surplus water and roads and their associated actors to enable this transport. As the operation increased in scale and changed in nature over time, the definition of these sets of actors – the number and nature of their elements – was expanded. During the height of the tankering operation over 600 lorries were required from local, national and international spatial scales (Brearley, 1995). Road use intensified and with it the enrolment of police and their police cars and helicopters. At one point the inside lane of the M62 motorway had to be closed to speed up supplies and police helicopters hovered overhead to monitor tanker movements.

Each of these actors is no more or less important than the others and each relies upon the others for their proper functioning in this new relational pattern. In contrast to the unsuccessful water-conservation strategy the tankering operation defined the nature of actors to be enrolled but did not define their nature in different ways from those they were accustomed to. Essentially, the actors were not being asked to change their role; reservoirs and water companies already supply water, lorries and lorry drivers already transport materials, roads exist to transport vehicles and one of the police's assigned duties is to ensure the proper functioning of that transport. The shaping of these actors coincides almost perfectly with the proposed problematization (Callon, 1986, p209). The tankering operation continued for a month. It ensured supplies and negated the need for water rationing but at a huge cost to Yorkshire Water of £47 million.

REORDERING SOCIO-TECHNICAL NETWORKS

Although the company's appeals to users to save water had failed, tankering only represented a temporary response that was not economically sustainable in the longer term. During 1996 an independent public inquiry examined the causes of the crisis and developed proposals for the longer-term reordering of the network. Recognition that the water network needed to be reordered to create a much more durable set of relational effects raised an important issue. How would the actors know that the network had been successfully reordered? The public inquiry identified new standards for the management of the water supply in Yorkshire. These standards are much more rigorous than those that existed before the drought and are tighter than those for water companies in the rest of the UK. Effectively the network now has to be able to maintain supply to users during the worst drought that could be expected to occur in 100 years. This standard involves 'new' evaluation criteria against which the reordering of the water supply network in Yorkshire will be judged.

Yorkshire Water considered a series of strategies which could operate to increase the water supply network's robustness by generating configurations of network durability, spatial mobility and calculability (Law, 1992, pp387–389). Importantly, each of these strategies could only generate its desired effect and, therefore, was only taken up by Yorkshire Water if a new or altered set of social relations was generated around it. In other words each strategy had to generate different social relations for its 'success' as a process through which to increase network robustness.

Mobility

Network robustness can be increased if relational patterns are extended through space by increasing network mobility (Law, 1992, pp387–388). Network mobility is about ways of acting at a distance. The building of a new pipe to transport water from the north east to Yorkshire increased the robustness of the overall water-supply network by effectively connecting the physical network of Yorkshire into a region with surplus water. The action as it was constructed defined a number of actors who were necessarily concerned with the action. This included a set of regulatory and governmental officials to grant permission for the infrastructure development to proceed, a set of interest groups who would not block the development by appealing to the regulatory and governmental officials, Lyonnaise des Eaux, the water company in Northumbria to provide the water to be transferred, and a set of engineers and pipes to effectively build the pipeline. The construction of the action therefore instigated the enrolment of both social and technical actors but crucially the motivation of these actors coincides almost perfectly with the proposed construction (Callon, 1986, p209). Yorkshire Water successfully extended the mobility, and therefore the robustness, of their network by connecting Yorkshire to the surplus-water capacity in the north east.

Calculability

Measuring and monitoring leakage rates was a further element of the strategy of Yorkshire Water. This would complement the effect of increased network mobility generated by the inter-regional transfer scheme. Reducing leakage is a complementary local strategy to foresee and predict the outcome of the water-supply network and to represent that outcome in a calculable form. Before the drought water supply was meeting demand so Yorkshire Water did not need to (and did not) accurately calculate and present leakage rates. New techniques for detecting leakage were developed and an increased number of technicians and engineers trained in new forms of knowledge and skills to use detection technologies. All these actors as they were defined by Yorkshire Water had to be enrolled into the leakage detection programme for that programme to be a success. Yorkshire Water could therefore increase the robustness of the network by more accurately calculating and representing the performance of the network.

Durability

Embodying relational patterns in durable materials so that they may last longer can also increase network robustness. Before the drought crisis, consumers were considered to be durable materials through which water would continue to be consumed and, conversely, water would continue to be saved in times of drought. In this way they were thought to help stabilize and increase the robustness of the water-supply network. During the drought crisis, therefore, Yorkshire Water pursued a vigorous campaign to encourage customers to reduce their water consumption. But durability is a precarious effect (Law, 1992, p387). Indeed the effects of customers did change when they were located in the new networks of relations under the drought crisis. They could no longer be counted on as durable materials: *they would no longer save water*. Appealing to the common good was unsuccessful in enrolling customers into the identity of 'water-saving user' defined for them by Yorkshire Water. A water conservation programme was therefore not chosen as part of

Yorkshire Water's strategy to increase network robustness in the long term because customers could no longer be relied upon as durable effects.

CONCLUSIONS

Although water networks appear to be relatively stable, this case study has shown that when an inanimate actor (rain) failed to perform its assigned role it severely disrupted the entire socio-technical network. As the network became destabilized, the complexities and the multiplicity of social and technical actors required to hold the network together was revealed. The fragility of the water network became apparent as Yorkshire Water quickly lost control over the network. The company responded by attempting to reorder the network using three strategies to increase the robustness of the network. There were clearly a number of different pathways along which the water network could have been reordered, provided that a particular set of technologies and social relations could be successfully enrolled into the company's construction of the drought.

Initially, the strategy focused on the enrolment of 'water-saving customers' to restabilize the network. While this had been a successful strategy in previous droughts customers now rejected the role that the company had assigned to them. The identity of a water-saving user did not mesh with the reality of privatized water provision, the commodification of water services and the transition from consumers to customers. Because customers could no longer be relied upon to act as durable water savers the company had to reorder the networks in other ways. The network was eventually restabilized by a parallel strategy of increasing network mobility and calculability. Each strategy was a complex socio-technical achievement involving the enrolment of many actors. But the relational effects of a water transfer pipe and the leakage detection programme were much more durable than water-saving users.

REFERENCES

Brearley, M (1995) 'Tanked up', *New Civil Engineer*, 30 November, p4

Callon, M (1986) 'Some elements of a sociology of translation: domestication of the scallops and the fishermen of St Brieuc Bay', in J Law (ed) *A Sociology of Monsters*, Routledge, London, pp196–225

Callon, M (1987) 'Society in the Making: The study of technology as a tool for sociological analysis', in W E Bijker, Hughes, T P and Pinch, T (eds) *The Social Construction of Technological Systems*, MIT Press, Cambridge, Massachusetts, pp83–103

Field, F (1996a) 'Water firm planned to move 1 million people', *Independent*, 19 March, p3

Field, F (1996b) 'Is this the UK's worst private company?', *Independent*, 18 May, p15

Harrison, J (1996) 'OFWAT "fines" Yorkshire Water £40 million', *Independent*, 4 June, p2

Haughton, G (1996) *Private profits – public drought: the creation of a crisis in water management for West Yorkshire*, Sustainable Urban Development Working Paper Series:5, Leeds Metropolitan University, Leeds

Hosking, A (1996) 'Yorkshire plods on', *Independent*, 17 March, p6

Hughes, T P (1983) *Networks of Power – Electric Supply Systems in the US, England and Germany 1880–1930*, Johns Hopkins University Press, Baltimore

Latour, B (1997) *On actor network theory: a few clarifications*, Centre for Social Theory and Technology, Keele University, Stoke-on-Trent

Law, J (1992) 'Notes on the Theory of the Actor-Network: Ordering, Strategy, and Heterogeneity', *Systems Practice*, vol 5, pp379–393

Pearce, S (1995) 'Water anger everywhere but no one stops to think', *Independent*, 27 August, p3

Varley, R (1992) 'When it rains it pours. How Yorkshire Water is dealing with the drought on North Humberside', *Water Bulletin*, p12

CONCLUSIONS

Simon Marvin and Susanne Balslev Nielsen

Looking across the urban case studies of network reconfigurations we can make three broad conclusions. The first is that infrastructure networks can undergo rapid and dramatic change in response to changed environmental conditions that represent a quite fundamental shift from the established style of network management. Second, a key feature of the reconfiguration process is the increasing complexity of infrastructure management as users are given new roles and a much extended set of social actors and new technologies become involved in the network. Infrastructure managers become more active in shaping the socio-technical development of their networks. Third, rather than a new logic replacing the existing logic, we can identify the emergence of multiple types of logic that can coexist. Network managers have to cope with considerable uncertainty about what constitutes sustainable network management so they build in increased flexibility through emerging and multiple styles of network management. We shall consider each of these points in more detail.

UNSTABLE NETWORKS

While the urban regions' experiences of network reconfiguration are quite diverse, it is clear that across the networks a complex set of environmental, economic, social and technical issues have contributed to the destabilization of the conventional logic of network development. In contrast to well-established assumptions that infrastructure networks are extremely stable and difficult to change, each of the networks is undergoing a highly contested shift towards new styles of network management. While the precise reasons for the destabilization of the networks vary over the case studies in each city, new environmental concerns over water quality, rainwater disposal and water resources have disturbed the conventional configuration of socio-technical relations that characterize stable networks.

Yet this is not the whole story. Changing environmental concerns have been paralleled by shifts in the social organization of infrastructure, the growth of social resistance to disruptive new developments, the increasing range of technological options and economic constraints on infrastructure expenditure. The network managers are also dealing with increasingly complex urban contexts where infrastructure is being asked to address often contradictory objectives of greater environmental quality, increased social equity, improvements in quality and reductions in cost to support competitive urban economic development strategies.

While the intensity of the crisis varies across the case studies, from almost complete breakdown of confidence and support in Yorkshire to incorporation of decentralized technologies in Copenhagen, it is apparent that the old style of network management characterized by large-scale technologies and a technocratic approach to relations with users is under increasing pressure. What would have seemed impossible just a few years ago – the incorporation of small-scale technologies, competing styles of groundwater management and the involvement of users with demand management – have become possible in the new context.

COMPLEX NETWORKS

The need for network reconfiguration raises fundamental issues for network managers. In response to competing and complex economic, social, environmental and technical shifts the management of networks becomes much more visible as new social interests compete to shape network reconfiguration. While the old logic was able to restrict the range of involvement of external actors, and users only operated within limits prescribed by the flow managers, the most recent phase of reconfiguration is characterized by a much more extended boundary of social and technical relations. Network managers are not able to simply address the challenges of environmental quality within the conventional limits of knowledge, user relations and technology.

Recognition of the increasingly complex ecological, social and technical dimensions of challenges to the centralized and technocratic approach of the past is opening up networks to new actors, social relations and technologies. Across the case studies there are examples of network managers attempting to engage with users to enrol them in the management of the networks through water-saving activities. New participants such as architects, planners, the building industry and employment officers have to be enrolled into the joint management of the network through the implementation and design of new technologies. At the same time interest in alternative technologies, especially decentralized systems, also means that new social actors have to be incorporated into more decentralized forms of network management. Such shifts raise increasingly complex questions for network managers who have to shift from the relatively simple social relations and organization involved in highly centralized technologies to the much more complex and negotiated relations involved when decentralized technologies are incorporated into the system. In this sense the notion of an infrastructure is widened significantly as the social character of network configuration becomes much more complex than the conventional logic.

Parallel Trajectories of Network Development

While network reconfiguration opens up a space for considerable environmental innovation, it is not clear given the uncertainty and complexity of the process what this may mean for the future development of the network. How will networks be re-established? Does reconfiguration point to a substantially different logic of network management? At this stage we can only offer tentative answers to these questions. Network reconfiguration is an intensely dynamic and uncertain process with new spaces opening and closing and strong echoes back to the original logic of network management. However, even at this stage we can begin to identify a number of issues that help to start mapping the new contours of a reconfigured infrastructure landscape.

Although network reconfiguration is a dramatic process, it does not mean that an old logic is simply replaced by a new one. While Yorkshire Water eventually extended the network with strong echoes of the supply logic, this still coexists with a renewed emphasis on leakage control and user demand management. At the same time, the new logic rolls out unevenly even within the same network. In the case of Copenhagen particular local contexts can facilitate the extension of a rainwater-percolation technology while other contexts do not create the social relations that allow the same technology to be developed. The old and new logic are then somehow held in tension; they seem to exist in parallel in contrast to the traditional notion of displacement or an entirely new phase of network development.

Reconfiguration is not then a simple shift from one style of development to another; instead it is about the development of multiple pathways of network development that are held together in tension. Demand side management can coexist with water transfers, decentralized technologies exist within centralized systems and changing styles of groundwater treatment are held together in parallel. While conventionally we might see a new style gaining momentum and overtaking the old logic there is considerable evidence that these styles will continue to coexist. The case studies show that the spaces for decentralized local systems are likely to be highly contingent on specific local conditions and they cannot simply be rolled out over a whole network. In this context decentralized and user-active systems are likely to coexist with, rather than replace, centralized networks. While decentralized technologies may give network managers increased flexibility in particular contexts, centralized technologies are much less socially complex.

With greater uncertainty about the context within which networks are developed, the coexistence of multiple pathways can give the network managers greater flexibility and resilience when dealing with unanticipated social and environmental conditions. An enlarged range of technologies and social relations gives greater understanding and flexibility when dealing with multiple and contradictory demands. Multiple pathways widen the base of potential options and responses open to the network managers as they respond to uncertainty. These options could be restricted if one pathway is followed. But not all pathways exist in all places. There is clearly a high level of path dependency. It is simply not possible to transfer styles of development between cities because new styles of network management develop in specific local contexts. A unique set of social relations and technologies cannot easily be transferred from one context to another.

Finally, flexibility is important because there is clearly no single notion of sustainable flow management. The case studies illustrate that the concept of a sustainable infrastructure varies across cities and is even heavily contested within a particular local context. We cannot define one optimal pathway towards sustainable flow management. Instead we have shown that a set of multiple pathways develops within a particular context and opens the route for more environmentally sensitive forms of network management. Sustainable flow management means different things in each context. The challenge is to develop increased sensitivity to the ways in which particular social contexts can both widen and constrain environmental innovation in network management.

PART 3

TRANSFORMING BUILDINGS

Credit: Jesper Ole Jensen

INTRODUCTION

Simon Guy

The potential for reducing the environmental impact of buildings is well documented. Energy-saving technologies and materials have been successfully identified and manufactured, energy-efficient building designs have been constructed, tested and widely promoted and extensive monitoring of local, national and international building stocks means we know more than ever before about the precise potential for improved energy performance. Ever more sophisticated, energy-conscious ventilation systems have also been successfully developed. Dynamic insulation now allows buildings to 'breathe', maintaining airflow, reducing energy costs and thereby minimizing CO_2 emissions and the potential for building 'sickness'. At the same time, advances in solar architecture and power are pointing the way towards self-sustaining buildings that consume little or no external energy, thereby radically reducing their 'ecological footprint'.

This technical performance approach to understanding environmental design has brought undoubted benefits in terms of highlighting the issues of energy efficiency in buildings. However, such approaches tend to be founded on a pre-defined conception of the environmental problem in which appropriate ends (sustainability) and means (technology) are simply assumed. In contrast, each chapter in this section adopts a social constructivist approach that explores the importance of social context for the shaping of environmental innovation. That is, each chapter views building design, like the notion of sustainability itself, as a fundamentally contested concept.

The case study by Simon Guy and Suzie Osborn offers a novel analysis of environmental innovation in buildings. The chapter examines the debate about 'greener' buildings by asking the key question: 'what do we mean by a green building?' The chapter highlights how the concept of a green building is, in fact, highly contestable, with competing definitions strongly linked to particular ways of seeing environmental design. Based on an extensive review of literature on green buildings and in-depth analysis of an individual green building in the north east of England, the chapter explores the competing logic shaping the design of green buildings. Each design logic is shown to vary in terms of perceptions of the environment it challenges and the temporal coordinates and the types of language, imagery, claims-making styles and rhetoric employed; thereby leading to different green building strategies. The strategies vary in terms of their own particular repertoire of technological choices (including varying views on connection to the physical infrastructure networks) and also in terms of the social relations of the development process (including user participation).

The case study by Regine Mauruszat explores the influence of differential modes of social organization of design and development on the technical or design features of a building. The chapter takes issue with the conventional assumption that traditional design solutions prevail, or fail, because they are more or less well adapted to the particular context of building development. The chapter explores the relationship between technology and social organization by analysing the difficulties encountered by selected green buildings in Berlin during their development process, and the strategies that were adopted to overcome them. The chapter argues that in order to understand the success or failure of the case-study buildings in a broader context, general observations on the social organization of green building are required.

The case study by Jesper Ole Jensen analyses the relationships between green buildings and infrastructure networks, and explores how each serves to shape resource flows while operating on different levels and being driven by different logics and rationales. The chapter argues that in the current debate of green buildings the relationship between the building design and the local infrastructure is often ignored. The increasing promotion of green buildings in Denmark has, however, put the focus on the role of infrastructure networks, which have often been seen as impeding green building innovation. The chapter explores the relation between the two dimensions of flow management by using a typology of interactions between buildings and networks, and through four case studies of buildings in the Copenhagen region, each demonstrating that infrastructure networks have considerable influence on the concept and location of the green buildings.

6 CONTESTING ENVIRONMENTAL DESIGN: THE HYBRID GREEN BUILDING

Simon Guy and Suzie Osborn

INTRODUCTION

What is a green building?

There is a wide consensus on the need to promote environmental innovation in building design. We are all now familiar with statistics that suggest that 50 per cent of CO_2 emissions derive from buildings, and we share a sense that the sealed, air-conditioned environments we commonly occupy can cause buildings and ourselves literally to become sick. Everyone, it seems, now wants to inhabit a greener building. All around we find talk of a 'green shift' (Farmer, 1996), a desire for 'natural' buildings (Pearson, 1989), the need for 'dialogue with the living earth' (Swan and Swan, 1996) and the viability of 'eco-tech' design solutions (Slessor, 1997). It is hard to escape the feeling that we are all committed to a common idea of what constitutes a green building. However, glancing through the many scholarly articles, in-depth reports and coffee-table books that promote green design we can find a whole host of different types or styles of green building.

Taking a brief scan through just three well-known books, *Green Architecture* (Vale and Vale, 1991), *Sol Power* (Behling and Behling, 1996) and *Eco-Tech* (Slessor, 1997), you can find:

- a house in New Mexico built with sun-dried mud-bricks and heated by solar warmth collected through south-facing openings;
- a high-rise apartment block in Turin utilizing hi-tech active solar collectors;
- a naturally ventilated bank's headquarters in Amsterdam the size of a small town, designed in consultation with its occupiers;
- Icelandic-inspired octangular domes which reduce heating-related energy;
- semi-buried houses in Catalunya that 'blend' harmoniously into their natural surroundings;
- a high-rise sky scraper in Frankfurt that has opening windows, sky gardens and natural ventilation throughout; and

- an array of other buildings with diverse technologies including photoelectric facades or blinds, integral wind-power generators and intelligent elevators that learn where they should be parked to reduce waiting times and minimize energy use.

Clearly what constitutes green design is open to very broad-ranging interpretations. Conduct your own survey and you will find a bewildering array of contrasting building types, employing a great variety of different technologies, materials, design strategies and construction methods.

Judging green design

Despite this enormous diversity in green design concepts, there are a growing number of green building competitions which try to 'judge' 'greenness'. For example, Groundwork Trust's 'Eco-Centre' in Jarrow, South Tyneside in the United Kingdom, which acts as a headquarters and demonstration facility as well as providing space for commercial rent, has won the British Royal Institute of Chartered Surveyors (RICS) 1997 Efficient Building of the Year award and was a finalist in the 1998 Green Building Award competition organized by the British Heating and Ventilating Contractors' Association (HVCA) and the British *Independent on Sunday* newspaper. The criteria for these competitions includes anything and everything from visual impact to standards of insulation, material conservation, control of harmful emissions, transport planning and the creation of a healthy, safe and 'user'-friendly environment.

So, in what ways was the Groundwork building considered 'green'? Surveying the numerous celebratory articles already published about Groundwork we can identify a familiar consensus about the technological efficiency and environmental and financial effectiveness of the design (Bunn and Ruyssevelt, 1996; Nicholson-Lord, 1997). We can note the way the building generates its own power from an on-site 80 kW wind turbine and the way solar panels on the roof provide hot water. Energy use is kept to a minimum through measures such as the triangular plan of the building, which optimizes passive solar gain; high levels of insulation; an automatically controlled heating system; natural air-conditioning; growing deciduous greenery next to the windows to shade the building; and the use of low-energy lighting and appliances. All this means that the building's energy target is set at 75 kWh/m^2/year as compared with 130 kWh/m2/year for typical non-air conditioned offices (Bunn and Ruyssevelt, 1996, p18). Overall, the building's focus on 'sound' energy usage means an annual saving of some 75–100 tonnes of CO_2 (ibid).

There are similar innovations in the handling of waste. All human sewage is digested on-site via three Clivus composters and a holding tank in the basement of the building. The resulting brew is used as compost to restore fertility and help recreate landscaped gardens on surrounding ground rendered toxic by mine waste. Water demand in the building is also minimized via the use of water-saving technologies such as low-flush toilets and low-water use sprinkler systems. There is an on-site borehole, which provides water for the building's non-potable water supply, and rainwater is collected from the roof. Moreover, as far as possible, all the materials used in construction are of sound environmental pedigree. For example, the building is constructed of second-hand bricks, all timber is from sustainable sources and there is almost no use of toxic paints, glues or varnishes. The Groundwork building is clearly a highly commendable example of innovative design and worthy of great interest and high praise. But are we any nearer to understanding the essence of what a green building represents? In what sense, or senses, does the Groundwork building or any other green building represent 'green' architectural values?

Understanding Green Buildings: From Technocentrism to Ecocentrism

David Pepper's well-known work on environmentalism identifies a dualistic debate which questions whether 'green strategies' should follow either what is termed an ecocentric or 'radical' approach, or a technocentric or 'reformist' approach to tackling environmental problems (Pepper, 1996, p7). Put simply, technocentrics adhere to a process of 'ecological modernization' which 'indicates the possibility of overcoming the environmental dilemma without leaving the path of modernization' (Spaargaren and Mol, 1992, p334), whereas ecocentrics believe a radical new way of living is the only way forward if we are to avoid the impending ecological crisis. This technocentric versus ecocentric debate is reflected in debates around green buildings where the 'diversity of responses displayed by contemporary sustainable architects ... tend to revolve around the issue of technology and its application within an ecological framework' (Steele, 1997, p285). For many, 'technology remains the answer to saving the environment', while other sustainable architects 'argue that technology ... is the primary cause of destruction of nature, and that expecting it to provide a solution for environmental ills is like using the cause of the disease to cure it' (Steele, 1997, p291). Here, design debates are split into competing social visions; on the one hand a sustainable urban economy in which technological innovation applied on a global scale mitigates environmental despoliation and, on the other, an anti-urban vision of community-based development which builds upon local technological knowledge. Below we take a closer look at some of these themes.

Technology: solution or curse

Technocentric approaches to green design would start from the belief that science and technology can provide the solutions to environmental problems. Consequently, a technocentric design strategy would be incremental and adaptive, focused around reconfiguring the design of, for the most part, recognizable, hi-tech buildings. As Cook and Bolton put it, 'technocentrics recognize the existence of environmental problems and want to "solve" them through management of the environment' putting their trust in 'objective analysis and a rational scientific method' (Cook and Golton, 1994, p677). This may mean, for example, the addition of the latest in high-tech structural and insulating materials, the utilization of complex energy-management systems and the development of new sophisticated design techniques. In contrast, ecocentrics tend to have less faith in technological innovation, calling instead for an alternative, socially radical approach to building design utilizing 'softer', 'small-scale' and 'appropriate' technologies. Here, the strategy is to 'learn from nature', taking ecosystems and the natural systems of sun, wind and water as the guiding principles of green design.

From urban to rural

Technocentric and ecocentric approaches to green design also tend to split along an urban/rural divide. Technocentrism is suggestive of an urban future in which a progressive process of technological innovation mitigates the adverse effects of urban development. Here, capitalism and economic priorities can be reconciled with environmental problems and the high-rise skyscraper can be retained as a symbol of progress while also symbolizing new green concerns. The work of international architects Norman Foster and Ken Yeang are good examples here.

In contrast, the belief system of ecocentrics tends towards a marked anti-urbanism in which skyscrapers symbolize 'defiance, not deference to nature' (Woods, 1992, p2). As John Short has suggested, 'for many people the city has become a metaphor for the decline of civilization' (Short, 1996, p5). Ecocentrics tend to promote a vision of skyscrapers and cities more generally as symbolic of a civilization out of control, greedily utilizing non-renewable resources and causing pollution to spiral. A direct link is made between what is seen as the over-development of our cities and the deforestation of tropical rainforests, the spread of acid rain and the rise of global warming. To ecocentric architects and designers the notion that an urban skyscraper can be merely reconfigured as a green building is almost a contradiction in terms. The city and skyscrapers are symbols of destruction and detachment from nature. Having decried urbanization of the planet as the root cause of the environmental dilemma, ecocentrics promote a vision of rural living in which buildings blend with their natural surroundings, becoming self-sufficient in water and energy and reflecting wider community values.

Between global and local

Finally, there appears to be a dualistic debate over the spatial context of design: technocentric 'global' or ecocentric 'local'. Technocentric designers take advantage of the environmental benefits to be gained from 'the information technology revolution and the globalization of the economy and of communication' (Borja and Castells, 1997, p1). The latest 'green' technologies and information from around the world are utilized, such as the latest in photovoltaics (PVs) from Turkey or the most up-to-date environmental management system (EMS) from the USA, taking advantage of innovations in other countries and the ease of global transportation and dissemination. New communication technology and subsequent new ideas, such as the paper-less office, working from home and hot-desking, are utilized to further reduce environmental impacts. The effect is to build relations between units that are far away from each other in terms of space.

In contrast and 'as a reaction against the globalism of the international style and the manic propositions of megacity', ecocentric designers argue that 'genius loci' must come back into 'architectural parlance' (Farmer, 1996, p169). Ecocentric designers dismiss the environmental benefits of 'globalization' and argue for a return to the notion of neighbourhood and 'locality'. What is needed is a new ecological life-cycle analysis that takes into account links between local action and global reaction. Ecocentric designs, therefore, concentrate on using local building materials so as to reduce transport requirements and thus lessen CO_2 emissions and global warming. There is also a particular focus on using local knowledge, techniques and skills, which have usually been passed down from generation to generation. In this way green design and construction is highly location specific. Whereas technocentric 'global' design is about connecting buildings into global homogeneous networks, ecocentric 'local' design is about containment within heterogeneous localities.

Of course the concepts of 'technocentric' and 'ecocentric' approaches to design are only ideal types of environmentalism that inhabit extreme ends of a spectrum; varying shades of green between technocentrism and ecocentrism exist. However, commitment to this approach means that analysis is reduced to locating examples of green building into fixed categories representing shades of greenness. This typology still suggests that we can all recognize the difference between more or less 'green' design and that individual buildings can be defined as reflections of pre-existing ideologies.

ANOTHER WAY OF SEEING GREEN BUILDINGS

This chapter suggests that we abandon the search for a true or incontestable definition of green buildings and instead treat the concept in a 'relative rather than an absolute sense' as a 'means of raising awareness of all the issues that can be considered' (Cook and Golton, 1994, p684). In this we follow John Hannigan and suggest that the concept of a 'green building' is a social construct whereby the aim of analysis is not to 'discredit environmental claims but rather to understand how they are created, legitimated, and contested' (Hannigan, 1995, p3).

The premise is, then, that individuals, groups and institutions possess 'a particular way of thinking and talking about environmental politics' reflecting their 'rather different social and cognitive commitments' which become reflected in the 'story-lines' each actor develops about what a green building is or is not (Hajer, 1995, p13). So, from this analytical standpoint we cease to view green buildings as merely differently configured technical structures. Instead, we will view green buildings as social representations of alternative ecological values, or material embodiments of the logics that frame the green buildings debate. In this sense, a logic, with Hajer, is 'here defined as a specific ensemble of ideas, concepts, and categorizations that are produced, repro-

Table 6.1 *Competing Logic of Green Buildings*

	Ecological	Smart	Logic Symbolic	Comfort	Community
Issue	Sustainability	Flexibility	Millennium	Sick buildings	Democracy
Image	Polluter	Asset	Symbol	Healthy	Home
Risk	Planetary	Market	Cultural life	Individual	Alienation
Rhetoric	Ethical	Commercial	Architectural	Medical	Societal
Design strategy	Reduce footprint	Maximize efficiency	Express nature	Living building	Create identity
Urban scale	Decentralized	Global–urban	Contextualized	Localized	Centralized
Technical approach	Local, renewable	Hi-tech, BMS	Organic	Non-toxic	Appropriate
Evaluative criteria	Holistic	Cost-benefit	Truth to nature	Productivity	Social cohesion

duced, and transformed in a particular set of practices and through which meaning is given to physical and social realities' (Hajer, 1995, p44).

Competing logic of green design

Careful analysis of an extensive literature of books, articles and reports covering issues related to 'environmental', 'ecological' or 'green' buildings resulted in a typology of five logics, which are illustrated in Table 6.1. These logics are not meant to be in any way exclusive. That is, competing logics may collide, merge or co-inhabit in the debate about form, design and specification. The main point is that the 'environmental problematique is hardly ever discussed in its full complexity' (Hajer, 1995, pp19–20). Rather, 'environmental discourse tends to be dominated by specific emblems: issues that dominate the perception of the ecological dilemma' (ibid). Each of the five logics presented in Table 6.1 highlight the way the green building debate is framed differently depending upon the particular 'emblematic issue' (Hajer, 1995, p20) promoted by the design participants. These 'emblems' 'mobilize biases in and out of the environmental debate' (ibid), thereby shaping the design strategy.

Building as ecological polluter

This is arguably the logic that would be popularly associated with the image of green buildings. Here we have visions of buildings greedily utilizing non-renewable resources and causing pollution to spiral. The emblematic issue here is 'sustainability'. The role of green architecture is clearly to limit the environmental impact of buildings; 'our all-encompassing goal is to create the best possible built environment, designed so that the strain on the natural environment is minimized' (Swedish Council for Building Research, 1990, p1). Nothing less than planetary survival and the survival of future generations are at stake according to the advocates of the ecological logic.

There is a deeply ethical argument here dominating any rhetoric of rationality. The overall design strategy of the ecological logic is to reduce the ecological footprint via the use of small-scale, soft and appropriate technologies and techniques, which depend upon local knowledge and resources and natural systems such as reed bed treatment for sewage. Having decried the urbanization of the planet as the root cause of environmental problems, the priority is decentralization with the emphasis on local, small-scale communities. There is a call for a new holistic ecological life-cycle analysis which takes into account links between local and global reaction.

Building as smart asset

In sharp contrast, the 'smart' logic is most familiar in the world of commercial property development, particularly in global cities. Here, environmental concerns are not the predominant issue but rather are wrapped up within wider commercial rhetoric and concerns for competitive advantage and survival in the global marketplace. In this way commercial organizations are increasingly adopting 'green' innovation as a means to reduce overheads and are seeing green buildings as a critical asset helping to fashion economic performance.

The design strategy is to maximize the efficiency of the building in resource use and space; the emblematic issue here is flexibility of the workplace 'required to move people and equipment in order to more readily respond to the demands of the business' (Health and Safety at Work (UK), 1993, p16–17). This is to be achieved through the use of cost-saving 'intelligent' technologies and organizational techniques that have environmental benefits. Sensory lighting, elevators that learn where they should be parked to minimize waiting times, hot-desking, the paper-less office and building management systems (BMSs) are all part of the smart building tool kit.

Building as symbol

It is the near invisibility of environmental issues in smart buildings which is anathema to those championing the symbolic logic. Building in this logic is a symbol of societal values and cultural life and the emblematic issue is how to represent the new millennium. So, having overcome the 'influences of modernist orthodoxy' with its association of energy-intensive growth for growth's sake, the challenge for ecological architecture is to 'identify a new language in the building arts' (Wines, 1993, p23). For Wines, architecture is the 'most visible and pervasive evidence of human intervention in the environment' and therefore should 'function as a visible demonstration of conservationist ideals' (ibid).

The smart approach to green buildings is increasingly critiqued by advocates of the symbolic logic for its emphasis on 'environmental' science and technology driven by 'numerical assessment of physical performance rather than on any expressive statement of organic empathy' (Farmer, 1996, p181). Instead, as Wines states: 'green architecture needs to go beyond just the current catalogue of environmental control techniques' and 'create architecture where both function and image celebrate the environmental message'. The design strategy emanating from this realization springs from the local context of development. Inspiration here is taken from vernacular and indigenous building strategies. Recycled materials, organic forms that reflect the image of nature and reflect the surroundings of the building are the priorities.

Truth to nature, as promoted by the 19th-century critic John Ruskin, is the final evaluative framework.

Building as healthy place

'Sick buildings' are a relatively recent yet already notorious emblematic issue. Here in the comfort logic we have a 'new' image of buildings as hostile local–internal environments in which individuals' health is put at daily risk from a variety of hazards. As the Vales put it, 'awareness of a range of indoor pollutants has turned the designers' attention to the need for healthy buildings' (Vale and Vale, 1991, pp 114–115). More psychological aspects are also drawn on in the comfort logic with critiques of buildings that isolate their inhabitants from the outside world and diminish their occupants' control over the internal environment.

This logic, then, utilizes a medical rhetoric which stresses a connection between a good working environment and productivity. Its building strategy is to create a 'living building' with a focus on the use of non-toxic and selective materials, enhancing 'links to nature' and increasing controllability. In particular, it stresses the advantages to physical and psychological well-being of opening windows as compared with air-conditioning. The approach envisages 'spaces in which environmental uniformity is replaced by variations, within limits, which maintain, in the occupant, a sense of dynamics of the natural climate, of the proper condition of mankind' (Hawkes, 1996, p18).

Building as democratic home

The final logic addresses the emblematic issue of democracy or the creation of buildings that embody and express the notion of community. This logic derives from a notion of building as home and seeks to challenge the feelings of alienation attached to many examples of modern architecture by striving for social cohesion. The rhetoric at work here is societal, whereby the overall strategy implies that buildings have the potential to help us to forge a sense of identity through the creation of buildings that express a sense of the 'organic' formation of society and links to the natural locality within which communities are developed.

The strategy prioritizes the involvement of occupants in the construction of 'appropriate' buildings that will serve their needs without impacting on the environment unnecessarily. In particular there is a focus on using locally produced materials and increasing the longevity of development by 'ensuring design is capable of adapting to users' changing needs' (Vale and Vale, 1991, p116). Mixing modes of home, work, leisure and welfare is also a feature of the creation of viable 'eco-communities'.

GROUNDWORK TRUST: CONTESTING ENVIRONMENTAL DESIGN

How far can this analytical approach help us in understanding Groundwork Trust's Eco-Centre? Looking back at the main features of the Groundwork design we have already noted the conventional attributes of 'greenness', such as its efficiency and use of renewable materials, which seem to situate Groundwork within an ecocentric logic of environmental design. However, when we start to look beyond a simple list of design features we start to discover some interesting paradoxes which refuse to sit neatly into a single logic – technocentric or ecocentric – and instead point to the coexistence of a number of logics of environmental innovation.

Autonomy: towards a compromise?

In the design process both the client and the architect shared a vision of a totally autonomous office building. The original aim was to design and construct a building which could generate all its own electricity, provide all its own water and dispose of all its own waste. As the architect states: 'the project is about constructing a building whose self-reliance can make a positive contribution to the environment' (interview). The original conception was of a building that did not have to rely on the external infrastructure services; a building that could be totally disconnected from the mains infrastructure networks, thereby not contributing to the sum growth of infrastructure demand. The RICS Efficient Building Award 1997 commends and celebrates the Eco–Centre for being:

> 'the first project of its kind to be built in an urban area where a commercial building does not have to turn its back on the usual infrastructure of grid electricity, mains drainage and gas, but chooses to do so.'

But in reality the building is not totally autonomous. Although the Centre is not connected to the external sewerage system or the external gas supply, it is connected to the external electricity and drinking water supply. When the logic of total disconnection meshed with the reality of actually constructing the office block 'the total self-sufficiency concept came unstuck. It was gradually chipped away bit by bit and eventually fell apart' (interview with architect). A whole array of economic, commercial, technical and planning factors combined to prevent the building being disconnected from the external, large-scale electricity and water supply systems. It was difficult to match the desires of the original all-embracing, self-sufficient, autonomous policy statement to commercial, technical and planning considerations.

For instance, in terms of the electricity-supply system the initial idea was for the wind turbine to provide all the electricity needs of the building. However, the Eco-Centre had to be connected to the main electricity supply for two main reasons. First, a wind turbine alone cannot guarantee a continuous supply of power required by commercial property developments for facilities such as computers, telephones, security systems, fire alarms and fire sprinkler systems. A back-up source of power is therefore required. The original plan was to install a back-up generator run on bio-diesel fuel which would mean that the power for the Eco-Centre would still be generated by 'renewable' means, enabling the Centre to remain disconnected from the mains power supply. However, a bio-diesel generator was not installed because it was not cost effective. The Eco-Centre, therefore, had to be connected to the grid to ensure a constantly maintained supply of electricity to the site. Second, after ordering the wind turbine, it was discovered that the refrigeration unit that provides the heating for the building had a very high starting current that could not be satisfied by the size of the wind turbine purchased. The Eco-Centre therefore needed to be connected to the grid so that energy from the main network could be used to start the refrigeration unit when required. When the wind turbine is not generating enough power for the building's needs, energy is imported from the National Grid for which Groundwork pays a fee. Conversely, when the wind turbine is generating more energy than is being used in the building, excess power is transported back onto the National Grid for which Groundwork receives an income. In this way Groundwork is forced to engage with the electricity utilities in the area.

A similar mixture of economic and technological issues prevented the building from being totally autonomous in terms of its water supply. The building does provide its own water for non-drinking water needs, but cannot provide water for tenants' drinking water needs. Non-drinking water needs are satisfied by two main systems. First, the water required for the underground heating and cooling system is provided by an on-site borehole. Second, hand washing and toilet flushing are aided by stored rainwater collected from the building's roof. It was originally envisaged that the building's drinking water needs would be satisfied by a second on-site borehole thus negating the need for mains connection. However, the water from the on-site boreholes turned out to be very salty and the desalinization system required to make the water fit for human consumption was again not cost effective. The building subsequently received its water from the mains water supply. In this way the purity of the ecological design logic is tempered by wider social and technical processes.

A technological hybrid

The client and the design team opposed 'high-tech', 'modern' green design in favour of more 'natural', 'organic' and 'holistic' solutions. Rejecting the notion of the Centre as an 'intelligent' green building, the design of the Eco-Centre is perceived as being 'analogous to a living thing that moderates itself to remain inherently stable' (interview with Director). And to a certain extent this is true. For example, the temperature of the building is moderated largely by the building's own large thermal mass. The idea of growing deciduous climbing plants up through netting on the outside of the building next to the windows is that during the summer the plants will provide an effective, natural filter to midday sun and act as solar shading. As the plants' leaves drop off in the winter more light will be let into the building.

The idea of the triangular plan of the building, whereby there are large south east and east facings but a very small north facing, acts to prevent overheating in the summer while maximizing light. The central atrium of the building draws air from the opening windows by convection (the stack effect) and expels it through the ventilation tower, thereby naturally ventilating the building. Occupants are free to open windows and a training programme is established so that all users understand the part they play in making the building work (interview with Director).

Somewhat surprisingly, however, given the claim that the client and architect rejected the notion of 'smart', high-tech building design, there are also highly sophisticated technological innovations incorporated into the building. As the promotional leaflet for the building states, for example:

> *'This is a unique opportunity to rent prestigious office accommodation in one of Europe's most innovative buildings. The Eco-Centre utilizes the latest technology to minimize the impact on the natural environment'.*

Alongside the more 'natural' features described above there is a highly sophisticated and complicated building energy management system. In the initial design phase, complex computer software and simulation packages were used to calculate the thermal lag of the building as well as the optimum orientation of the building, ceiling heights, room depths and size of windows (to maximize daylight and have minimum heat loss). Artificial internal lighting has been computer designed to be glare-free and flicker-free and the latest in high-tech insulation materials has been utilized (interview). A sophisticated heat pump feeds warm water from underground to underfloor radiators. Perhaps the most visible demonstration of the incorporation of the smart design logic is the wind turbine, which represents the latest in wind turbine technology (interview with consultant).

Local/global technologies and skills

In the original, conception stage of the project there was a very strong focus on using 'local' technologies and materials. Here, again, the purity of the ecological design is tempered by the use of more global technologies and materials. On the one hand, all bricks used are recycled from a nearby source, the external paving slabs are recycled from Gateshead Metrocentre, the car park is made from recycled road surfacing from the streets of Newcastle, and three defunct railway lines from the local transport system, Tyne and Wear Metro, hold the roof aloft. On the other hand, renewable power is generated from a wind turbine that has been specially imported from Denmark because it represented the quietest turbine available for its output, an important consideration because of the urban location of the Eco-Centre. This mixing of 'local' and 'global' technologies is also reflected in the knowledge and skills base underlying the design and development of the building. For example local architects and builders were chosen to design and develop the building. Furthermore there was a particular focus on using the artistic talents of local craftspersons to visually enhance design. In contrast, the wind turbine requires the specialist knowledge of a geographically distant specialist engineer who has to fly over from Denmark in the event of a technical breakdown.

Community vs commercial concerns

It was originally conceived that the Eco-Centre, because of its ecological design, would be more suitable and beneficial for community and environmental groups and would therefore attract these groups as compared with commercial businesses. 'We were expecting to get the green welly and woolly jumper brigade in there as potential tenants because it had so few conventional facilities that people would normally expect to find in a normal conventional office block' (interview with estate agent). However, the feasibility study suggested that, because of the way the building is funded and because of the current tax regime, it made commercial sense to rent office space to organizations that are registered for VAT (ie commercial firms as compared with community-based organizations, which are not registered for VAT). For this reason it was found that 'community groups don't fit easily with the commercial agenda of the Trust' (interview with agent).

Therefore, in terms of promoting the building, Groundwork approached commercial enterprises. In particular, they promoted the building to local, start-up business enterprises, especially computer firms and office equipment companies with environmentally friendly attitudes. Groundwork thought that these firms would be interested in the Eco-Centre because it could help them to promote their environmental image (interview with Director). And it is companies like these, rather than community groups, that are now letting space in the building.

Moreover, despite a rhetoric of consideration of community in the original conception of the Eco-Centre, it is perhaps surprising to note the lack of consultation with the local community during the design of the building and the lack of involvement of the local community in the actual construction of the building. Rather the building design was largely informed by the Managing Director of Groundwork and the architect and was constructed by professional contractors.

Public vs private transport

The client and the architect are both committed to reducing car usage and increasing the use of public transport and wanted to manifest this commitment in the Eco-Centre. For example, it is hoped that any surplus out-of-hours electricity generated by the Eco-Centre's wind turbine will be used to develop electric powered community based transport (interview). In addition, the Centre provides cycle stands and aimed to limit the number of parking spaces legally allowed for a commercial office development of its size by the planning system. Furthermore and most importantly, when selecting the site for the Eco-Centre the client and the architect wanted to locate the Centre ideally not more than five minutes walk from the nearest station on the Tyne and Wear Metro rapid transit system and a major bus route (interview). However, proximity to public transport was not the only factor that was important in terms of the location of the Centre. The location of the Centre also had to satisfy other 'criteria' including:

- *Physical criteria:* The site needed to have good borehole access to provide the building with on-site water. It also needed to have good wind and energy regimes. In particular, coastal and riverside locations were favoured.
- *Planning criteria:* For the wind turbine the Eco-Centre not only had to be located in an area with a good wind regime but it had to be located at least 200 metres from any housing so that noise disturbance to local residents would be minimal (interview).
- *Economic criteria:* If the project was to qualify for funding from the Tyne and Wear Development Corporation then the Centre would have to be located in one of the Corporation's designated urban regeneration areas.
- *Commercial criteria:* The Centre had to be located in an area that was going to be attractive to commercial firms.
- *Organizational criteria:* The site had to be in South Tyneside for the Managing Director to meet his charitable objectives.

To meet these criteria, the Eco-Centre has been located in an urban regeneration area on the banks of the River Tyne in Hebburn, South Tyneside. It is a former industrial area of South Tyneside that has been in decline since the closure of its shipbuilding and heavy engineering activities and as such is located in the Tyne and Wear Development Corporation's area. It is at the forefront of the up-and-coming Viking Business Park. In particular it is hoped that the Eco-Centre will attract businesses that have started up in the nearby Techno Business Park and are 'now looking to raise their profile by moving into more prestigious office space' (interview with estate agent). The site is away from housing and thus negates the issue of noise disturbance from the wind turbine. Being located next to the river Tyne the site has good borehole access/groundwater sources (good riverside location), is windy and, being open to the south, east and west, has good access to solar power.

What this has meant in reality is that the Centre has been located in an area that is arguably difficult to reach by public transport. Moreover, to facilitate the commercial attractiveness of the building more car parking has had to be provided. As the Managing Director of the Eco-Centre himself states, there is a 'trade off between location being its [the Eco-Centre's] weakness and its greenness (for example use of renewable energy and resources) and attractiveness to businesses being its up-thing' (interview).

CONCLUSION: THE HYBRID GREEN BUILDING?

It is important to note that we are not highlighting the paradoxes of green design to question whether or not Groundwork Trust or their Eco-Centre is a good or bad example of a green building. We are not disputing that Groundwork is a highly commendable environmental organization, nor that their Eco-Centre is a worthy example of green architecture. Rather, we use Groundwork Trust's green building to highlight the fact that the ecocentric/technocentric analytical approach appears to oversimplify the production of green design. It is clear that

Groundwork Trust's environmentally innovative building defies easy definition; each element of its design strategy incorporates its own logic and can be justified in environmental terms by different arguments. While the initial design philosophy was driven by an ecological logic, a combination of technical, organizational and commercial considerations necessitated the use of smart logic innovations. A symbolic logic has driven the use of recycled materials in a decorative role, but commercial need shaped the design of space and form to maximize floor-space. Similarly, economic and commercial factors limited the influence of the community design logic.

The Groundwork Trust building is an illuminating example of the apparent paradoxes which inevitably face planning and design strategies aimed at promoting 'green buildings'. How, for instance, are we to handle the challenges of location – the priority of accessing public transport nodes and the ideal of mixing living and working space with the need for windy sites for power generators and the need to satisfy commercial expediency in cost terms? What is the right balance of basic, locally available technologies and the opportunities presented by high-tech innovations? Should we prioritize the use of local labour and expertise or make use of wider knowledge even if there are transport and communication costs? Is it more effective to encourage highly motivated individuals or energize the local community in the design process? And so on. Of course these are not all either/or choices. But if we are to seriously attempt to green our cities through a coherent planning strategy we surely need to develop a better understanding of what we are trying to achieve and what we might mean by ecological design and greener buildings. Analysis of the Groundwork Trust building would suggest that commitment to green design clearly does not simply revolve around attitudes to technology. Clearly, green buildings cannot be simply classified in terms of a series of pre-defined dualisms.

To understand why a building is designed in a particular environmental fashion we have to understand the strategic priorities of those involved in its design and construction. As Paul Murphy suggests, 'different eco houses reflect the different priorities of their designer and/or inhabitants' (Murphy, 1997, p25). If we want to locate opportunities for environmental innovation then we have to identify the ways in which particular logics of environmental innovation (as identified above) take root in changing development practices. This means rejecting any notion of buildings as simply technical structures that can be more or less well designed in relation to an external definition of accepted environmental standards. Instead we must accept that 'architecture is part of the conflicting and contradictory struggle of differing forces, interest groups and movements' (Borden and Dunster, 1995, p4) and therefore contingent on the particular strategic objectives of those design and development actors with the power to implement their chosen design strategy. In unravelling those strategies may lie the key to understanding competing strategies of green design and judgements about the 'greenness' of buildings. Seen this way, Groundwork Trust would perhaps be better classified as a complex hybrid in which design incorporates competing social visions, differing ideas about our relationship to nature, work, organizations, aesthetics, finance and so on. The Groundwork Trust building is then the product of contrasting green logics which collide, clash and mesh to produce a hybrid design, a situationally specific response to the global environmental challenge.

REFERENCES

Behling, S and Behling, S (1996) *Sol Power. The Evolution of Solar Architecture*, Prestel, London

Borden, I and Dunster, D (eds) (1995) *Architecture and the Sites of History*, Butterworth Architecture, London

Borja, J and Castells, M (1997) *Local & Global. Management of cities in the Information Age,* Earthscan, London

Bunn, R and Ruyssevelt, P (1996) 'Ecological?', *Business Services Journal,* December 1996, pp14–18

Cook and Golton (1994) *Sustainable Development Concepts and Practice in the Built Environment – A UK Perspective*. Sustainable Construction, CIB TG 16, Nov 6–9, pp677–685

Farmer, J (1996) *Green Shift: Towards Green Sensibility in Architecture*, World Wildlife Fund, London

Hannigan, J (1995) *Environmental Sociology: A Social Constructivist Perspective*, Routledge, London

Hajer, M (1995) *The Politics of Environmental Discourse: Ecological Modernisation and the Policy Process*, OUP, London

Hawkes, D (1996) *The Environmental Tradition: Studies in the Architecture of the Environment*, E & FN Spon, London

Health and Safety at Work (1993) *Smart Buildings*, February, vol 15, no 2, p16

Murphy, A (1997) 'Any Colour as long as it's Green', *The Observer,* 2 February, pp24–25

Nicholson-Lord, D (1997) Ecology at Work, *Independent on Sunday,* 17 August, pp46–47

Pearson, D (1989) *The Natural House Book,* Conran Octopus, London

Pepper, D (1996) *Modern Environmentalism: An Introduction*, Routledge, London

Short, J (1996) *The Urban Order: An Introduction to Cities, Culture and Power,* Blackwell, London

Slessor, C (1997) *Eco-Tech: Sustainable Architecture and High Technology*, Thames and Hudson, London

Spaargaren, G and Mol, A J P (1992) 'Sociology, environment and modernity: ecological modernization as a theory of social change', *Society and Natural Resources*, 5, pp323–344

Steele, J (1997) *Architecture Today,* Phaidon Press, London

Swan, J and Swan, R (1996) *Dialogues with the Living Earth,* Quest Books, Illinois

Swedish Council for Building Research (1990) *Research on the Built Environment of the Future*, Swedish Council for Building Research, Stockholm

Vale, B and Vale, R (1991) *Green Architecture*, Thames and Hudson, London

Wines, J (1993) 'Architecture in the Age of Ecology, *The Amicus Journal*, Summer, pp22–23

Woods, C G (1992) 'A Philosophy of an Organic Architecture', in C G Woods and M Wels (eds) *Designing Your Natural House*, Van Nostrand Reinhold, New York

INTERVIEWS

The Director of Groundwork South Tyneside Eco-Centre, 20 February 1997
An architect from Earthsense, 20 February 1997
A letting agent from Chestertons, 27 February 1997
A representative from Mechanical and Electrical Consultants, 26 February 1997
A consultant from McAlpine, 13 March 1997
A representative from Hutter, Jennings and Tickmarsh, Structural Engineers, 17
   March 1997

7 THE SOCIAL ORGANIZATION OF ENVIRONMENTAL DESIGN: RESIDENTIAL BUILDINGS IN THE BERLIN REGION

Regine Mauruszat

INTRODUCTION

The many 'green' buildings built over the last two decades present a striking variety of resource-saving technologies. What can be observed beyond this diversity is that the technologies actually implemented often fail to exploit the potential for green building, either overlooking best available techniques or else focusing on only one aspect of resource saving, such as water or energy. As any architect engaged in green building will confirm, the end result – in terms of the 'in-house' infrastructure actually installed – often differs substantially from the original green design. On the passage from the drawing board to the final product many components of the original design fall by the wayside.

In some cases the downscaling of the original green design is clearly a result of technical deficiencies. It is becoming increasingly apparent, however, that this is not the whole story. Major restrictions for implementing green building technologies are located within the complex social processes necessary to design, construct and subsequently manage a building. These processes involve a large number of different actors, such as the proprietor, architect, technical consultants, construction companies, utilities, suppliers and state regulators, who need to reach agreement over green technologies before the building can be constructed or refurbished. At a later stage, users and facility managers add to the list of actors influencing the way the technologies are used once installed.

This process of interaction, though, is not dependent solely on the preferences of individual actors but also on the institutional context within which they operate. Architects and engineers, for instance, have to comply with regulations and building standards as well as financial incentives and environmental policy. These institutional settings have been established by society to rationalize the activity of building, comprising not only government specifications – very important for building – but also in a much broader sense the scope of actor influence and the patterns of interaction which have developed out of traditional practices.

This chapter is a study of the social organization of green building. By social organization we understand the constellation of actors engaged in regulating, designing, financing, installing and using environmental technologies as well as the institutional context within which these actors operate (for example regulation, ownership structures and market forces, political influence). The chapter explores the relationship between technology and social organization by analysing the difficulties encountered in selected green buildings in the Berlin region during their development process and the strategies that were adopted to overcome them. First, however, the case studies need to be placed in their institutional setting.

The Political, Economic and Organizational Framework to Green Building In Berlin

The following section provides an overview of the political, economic and organizational forces which determine the scope for action of the actors involved in decision-making processes on a particular green building. It indicates further how these forces have changed in recent years, creating new contexts for green building. These shifts are particularly pronounced in the Berlin region, where over a period of 15 years several components of this framework have changed, altering the opportunities or restrictions faced by the decision makers on building projects. This, in turn, has had considerable impact on the possible ways of arriving at a green building, suggesting the existence of multiple pathways depending on the social organization.

Institutional disincentives to green housing design

The implementation and use of resource-saving technologies is subject to the rules and structures that apply to the design and management of in-house infrastructure in general. In Berlin, as elsewhere, the institutional framework – comprising issues of ownership, regulatory standards and cost mechanisms – has a direct impact on the motivation of key actors in housing to become involved in green design.

Pipes and appliances distributing resources within a building are the property of the house owner, who is, therefore, responsible for investing in these installations and for maintaining and operating them. The basic freedom of the proprietor to determine the features of his or her building is limited considerably in practice, as house owners have to comply with detailed regulations regarding in-house infrastructure. These regulations are mainly intended to ensure that in-house infrastructure corresponds with the existing regional/urban technical network. Since such networks tend to be highly standardized, the regulations as a rule leave little scope for individual negotiations between house owner and utility on the technical specifications of a building. The regulations are mainly issued by the municipalities or counties legally responsible for the networks, who, being owners of the utilities in many cases, have an interest in the compliance of private actors with the centralized system.

For rental accommodation, the owner and the user of in-house infrastructure are not one and the same person. In this case the house owner functions as provider of the physical links between the urban/regional networks and the users. This intermediary function of the house owner is present also in the methods of payment for utility services. Except for electricity, tenants in Germany generally do not have direct contact with the utility, as they are not directly invoiced for these services by the utility. The house owner is presented with an overall bill for the whole building by the water or waste utilities and passes these expenses on to his tenants as so-called 'running costs' paid together with the monthly rent. The overall expenses of a tenement block are in most cases distributed among tenants in proportion to the size of flats and not according to individual consumption (Schmid and Wetekamp, 1996, p116).

As tenants do not usually have any influence over the choice of technologies, their efforts to reduce consumption are limited to the way they use the existing installations. Given the method of paying for utility services, they have little financial interest in reducing consumption as they can benefit from free-rider incentives. Every tenant in a house will benefit from one particular tenant's reduced consumption and the advantages for each decrease the more apartments the building comprises.

At the same time there is no incentive for the house owner to invest in resource-saving technology as he is legally bound to pass on to the tenant the exact sum charged for resource consumption within the building. Reduced resource consumption would therefore result in lower running costs for tenants without offering the house owner an opportunity for return on investment. House owners have, therefore, traditionally displayed a low interest in any technologies affecting running costs.

Thus, the institutional setting serves to discourage resource savings in residential property for both user and house owner. The scope for applying green technologies voluntarily in rental housing is thereby limited considerably.

Green building as a political objective

In response to inadequate private engagement in introducing green housing technology – at least in tenement housing – federal, state and municipal authorities in Germany elevated green housing to a policy field requiring government attention, a move in accordance with the general shift in political priorities towards environmental issues. Since the 1980s, public authorities have launched a number of initiatives to promote and disseminate green building technologies.

In the early days, ambitious model projects were initiated all over Germany, but Berlin was a clear pioneer in this field (Foerster-Baldenius, 1995). The model projects were the core of a political strategy that assumed that establishing and publicizing positive examples was the most effective way to disseminate the relatively unknown and untried technologies. Experience gained in the model projects would flow into mainstream building know-how resulting in a wider application of green technologies (Hahn, 1993). To pursue this objective the Berlin Senate committed considerable funds to selected, ambitious green housing projects (Abgeordnetenhaus, 1994).

The limits of this policy approach soon became apparent. The funding necessary to overcome resistance from development companies and other involved actors in order to successfully establish the projects proved higher than initially expected. In the early 1990s Berlin's severe budget crisis made further generous project funding impossible, resulting in a marked decline in new green housing projects. Moreover, the expectations with respect to raising awareness for environmental technologies among architects and developers via the projects were not fulfilled. A noticeable influence on ordinary building activity could not be observed as green building in rental housing continued to be limited to highly subsidized projects.

Nevertheless, the model projects successfully contributed to preparing the ground for another political instrument: including green building technology into building regulations. The Senate decided to add several 'uncontroversial' green technologies, such as water-saving appliances and waste-separation bins, to minimal requirements in state-funded residential building (WFB, 1990). A further extension of environmental building regulations (for example on solar heating), however, no longer seems an attractive policy instrument given recent political orientation towards greater deregulation.

Not willing to give up green building as a policy objective but unable to pursue conventional strategies further, the Senate has started to experiment with new policy instruments, including voluntary agreements with business organizations and shifting responsibility for dissemination of green housing technologies on to utilities, partly in exchange for new commercial opportunities. Nevertheless, politics now plays a less decisive role in promoting green buildings than it did ten years ago.

New market opportunities

Although political activity in supporting green building has been reduced substantially, a respectable number of new projects have been started in the region since the mid-1990s. This indicates that new factors must be coming into play, opening up new opportunities for green buildings despite the reduced availability of public funding. These factors, it would appear, include, primarily, shifts in the housing market and the maturation of green technologies from experimental status to marketable goods.

The housing market: changes in scarcity relations

For decades the region's housing market was characterized by a severe lack of supply in accommodation. Dramatic rent increases were prevented by rent regulation, but landlords did not need to make great efforts to find a tenant so long as the accommodation they offered fulfilled basic requirements in comfort. After the opening of the Berlin Wall, expectations of a major population increase for the Berlin region induced massive new building activity. However, these predictions have proved ill-founded till now, creating the highly unusual situation of a surplus of accommodation.[1] For the first time in many years house owners are having to compete for tenants. The result is a stronger consideration of user preferences by housing companies and private house owners.

Among other improvements, the house owner can be motivated to install green technologies to attract tenants who are interested in an ecological lifestyle. These people – in the eyes of the house owner – tend to be well educated with a reliable source of income, thus making them attractive tenants. A more important factor for considering green technologies to attract new tenants is potential reductions in utility service costs achieved via resource-saving technologies. In recent years, prices for utility services, mainly for the disposal of sewage and solid waste, have risen substantially (Bundesbaublatt, 1998). Financial burdens on consumers have risen correspondingly. House owners see their own financial interests involved as the scope for rent increases diminishes and the risk of non-payment of utility bills by poorer tenants increases (Das Grundeigentum, 1997b). Furthermore, in times of a relaxed housing market, the level of running costs becomes an important factor in determining the attractiveness of a building for (potential) tenants. Therefore the cost of utility services has caught the attention of housing companies and private owners after a long period of neglect. Although a significant shift towards green technology cannot, as yet, be observed, some resource-saving technologies are now being seriously considered by housing companies as an attractive means to cope with the problem of ever-increasing running costs (Verband Berlin-Brandenburgischer Wohnungsunternehmen, 1997).

Green technologies as a business opportunity

In the early period of green housing technology the installations had to be custom made owing to the early stage of development of many of the techniques. For this reason these technical appliances were also comparatively expensive. Additionally, it sometimes proved difficult to find companies willing to produce or install these new technologies rather than market their customary products. This lack of motivation among the relevant production companies even contributed to severe quality problems with these technologies (complan, 1994, p43).

Since then, the situation has changed markedly. Specialized companies now count for the most committed promoters of green housing technology. Over time, a large number of small firms have sprung up, focusing their business attention on technologies of this kind. These firms contribute to the spread of the technologies by achieving specialist know-how, standardizing products and routinizing processes, thus reducing both the risk and the unit costs for the customer. At the same time these companies actively promote projects involving these technologies in order to publicize their competence and increase demand for their products.

Most of these companies rely primarily on the owner-occupier market, where green housing technology is better established than in rental apartments owing to the absence of the user–owner divide. Nevertheless, most of these companies did not react to an obvious market demand when developing their products, but were either motivated by environmental concerns themselves or were looking for innovative markets as a niche for commercial survival.

Not only in the production of technologies but also in services connected with their use, new enterprises are playing an important role in creating new options for green technologies. The most prominent of these innovations is the so-called 'operator model' for decentralized cogeneration, which has facilitated a wider implementation of the technology. Its main feature is to externalize decentralized heat production, previously carried out by the house owner, by contracting a specialized company (Das Grundeigentum, 1997a). These new paths have also attracted the attention of the utilities (mainly electricity and gas), who in an environment of increasing competitiveness and commercialization are exploring new fields of activity, including new services connected with the provision of natural resources (Senatsverwaltung für Stadtentwicklung, Umweltschutz und Technologie, 1998).

CASE-STUDY BUILDINGS FROM THE BERLIN REGION

On the basis of the institutional framework, past experiences and emerging trends outlined above we now turn to the cases of selected green buildings in the Berlin region, which can reveal in more detail knowledge on the social organization and processes of introducing green technologies. Specifically, we are interested in determining the kinds of actors involved, their motives for supporting (or rejecting) green technologies, the forms of interaction between the actors and the lessons which can be drawn on the forces shaping technology innovation in the housing sector.

The selected buildings represent different types of housing, different eras of green building and both new and refurbished properties. The case study buildings, Berliner Straße, Yorckstraße and Greifenhagener Straße, are all large tenement blocks, characteristic for Berlin, in contrast to the small terraced estate of user-owned homes in Schöneiche. Two of the buildings are new (Berliner Straße and Schöneiche), the other two are refurbished blocks built at the turn of the 20th century, included in order to reflect the importance of refurbishing the existing housing stock in improving environmental quality. While Berliner Straße and Yorckstraße represent the early phase of green building in Berlin, dating from the late 1980s, the cases of Schöneiche and Greifenhagener Straße are examples of very recent green buildings (see Figure 7.1).

Berliner Straße: A model project in green housing design

Berliner Straße belongs to the series of model projects launched by the Senate of Berlin during the 1980s to gain experience with green housing design and promote green technologies by demonstration (see above). Among these, Berliner Straße was intended to demonstrate and evaluate green housing technologies for larger blocks of rental apartments. The original green design included water-saving appliances, individual water meters as well as grey and rainwater use to reduce water consumption, a low-heat district heating system

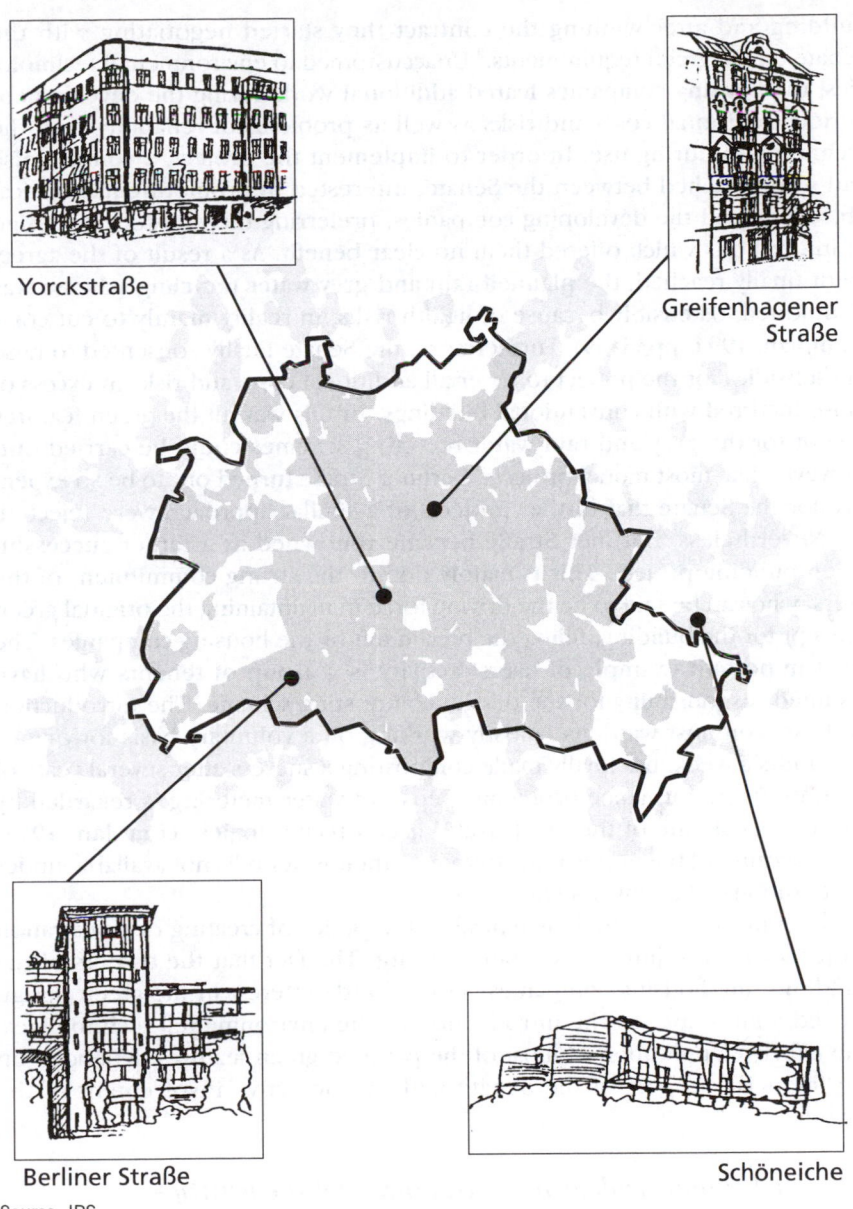

Yorckstraße

Greifenhagener
Straße

Berliner Straße

Schöneiche

Source: IRS

Figure 7.1 *The Case-study Buildings in the Berlin Region*

and the composting of organic waste on site. For social reasons, municipal housing companies were preferred as developers and subsequent owners of the buildings.

Unexpectedly, the Senate met considerable resistance on the part of the housing companies involved. While the building site had been an attractive object for the companies to bid for, they did not favour the idea of a green building and after winning the contract they started negotiating with the Senate on the green requirements.[2] Unaccustomed to environmental technologies, the housing companies feared additional work during the development period, additional costs and risks as well as problems of reliability with the technologies during use. In order to implement the project, a compromise had to be reached between the Senate, interested in promoting its political objectives, and the developing companies, preferring their customary design to innovations which offered them no clear benefit. As a result of the agreement finally reached, the planned rain and grey water recycling scheme was abandoned, ostensibly because of health risks, in reality mainly to cut costs (complan, 1994, pp38–39). Furthermore, the Senate finally consented to raise the subsidies for the project to cover all additional costs and risks in excess of those incurred with conventional buildings. In this way all the green features except for the grey and rain water recycling schemes could be carried out. However, like most model projects, Berliner Straße turned out to be so expensive for the Senate that further projects of a similar approach were rejected.

Nevertheless, Berliner Straße became renowned as a rather successful green building project. This is mainly due to the strong commitment of the users, who can be said to be the driving force in maintaining the original green concept for the building, filling the breach left by the housing companies. The most important example of users' activity is a group of tenants who have assumed responsibility for the on-site composting scheme. The introduction of these 'compost wardens', mostly working on a voluntary basis for one or two hours a week, has finally made composting a success after several years of continuous performance problems. Separate water metering is regarded by the tenants as one of the most useful green technologies (complan, 1994, p95), because of the opportunity to reduce their water bills not available under the traditional charging system.

Overall, Berliner Straße is typical of the policy of creating demonstration projects which require heavy state funding. The fact that the owners of the buildings, the housing companies, showed little interest in the green design proved a hindrance to the introduction of the environmental technologies. The effective application of most of the planned green features depended on the financial support of the Senate and on the active involvement of the tenants.

Schöneiche: independent infrastructure and the utility – the classic conflict

The selected building in the small municipality of Schöneiche, close to the edge of Berlin, is exceptional among the case-study buildings because it is a group of 13 terraced houses owned by the users. Apart from the green approach, a strong community spirit underpins the rationale behind the building. It was built between 1994 and 1997 by a group of families within a self-help programme. The families decided on all specifications for the building in a collective discussion process in consultation with an architect, committing considerable free time to acquiring the necessary knowledge.

Thus, user involvement in the planning and design phase was unusually intensive, even compared with the development process of conventional owner-occupier houses, where user influence is generally higher than with rental buildings. The ideas for green technologies for the building were introduced in the course of this decision-making process.

The most noteworthy aspect of green technology is the independent sewage disposal system. A reed bed treatment plant is used for grey water treatment, while composting toilets reduce the amount and polluting content of sewage to be treated. The selection of the sewage system was motivated not only by environmental convictions, but also by the desire to save on the investment and disposal costs incurred if the houses had to be connected to a planned central sewerage system at a later date. Being both investor and user, the owner-occupiers were not limited by the financial disincentives predominant in the rental sector when calculating investment and future disposal costs.

Independent sewage disposal, though, came into conflict with the local water utility's strong preferences for comprehensive and uniform sewage disposal, as substantiated in their technical regulations. In Schöneiche, the local utility's statutes initially prohibited decentralized sewage disposal if a connection to the central sewer network was possible. However, the project initiators found powerful support in the municipality, which was able to exercise its influence as part-owner of the utility in favour of the project, effectively resulting in a change in the regulations. However, the financial burden resulting from the decentralized solution for the owner-occupiers proved much higher than originally foreseen. While granting exception from connection obligations the utility was not willing to extend this exemption to on-site infrastructure, obliging the owner-occupiers to lay sewers on their premises in preparation for possible connection to the central sewer system in the future (Wasserverband Strausberg-Erkner, 1997). This necessitated costs that were so high that the owner-occupiers claimed afterwards that they would not have considered a green sewage treatment plant had they known the final sum in advance.

This case illustrates that the prevailing relationship between house-owner and utility becomes destabilized when green technology is involved. The necessary exemption from technical guidelines leads to extensive negotiations with the utility, even involving additional actors (in this case the municipality) as mediators. This is a very untypical form of interaction between utility and house owner, departing from the conventional top-down relationship.

Originally, the building group also pursued a green energy concept, envisaging a common heating facility. Ultimately, however, each house was provided with ordinary central heating. The reason for this change of mind lay in the inability to strike a compromise agreement among the participants of the group who were not prepared to endure a further complicated and lengthy discussion process. This development indicates the limits to collective decision-making processes in user involvement,[3] which are nevertheless indispensable in all houses with a large number of users. The burden on owner-occupiers who take on work that is normally done by paid professionals can, clearly, limit their capacity to be actively involved in the planning process.

Yorckstraße: the aims and the reality of 'green urban redesign'

The Yorckstraße building is the older of the two green refurbishment projects presented here. The idea for the project was developed by the Berlin borough of Schöneberg in 1987. The original intention was to refurbish the whole neighbourhood – officially declared as an area of urban renewal – according to the principles of urban ecology (Senatsverwaltung für Bauen und Wohnen, 1992). The building in Yorckstraße was to act as a pioneering project to gain experience and knowledge which could be applied to other buildings of the same kind: that is, typical inner-city tenement blocks built around the year 1900 with a high population density.

The green in-house infrastructure for the Yorckstraße building was supposed to consist of solar heating and the use of rainwater for toilet flushing. In addition, a computer-based control system for the heating facilities was intended to reduce the tenants' energy consumption to a minimum. Special noise-resistant windows absorb most of the traffic noise from Yorckstraße.

After the features of the green design were agreed upon by the borough and its consultants, the project met resistance very similar to that of the Berliner Straße case. Although the municipal housing company that owned the building was legally bound to follow the political objectives of the borough,[4] it opposed the idea of a green building. The housing company's resistance was appeased by additional generous funding for the project which enabled all the planned green technologies to be installed. Once again, considerable concessions from the Senate and borough, taking on additional financial burdens and risks, saved the project.

Despite the installation of all the technologies from the original design, major problems have arisen with their use which are so serious in the eyes of both the borough and the housing company that the borough has cancelled all further plans for green refurbishment in the neighbourhood. In part, the appliances introduced have been technically deficient, requiring considerable expense for frequent repairs. The main reason for abandoning further plans for the neighbourhood as a whole, though, is attributed to the incorrect use of the green technologies by the residents. Housing company and borough both see the root of the problem in the social situation of the inhabitants, who are mainly immigrants. They regard the inhabitants as not sufficiently interested in their housing environment to take greater care of the technologies, and not literate enough in the German language to understand written directions on how to use them properly. As a result the housing company has reduced its efforts to explain the technologies to the users.

Although the immigrant inhabitants do not appear – according to our research – to be as indifferent towards their housing environment and neighbourhood as is assumed by the housing company and borough, cultural differences have obviously prevented the conventional information strategies of the housing company from working effectively. Thus the 'failure' of the house can be said to be at least as strongly rooted in communication and social problems as in technical shortcomings.

Greifenhagener Straße: new opportunities through new organization

The Greifenhagener Straße building is in age, size and characteristics very similar to the Yorckstraße case but, in contrast, the project was not initiated by the political administration nor did it receive major additional funding for its green technologies. By the mid-1990s, green building had ceased to be a political priority worth devoting considerable funds or attention to. But several actors who had contributed to the development of model projects in the late 1980s were still professionally active. Thus the Greifenhagener Straße project originated on the initiative of an urban renewal agency responsible for the building and actively involved in green refurbishment during the earlier period, acting together with a group of motivated tenants. They decided the building should be provided with a decentralized co-generation plant, producing heat, warm water and electricity on site, a photo-voltaic panel for peak demand in summer, a central warm water supply for washing machines and dishwashers and rainwater flushing in the toilets.

Similar to the Yorckstraße case, the owner of the building, an individual not resident in the building himself, was not involved when the ideas for the green specifications of the building were developed, but had to be persuaded afterwards. One might have expected serious reservations on his part, given the limited incentives for house owners to invest in green technologies (see above) and previous experiences with similar projects (see Yorckstraße). Instead, the owner accepted the idea even though he had no previous interest in environmental technologies. The decisive factor for his consent was that his overriding interest in the commercial viability of the project could be assured by contracting the co-generation out to an external operator, a novel organizational practice recently gaining ground in Berlin. The owner financed the plant, then leased it to the Berlin gas utility, which now performs the function of an independent operator. The users have to buy heat as well as electricity from the gas utility, which itself undertakes all the necessary interaction with the tenants, thereby reducing the house owner's duties in running his building and giving him an acceptable financial return on investment at the same time – an attractive scheme for the house-owner. Additional financing was secured by redirecting refurbishment funds for green technologies, keeping to the upper limits of refurbishment funding by cutting down on other specifications.

The Greifenhagener Straße building demonstrates the growing role of specialized suppliers and their commercial motives for the development of green building; not only the gas utility but also the technical consultant and the installation company viewed the project as a means to acquire experience in green technology. This, they consider, might give them a decisive advantage over competitors in the future and even contribute to the development of additional demand in the field by demonstrating the successful application of new technologies.

In comparison with the Yorckstraße case, Greifenhagener Straße shows that a project with very similar technical characteristics can develop in a different direction as a result of differences in the social environment. The changing contextual framework of green building in the mid-1990s created for the Greifenhagener Straße project a new actor constellation, an example of setting the social organization of in-house infrastructure on a fresh footing.

CONFLICT AND COMPROMISE BETWEEN ACTORS IN GREEN BUILDING

Conflicting interests

The role and motives of actors are thus important determinants in the application of green technologies in housing. Although each of the case-study buildings is characterized by a distinctive actor constellation, certain actor groups are represented in almost all cases. Table 7.1 compares the attitudes of the actor groups relevant to the decision-making process. The last column draws on the findings from the case-study buildings, as well as those from the earlier analysis of the social organization, to express viewpoints on green technology typical for the respective actor group.

The comparison reveals that the principal interests of the different actor groups in respect to housing technology generally do not coincide. As the various actors expect very different kinds of benefits from a building, they have to reach agreement on the features of a particular building that are able to fulfil the expectations of all actors involved. Traditional buildings can be regarded as a routinized version of finding a compromise, drawing on long-term experience in cooperation. The implementation of new technologies questions the balance of actors' interests inherent in traditional buildings. A new balance of actors' interests has to be sought for every unconventional building; in other words for each green building.

Paths to a consensus

To produce a green building, some kind of compromise has to be achieved. This applies to the case-study buildings as well. Reviewing the outcomes of the decision-making processes in the case-study buildings, several distinct paths for reaching a consensus can be discerned.

Downscaling the technological design

In those instances when, even after intense negotiations, a proposed technical concept could not find universal approval among the actors, the design was adapted. This means, in general, dropping or simplifying some of the technologies originally proposed in order to save the rest of the project. This is the familiar, but unsatisfactory solution encountered in many green building projects, including Berliner Straße and Schöneiche. Equally unsatisfactory from an environmental point of view is when the original design is implemented to the full but the technologies are either not used or not used correctly (eg Yorckstraße).

Table 7.1 *Actors' Interests in Respect to Green Technologies in the Berlin Region*

Actor group	*Berliner Str. – A model project in green housing design*	*Schöneiche – Independent infrastructure and the utility – the classic conflict*	*Yorckstr. – The aims and the reality of 'green urban redesign'*	*Greifenhagener Str. – New opportunities through new organization*	*Prevailing viewpoint within actor group*
Owner	No additional costs and risks accepted, avoid change in accustomed planning and work procedures	Personal preference for green lifestyle, reduce costs (running costs for resources, investment costs for installing facilities)	No additional costs and risks accepted, avoid change in accustomed planning and work procedures	Maintain financial viability of project, secure long-term attractiveness of accommodation with tenants via low running costs	Investment: additional investment costs must produce equivalent commercial benefit
Users	Save on running costs for resource consumption, improve housing conditions, no reduction in accustomed housing comfort accepted	as for Owner	Some users ignorant of the green technology: too complicated to use and no information available	Personal preference for green lifestyle, reduction of running costs	Consumption: housing comfort, personal lifestyle, costs of resource consumption
Local government	Demonstrate feasibility, gain experience for wider dissemination of technology	Municipality supported user-owners	Demonstrate feasibility, gain experience for wider dissemination of technology	Neither explicit political support nor resistance	Public welfare: environmental protection as political objective, but subject to higher political priorities
Contractors: architects, technical consultants	Uncomplicated fulfilment of contract, ie without unaccustomed green requirements	Offer standardized technology, develop expertise in green building in order to get additional contracts	Execute contracts	Offer standardized technology, develop expertise in green building in order to get additional contracts	Product: niche market strategy to promote business
Utility	Not affected by single model project, secure good cooperation with Senate	Increase number of users of central sewer system for commercial reasons	Not affected by single model project, secure good cooperation with Senate	Exploit new possibilities to diversify commercially	Urban/regional networks: maintain functioning of networks technically, economically and organizationally

Compensatory solutions

The buildings from the case studies present, however, other examples of how to secure a consensus while maintaining the original green approach. A common strategy to reach agreement among the actors in the case-study buildings was to introduce compensatory schemes. Compensation implies, in most cases, financial concessions by those actors favouring the original green design. The consent of actors who see their interests negatively affected is literally bought. The Berliner Straße case demonstrates this consensus strategy; the housing company, originally resisting green technology demanded by the Senate, finally consented when additional funding was granted such that the company's costs and risks were no higher than for an ordinary building. In Schöneiche, the owner-occupiers had to appease the water utility by installing extra sewer pipelines at their own expense – here, again, additional payments to a reluctant actor served to secure the necessary approval. Non-monetary kinds of concessions could theoretically play an important role as well, but were not used with the case-study buildings.

Organizational innovation

Compensatory solutions are of an individual nature, devised for a particular case, with the amount of the compensation depending directly on the individual perception of damage on the part of the compensated party. Organizational innovation, in contrast, changes the organization of a building or the building process in such a way that the green technology will not produce significant negative effects for any of the actors involved. The basic interests of all actors are maintained.

Among the case-study buildings, one example of how organizational innovation can work stands out in particular. In the Greifenhagener Straße building the financial interests of the house owner, who regards the building primarily as an asset, could be protected by shifting the responsibility for daily management of the energy supply on to an external operator – a form of organization not present in the traditional management of in-house infrastructure. Externalizing heat production overrides traditional institutional disincentives to installing green technology, as independent operators can profit from resource-saving investments in in-house infrastructure. External operators, therefore, often apply co-generation, this way entering the electricity market in competition with the utilities. This new scheme also overcomes severe administrative barriers by circumventing the licensing procedure, otherwise necessary for a house owner intending to sell electricity to his tenants.

Organizational innovation can even become a precondition for the successful operation of a green technology. This was the case with the composting facilities in Berliner Straße. Whereas at the onset the composting was said 'not to work', evoking the notion of technical failure, it turned out simply to need basic regular care. As this kind of work is not needed for conventional waste disposal, it had not been provided. A new form of organization for operating the compost bins had to be invented which succeeded in making the technology 'work'.

Institutional innovation has the advantage that it can usually be readily copied in other green buildings and may this way encourage the development of new, widely accepted organizational standards which create new routinized balances between actors' interests. Hence, organizational innovation has great potential to contribute to the wider dissemination of green housing technologies.

CONCLUSIONS

This chapter has contributed to the debate on diversity in green buildings by examining the pathways towards a green building, concluding that these, too, can be very diverse. These pathways appear to be shaped less by the environmental technologies selected and more by social processes and institutional arrangements. The path from the original green concept or design to the installation and use of green technologies can be long and arduous, involving many acts of negotiation between the various actor groups involved at different stages along the way.

These social interactions occur not in isolation but within the framework of political, organizational and economic conditions which can create either openings or disincentives for green buildings. In the early phase of green building in Berlin, in the late 1980s, financial incentives were used by the state to overcome house-owners' reluctance to introduce experimental environmental technologies. More recently, shifts in the housing market and rising utility charges have encouraged house-owners to view environmental technologies as an asset for raising the attractiveness of their property. In addition, new organizational models for operating certain green technologies (eg co-generation) are offering ways of bridging the gap between tenants and house owners over their introduction and use.

These findings hold important implications for policies to promote green buildings. It would seem that the provision of state subsidies for model projects, although an important stimulant for green building, also has its limitations, in terms of disseminating technologies and ensuring their correct use. Given the decline in public funding in recent years, government bodies could improve policy impact by considering the institutional settings which encourage green building, directing policy action towards the better exploitation of existing opportunities. This is particularly important today, when major shifts in the organization of utility services and their associated technologies are creating new incentives for the various actor groups to consider green buildings. Directing policy initiatives at exploiting these new openings would be a more cost-effective way of establishing green building on a wider scale.

NOTES

1   Between 1990 and 1997 the population of the whole metropolitan area of Berlin grew by 24,735 persons (statistical offices of Berlin and Brandenburg). The number of new dwellings within the administrative boundaries of the city of Berlin alone

grew by 111,321 over the same period (own calculation according to Investitionsbank Berlin, 1998, p15).

2 See complan, 1994.

3 User involvement is frequently seen as the 'main route' to a wider implementation of green building technologies; see, for example, Schulze Darup (1996, p96).

4 Political influence on refurbishment is high, as it relies heavily on public funding.

REFERENCES

Abgeordnetenhaus von Berlin (1994) *Bericht des Senats an das Abgeordnetenhaus von Berlin: Ökologisches Planen und Bauen*, Drucksache 12/4763, Berlin

Bundesbaublatt (1998) *Monatsdaten zur Wohnungs- und Bauwirtschaft*, vol 3, pp 85–88

complan GmbH (1994) *Berliner Straße 88: Städtebauliche Qualitäten im Wohnungsneubau*, Abschlußbericht Begleitforschung im Rahmen des Experimentellen Wohnungs- und Städtebaus (ExWoSt), Berlin

Das Grundeigentum (1997a) *Wärmelieferung als Dienstleistung*, vol 5, pp296–298

Das Grundeigentum (1997b) *Jahn: Mehr Transparenz bei den kommunalen Gebühren*, vol 12, pp706–707

Foerster-Baldenius, P (1995) 'Stadtökologie – Ansätze, Probleme und Ergebnisse: das Beispiel Berlin', in E-H Ritter (ed) *Stadtökologie: Konzeptionen, Erfahrungen, Probleme, Lösungswege*, Analytica (Sonderheft der Zeitschrift für angewandte Umweltforschung Nr. 6), Berlin

Hahn, E (1993) *Ökologischer Stadtumbau: Konzeptionelle Grundlegung*, Peter Lang, Frankfurt a.M.

Investitionsbank Berlin (1998) *Tätigkeitsbericht 1997*, Berlin

Schmid, M and Wetekamp, A (1996) *Mietzins für Wohnraum: Das Gesetz zur Regelung der Miethöhe*, Luchterhand, Neuwied

Schulze Darup, B (1996) *Bauökologie*, Bauverlag, Wiesbaden/Berlin

Senatsverwaltung für Bauen und Wohnen (1992) *Ökologisch orientierte Stadterneuerung in Berlin-Schöneberg*, Berlin baut 11, SenBauWohn, Berlin

Senatsverwaltung für Stadtentwicklung, Umweltschutz und Technologie (1998) *Energiebericht*, SenSUT, Berlin

Verband Berlin-Brandenburgischer Wohnungsunternehmen e.V. (1997) *Betriebskostenmanagement: Ein Leitfaden zur Erschließung von Kostensenkungspotentialen*, BBU, Berlin

Wasserverband Strausberg-Erkner (1997) *Satzung über die Abwasserbeseitigung und den Anschluss an die öffentliche Abwasserbeseitigungsanlage des Wasserverbandes Strausberg-Erkner*, Wasserverband Strausberg-Erkner, Strausberg

WFB (Wohnungsbauförderungsbestimmungen) (1990) 'Richtlinien für den öffentlich geförderten sozialen Wohnungsbau in Berlin' (Guidelines for publicly funded social housing in Berlin), *Amtsblatt für Berlin*, vol 40, pp 1289–1390

INTERVIEWS

General

Representatives from the Berlin Senate Department for Building, Housing and
Transport responsible for ecological building, 5 February 1997

Berliner Straße

Representative from the housing company, technical department, 7 March 1997

Tenant and compost warden from Berliner Straße 84, 28 August 1997

Representative from private consultants on the management of the ecological
technologies, 9 October 1997

Yorckstraße

Representatives from the housing company of the borough of Schöneberg, 17
April 1997

Four tenants (selected at random) from Yorckstraße 51/52 and Katzlerstraße
19/20, 9/10 September 1997

Representative from the borough of Schöneberg, department for town planning
and refurbishment, 24 June 1997

House warden for Katzlerstraße 18/19, 22 September 1997

Schöneiche

One of the architects, also a house owner in the green settlement, 16 June 1997

Greifenhagener Straße

The architect, 28 July 1997

The house owner, 11 September 1997

Representative from the tenants' consulting agency for the borough of Prenzlauer
Berg, 3 July 1997

Representative from the private engineering office responsible for planning the
energy concept of the building, 16 September 1997

Representative from the urban renewal company responsible for the borough of
Prenzlauer Berg, 13 March 1997

8 GREEN BUILDINGS IN AN INFRASTRUCTURE PERSPECTIVE

Jesper Ole Jensen

INTRODUCTION

Recent years have been marked by a rising number of green residential buildings in the Copenhagen region and throughout Denmark, both in terms of new buildings and those renovated under the Urban Renewal Act. The green buildings have been seen as an important way to achieve sustainable cities and have a central role in various national environmental programmes. A focal point of green buildings has been the ability to reduce flows, that is, minimize consumption and outputs of water, energy and materials by using different technical devices. Flow management in green buildings has mainly been understood in terms of 'closing the circuits of flows locally' and 'creating a circular metabolism', often with an implicit understanding of self-reliance for the building as the ultimate in greenness. This understanding has primarily been demonstrated by a number of self-sustained eco-communities, sited in rural environs, using a vast variety of green technologies for managing flows locally. These ideas have largely been copied by many urban projects for green buildings in Denmark. However, the use of the same green elements in buildings has met with several difficulties.

One of the main problems has been that the existing infrastructure networks in many cases have been experienced as an obstacle, not only in a technical sense, but also due to organizational, economic and cultural differences (Andersen et al, 1993; Jensen, 1993). One reason for this is that the question of how the green buildings should relate to the infrastructure networks has been largely ignored. To some extent it has been assumed that the maxim of 'act locally – think globally' would work in such a way that local reduction of flows would automatically help the infrastructure networks to achieve a more efficient flow management, and thereby environmental improvements. However, things are not as simple as that.

Over recent decades technical infrastructure has developed remarkably in Denmark. In almost all sectors large centralized networks have been established, including systems for sewage treatment, waste treatment and combined heat and power (CHP) production, with most cities exploiting the heat surplus for district heating. Moreover, waste incineration is often combined with CHP, which makes heat a waste product in a double sense. These systems, however, have their own logic of flow management (Balslev Nielsen, 1997). Due to the investments in and the efficiency of the systems, almost all households are meant to be connected. Therefore many traditional green technologies like local heat production, reed bed plants, waste composting or recycling of grey wastewater are generally disapproved of by local authorities and network managers. Certain technologies, like solar collectors, are even regarded as harmful for the CHP system.

Increased attention to sustainability and green buildings has, however, started to question this logic. For the green buildings, the potential conflicts might affect both the concept and the locality, as one of the initiators of a renowned eco-village in Denmark (Hjortshøj in Århus) stated in an interview. Asked why the eco-villages have all established themselves in rural areas, and not in the cities, he explained:

> *'I think it is because it is very difficult to do anything about these ideas in the cities. I have a background myself in trying to establish everything in the centre of the city, but we had to realise that those structures in there are so powerful and set in the mould that is our industrial culture, that you can't change it. So to make some of the ideas grow and test them here and now you have to go outside the cities. Once we have made it work here it becomes an image you can transfer to the cities'* (Jensen, 1996).

Although this view represents a rather radical attitude, it underlines the potential conflict between green buildings and the infrastructure networks, and also suggests a reason for the difference between green buildings in urban and rural contexts. To understand the role of green buildings in sustainable development it is necessary to understand how they relate to the technical networks. Do they reconstitute the existing infrastructure networks by following their logic and rationale or do they actually represent new pathways in flow management, for example, a transfer of technical solutions from rural to urban environs as indicated above? In this case, not only technical but also cultural barriers are involved. Studies of the transformation of large technical systems show that cultural biases or incompatibility between the system and its socio-cultural milieu can be just as strong a barrier as technical incompatibilities for implementing alternative technologies into existing systems (Summerton, 1994). The scope of this chapter is to answer some of these questions about the relationship between green buildings and technical infrastructure. This will be done, firstly, by outlining a model of different principal modes of interactions between buildings and networks and, secondly, by presenting the findings of case studies of four buildings in the Copenhagen region.

Buildings and Networks: Different Types of Interaction and Conflicts

Although infrastructure networks and green buildings operate with flow management on different scales and from different rationales, they might not exclude each other. As green buildings can utilize many different concepts of flow management and the networks have developed differently, many combinations are possible. With inspiration from Mary Douglas' grid/group theory (Douglas, 1992, 1996), the principal different modes of interaction can be illustrated by representing the infrastructure networks and the buildings each on its own axis.

Weak and strong grid infrastructure

Within the same region the infrastructure can be developed to various degrees. In some parts of the region the infrastructure can be strongly developed, using centralized and large-scale solutions like district heating based on CHP, regionally based water supply and extended sewerage systems, typically in urban areas. This type of 'strong grid' infrastructure is principally meant to take care of all infrastructure services for all buildings. In other parts of the region, typically in rural environs, the infrastructure can be less developed, only covering the most basic facilities, like electricity and water supply, representing a 'weak grid' infrastructure. 'Strong grid' and 'weak grid' represent ideal types which do not necessarily exist in reality but for this purpose illustrate different features of infrastructure systems, both in technical terms and in terms of organization, capacity and views on the relationship between users and suppliers. Systems with well-developed infrastructure – technical and physical – are likely to have a more bureaucratic organization, leaving less flexibility for individual solutions than systems with less developed infrastructure. The different modes 'strong' and 'weak' are not necessarily permanently stable infrastructure environs but may change with the capacity of the system or the organizational mode. Increased liberalization of the infrastructure networks represents a move from strong to weak grid, with supply services increasingly working under market conditions. As the British experience with liberalized utilities demonstrates, this might give room for more individual performances for both suppliers and customers (Guy et al, 1997), but it also removes the traditional security of supply of energy and water (Graham, 1997).

Light and deep green buildings

As discussed in the introduction, green buildings are often understood in terms of their ability to use technical devices that can 'close the circuits' and reduce the flows of energy, water and materials in and out of the buildings. The differences in metabolism, from linear to circular, can also be understood as light green in contrast to deep green (Haughton, 1997). In light green buildings the minimum environmental standards, as defined in national and local building regulations, are observed but nothing is done to exceed those regula-

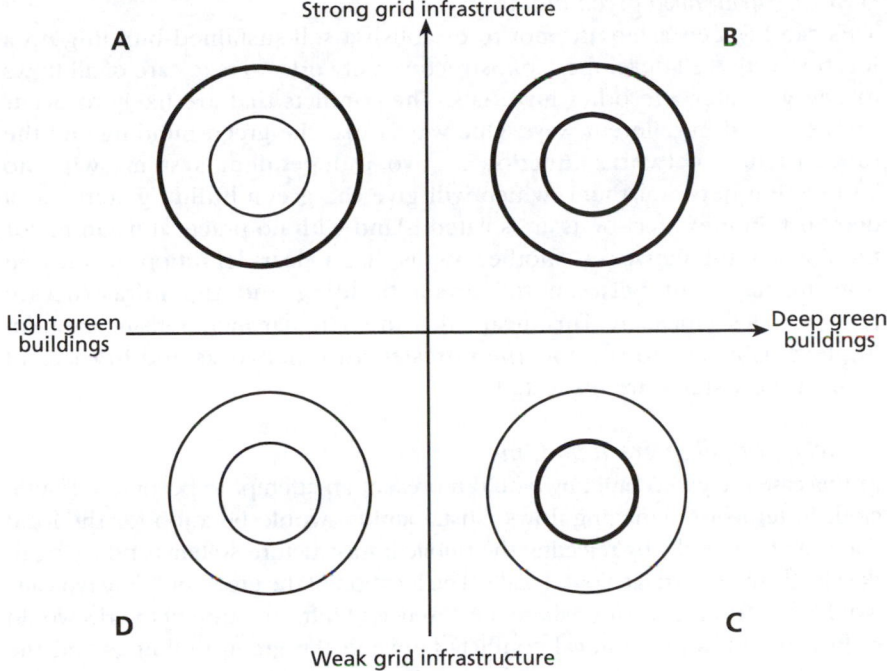

Source: DTU (Technical University of Denmark)

Figure 8.1 *A Typology of Flow Management*

tions. The other end of the scale is represented by a 'deep green' approach, using different technical devices to create a circular metabolism of the building, including local heat and electricity production, collection of rainwater, recycling of grey water, local sewage treatment, extensive waste sorting and waste reduction.

A typology of flow management

Combining the two dimensions gives four principal types of interaction between the infrastructure networks and the buildings, as illustrated in Figure 8.1. The types A–D illustrate principally different models of managing flows in buildings, with different modes of responsibilities between the building and the infrastructure. More detailed characteristics are suggested below, based on the experiences from typical buildings, green and traditional.

A *Strong grid, light green building*

This represents the traditional building, where the green efforts follow the minimum standards defined in building legislation and regulation. In this case the infrastructure networks take care of practically all flows to and from the building. Strong regulation on the one hand ensures that minimum environmental standards are respected, but on the other hand it prevents the building actors from implementing green solutions that exceed minimum standards.

B *Strong grid, deep green building*

This can be seen as an attempt to establish a self-sustained building on a location with well-developed infrastructure networks to take care of all flows of energy, water and other materials. The conflicts that are likely to occur can be solved in different ways. One way is that the green building and the infrastructure networks function as two independent systems with no connection between them, which will give the green building status as a demonstration project or as an isolated island with no practical meaning for the flows of the networks. Another way is that a clear definition of roles on flow management between the green building and the infrastructure networks is established. This means that the 'circular metabolism' at build-ing level is meant to support the infrastructure networks and in cases of conflict the systems are respected.

C *Weak grid, deep green building*

In this case the green building would represent an attempt to become self-suffi-cient in terms of managing flows. Sustainability would be a job for the local community, typically by rejecting the public infrastructure systems and trying to develop ways to manage flows locally. The location of the green building typically would be in rural environs, where the absence of infrastructure networks would reduce the risks of technical conflicts between the green buildings and the networks. A typical representative for this situation could be an eco-village, trying to establish a self-sustained community in rural surroundings.

D *Weak grid, light green building*

Translated into terms of buildings this would mean rather uncontrolled flow management, with the absence of a public infrastructure system and a lack of awareness of local flow management, which is likely to cause both hygiene and environmental problems. Although this situation is rather rare, it is to some extent represented by buildings located in sparsely populated areas with no public infrastructure (for example, sewer systems, heating infrastructure and waste management) and where local flow management is seen as pollut-ing, or health threatening. The environmental regulators pay a lot of attention to these types of buildings, typically planning to solve the problems by improv-ing the public infrastructure, leading towards a situation like that in A.

As described above, the typologies should be thought of as models, which can be used as tools to understand the flow management of a building, including the relationship between local and public networks. In the following section case studies of four different buildings are presented. The buildings in Skotteparken, Torup Ecological Rural Community (TERC) and the Horse Stables Block represent renowned examples of green buildings in the Copenhagen region, while the building in Dagøgade represents a traditional new building. The buildings are different not only in concept but also in their location, including the local infrastructure. Relating the models of Figure 8.1 to the ideas behind the buildings, Dagøgade represents model A, the Horse Stables Block model B, TERC model C, while Skotteparken represents a step from A towards B. From these case studies it is possible to discuss different relationships between the buildings and the networks and what influence the infrastructure has had on the green elements of the building.

FOUR CASE STUDIES ON BUILDINGS AND INFRASTRUCTURE

Dagøgade: the traditional building (type A)

The building in Dagøgade, close to central Copenhagen, is an example of a traditional building and in many ways typical of newer non-profit housing projects. What makes the building traditional is, firstly, that it is subject to very extensive regulation including a well-developed infrastructure and, secondly, that efforts to go beyond the minimum environmental standards have been very limited.

As a non-profit housing estate the building has been exposed to extensive regulation in all phases: planning, design, construction and use. This includes strong economic regulation, with a maximum price range not to be exceeded, which meant that potential green solutions had to compete with other additional elements, like better quality materials and construction, and therefore were discarded. The location in an area with a 'strong grid' infrastructure (district heating based on CHP technology, a well-established sewer system, waste used for incineration, etc) meant that the economic benefits from the green solutions would be rather small:

> 'You are normally in urban areas where the district heating fee is so low that investments have to be fairly low in order for the projects to pay for themselves. The exception is if there are subsidies involved, for instance from the EU ... I still haven't experienced people ready to pay for environmental solutions themselves' (business manager, interview).

Also, the initiators had experienced strong bureaucracy in other cases where additional environmental efforts had been included. Other obstacles for green solutions relating to the location include the administrative burden on the authorities and the physical context, especially the lack of space for alternative solutions (business manager and architect, interviews). What seems to be characteristic in this case is the experience of limited options for individual choices, where all actions are regulated by 'the system' and where just to complete a building is seen as a challenge in itself (business manager, interview).

Skotteparken: an eco-modernist approach (type A/B)

Skotteparken can be said to represent an example of what Marteen Hajer calls 'ecological modernization', with a green concept based on a rejection of both the traditionalist's end-of-pipe solutions and the radical environmentalists', instead believing in the 'rationalization' and 'technicization' of ecology (Hajer,

1996). Although the project in Skotteparken is strongly influenced by the same conditions that were present for the traditional building in Dagøgade (strong regulation in a declining housing market), several steps have been taken towards a stronger local metabolism. With respect to heat consumption, solar panels, ample insulation, passive solar heating and periodical heat supply from a local CHP plant have been applied. As for water consumption, various simple water-saving devices have been installed. Due to these measures, Skotteparken has been internationally acclaimed, awarded the 'World Habitat Award' by the UN in 1994 and 'The European Sun Award' in 1995.

What enabled Skotteparken to take this step is a combination of different factors. Firstly, as the local heat infrastructure in Ballerup is based on decentralized combined heat and power production with natural gas as the fuel, heat savings in buildings are welcome. Secondly, KAB (the non-profit-making housing association of Copenhagen) has, through several environmental projects, tried to distinguish itself as a 'green' non-profit housing association. One of the main reasons for this has been to acquire a special quota for development projects which, unlike the traditional non-profit-making housing quotas, have not been reduced in recent years. This also allowed KAB to exceed the traditional maximum price range by 10 per cent which, along with additional EU funding, helped avoid strong economic regulation that normally would have prevented the extensive use of solar heating. Finally, the concept behind Skotteparken is largely copied from another green building project (Tubberup Vænge I and II). Having Skotteparken defined as a development project enabled collaboration with the same team of consultants and business managers since an EU-wide tender was not required.

One main reason for the implementation of green elements in Skotteparken, unlike in Dagøgade, lies in the ability to avoid different types of regulation: technical (infrastructure networks), economic and administrative (EU regulation). The effort to reduce flows has, however, primarily dealt with heating, while the efforts to reduce flows of water, electricity and waste have been more limited, partly because some green elements had to be abandoned for economic or technical reasons. In addition, the low price of heat provided the residents with very little incentive to limit heat consumption (Honoré, 1997), a further form of influence by the infrastructure networks.

The Horse Stables Block: self-sufficiency in an urban context (type B)

Urban renewal in the Horse Stables Block represents an attempt to establish a self-sustained block as part of the urban renewal of Inner Vesterbro in Copenhagen. The goal is to demonstrate that 'the goals of the Brundtland Report also can be achieved in a urban residential block' (project material from the Ecology Group of the Horse Stables Block). As with the projects in Dagøgade and Skotteparken, the Horse Stables Block is located in a 'strong grid' infrastructure and as an urban renewal project it was also strongly regulated, legally, economically and organizationally. The difference is that the goals to establish circular metabolism at a local level have been far more ambitious and that the residents have had a much more central role.

The project 'Visible Resource Balance' is regarded as a flagship project for ongoing urban renewal. The project contains plans for a common central facility with different environmental devices (a shared central heating system, a common PV plant, plants for rainwater collection, etc) combined with green solutions for the individual buildings. The green elements have been funded through additional financing from the EU and the Ministry of Housing and Building. The residents have been a driving force in the project, however, collaborating closely with consultants, the Urban Renewal Company of Copenhagen (URCC), municipal bodies, local utilities and the Ministry of Housing and Building. Among the green solutions first suggested by the residents and their consultants were windmills, solar panels, energy towers, composting toilets, reed bed plants and local waste sorting. Many of those were, however, changed or abandoned due to incompatibility with the existing networks. The solar panels were excluded because of the policy of the municipality and Copenhagen Lighting Department (CLD) of not combining solar heating with CHP production. Prior sorting of waste into 18 categories was discarded owing both to the small size of the apartments and to the waste utilities' inability to handle so many types of waste. However, the residents generally accepted this:

> 'Would they [R98, the municipal waste manager] want to collect 18 different types and deliver them? Where to? And if they do collect it and put it all into the same bin then it's all ridiculous, and that's what they'll probably do anyway because they haven't got the facilities for handling 18 different types' (resident, interview).

This view emerged in part from face-to-face negotiations with the utilities. Furthermore, the backbone of the project, a central boiler for the whole block, is a result of direct negotiations with the CLD, which saves both money and administrative tasks by having to install and manage only one common central boiler instead of one for each building.

What is characteristic about the project is the emphasis on visibility and on the process rather than on the final result. The visibility of the flows of energy, water and waste in the block is meant to make the residents more aware of environmental issues. It has been realized that long-term changes in the lifestyles of the residents have to be made before more advanced technical solutions can be implemented and the goal for self-reliance can be achieved.

Torup Ecological Rural Community (TERC): self-sufficiency in a rural context (type C)

The Torup Ecological Rural Community (TERC) represents another renowned settlement of green buildings. The community is located in the Municipality of Hundested in the north-western part of Zealand, on the fringe of the Copenhagen region. It consists of 30 dwellings, primarily privately owned houses. The green elements include the use of solar panels, additional heat insulation, PV panels, composting toilets, waste sorting, a reed bed plant for local sewage treatment, a windmill and a large area reserved for organic farming, livestock and vegetable gardens. The residents have to a large extent taken care of the planning, design and construction of the houses themselves. The community dates back to 1982 when a group of people decided to form their own community, integrating work, housing, institutions, leisure activities and other functions. Later, sustainability was made a central theme as well. The dissociation from urbanization and the city, which are seen as the main factors for unsustainability – ecological and social – in our society, was one of the driving forces for shaping the community.

The location of the community fulfils several practical goals. The long distance from Copenhagen makes work in Copenhagen less attractive, increases the opportunities for creating local jobs and reduces the segregation between work and home. Also, the low price of land and property taxes was seen as an important factor in the initial start-up phase. Finally, the limited public infrastructure and the positive attitude towards the concept of TERC from the municipal administration of Hundested were other reasons for choosing this location. As there was no public heat supply, no sewage system or any CHP production based on waste incineration, the green features of TERC fitted well into the existing infrastructure context. Indeed, TERC was rewarded in 1994 with the European Solar Prize for being the first local plan in Denmark based on solar heating. In spite of the location, some green initiatives collided with public infrastructure management. Waste treatment and disposal facilities were shelved due to national waste regulations and the plan for using waste water from the reed bed plant as a fertilizer for growing vegetables was prohibited by EU legislation on organic farming. Finally, the existing reed bed plant was transformed into a percolation facility as it was unable to meet the new demands on outlets following the establishment of a municipal sewer system in Torup.

DIFFERENT NETWORK RELATIONS, DIFFERENT SUSTAINABLE PATHWAYS?

In the following section, different aspects in the cases will be discussed regarding the interrelationship between buildings and networks. The discussion will be conducted around two main subjects:

- the different understanding of and attitudes towards the networks, and how these affected the concept and the localization of the building; and
- the conflicts between the buildings and networks that occurred in these cases.

Finally, the different interrelationships between buildings and networks are considered as three different pathways towards sustainable development.

Different understanding of network rationales

Firstly, the actors have taken very different accounts of the infrastructure when planning the building. A general characteristic in the shaping of the buildings is that the initiators in all phases have tried to avoid conflicts in the choice of collaboration partners, typically by using existing social and professional networks. This way the actors tend to reproduce existing concepts on green buildings instead of inventing new ones. This is most clearly demonstrated in Skotteparken, where the whole concept, including the consulting team, was largely copied from an earlier project; the other cases also include this type of network building. The choice of location can also be seen as a way to reduce potential conflicts between the building and the local context, including the infrastructure. Especially for the actors of Skotteparken and TERC, the compatibility between the local infrastructure and the concept of the green building as well as the positive attitude of the municipality were important reasons for choosing a location there. Avoiding conflicts, however, presupposes knowledge of the rationales of the networks and knowledge about technical incompatibilities between different green technologies and different infrastructure networks. Obviously, the more experienced actors are aware of this and are able to take the necessary steps, as the quote from the eco-village representative above indicates and as demonstrated in the cases of Skotteparken and TERC. In the Horse Stables Block the initiators were practically unaware of the rationales of the networks and of the technical incompatibilities between the suggested green solutions and the local networks.

Secondly, attitudes towards the networks have been very different, which is reflected in the concept and in the choice of location. For the traditional building in Dagøgade the views of the business manager reflect an acceptance of the rationales of the networks and at the same time resignation in the face of the major obstacle they represent for green solutions in terms of economics, regulation and bureaucracy. A typical statement reflects earlier experiences with the implementation of green solutions:

> 'There are so many bodies involved that you think, "I wish I had never got involved in this, it would have saved me a lot of time"' (business manager, Dagøgade).

The case of Skotteparken, however, illustrates how these regulations can be circumvented by skilfully exploiting different rules/orders of exception provided by the system itself. This is expressed in the way building projects are created:

> 'We would prefer to do it as a development project, because there you can use the same contractor and design team and you don't have to send it to EU tender. This is one way; another way is to keep your eyes open for architectural competitions or even arrange them yourselves' (Head of the Building Department in KAB, Honoré, 1997).

This manipulative and opportunistic approach is reflected in the green building concept, which follows the rationales of the networks, recognizing that it is no use locating where the building is not compatible with the local networks.

In TERC, attitudes towards the infrastructure are also embedded in a perception of society, in this case an anti-urban view.

> *'We want to create a social and sustainable alternative to urbanization. We all know that there is urbanization going on, where people are moving to larger and larger cities, and metropolises are anything but ecological'* (former chairman of TERC).

The existing infrastructure is seen as a major reason for the ecological degradation of cities and therefore the more independent from the networks, the more sustainable. Public regulation that acted as a barrier to some of the green initiatives (EU regulation on the use of waste water on organic crops and national regulation on sewage) confirms the view of infrastructure regulation as being unsustainable.

Although the actors in the Horse Stables Block put the same emphasis on local self-supply as in TERC, the view towards the networks is characterized by loyalty and by a will to find compromises that will satisfy both parts.

> *'... We can't see any ecology in producing our own heat when they're pouring heat out into the Øresund... And we are in a district heating area, it would be much more ecological to get together and use the heat they produce. We would rather produce electricity and help the utilities to get rid of their heat, we think that's much more ecological'* (resident in the Horse Stables Block).

The network managers are seen here, unlike in Dagøgade where they were experienced as remote and bureaucratic, as 'partners in negotiation' with whom it is possible to establish meaningful compromises.

In Table 8.1 the findings of the case studies are presented according to the typology from Figure 8.1, the dominant attitude towards the networks and how the infrastructure influenced the green concept and its location.

Conflicts between buildings and networks

Conflicts between buildings and networks appeared not only in the case of the Horse Stables Block but also in Skotteparken and TERC. In the last two cases, however, the conflicts were more due to unexpected expansion of the local infrastructure networks than to a lack of knowledge about the logic of the networks. This underlines the paradox that increasing environmental regulation and infrastructure development can become a barrier to local green initiatives, although both claim to be working for sustainable development. Although technical incompatibilities are the main reason for the conflicts in these cases, they can be emphasized by cultural bias, as in TERC where the local political attitude towards TERC apparently influenced the decisions on whether dispensations should be given to the reed bed plant.

Table 8.1 *Summary of the Main Findings from the Case-study Buildings in the Copenhagen Region*

	Typology	Attitudes towards infrastructure and regulation	Influence of infrastructure on buildings
Dagøgade The traditional building	A. Strong grid (central Copenhagen), no efforts to reduce flows beyond minimum standards	Systems seen as remote and bureaucratic, resignation towards strong regulation	Green solutions seen as unprofitable and time-consuming due to infrastructure and bureaucracy
Skotteparken An eco-modernist approach	A/B. Less strong grid (suburb of Copenhagen), extensive heat savings, some water savings	Acceptance of the infrastructure rationality, but an opportunistic approach and ability to find ways to avoid strong regulation	Infrastructure important for location, limited conflicts between buildings and networks
Horse Stables Block Self-sufficiency in an urban context	B. Strong grid (central Copenhagen), many green initiatives (water, sewage treatment, electricity production, waste sorting)	The network managers seen as negotiation partners, loyalty towards the logic and rationales of networks	Technical incompatibilities not considered, many green solutions abandoned or changed due to conflicts with networks
TERC Self-sufficiency in a rural context	C. Weak grid (rural environs), many green initiatives (heat savings, sewage treatment, electricity production, water savings, waste sorting)	Suspicion towards infrastructure, seen as representative of urbanism, unchangeable and should be avoided	Infrastructure important for location, some conflicts due to expansion of existing networks and national and international regulation

Source: DTU (Technical University of Denmark)

The cases demonstrate that the network managers generally accept green technologies if they support the logic of the systems. If used in sympathy with the local infrastructure some technologies, like solar panels, are accepted by the network managers. This indicates that the views on green technology are not decided by a general bias but rather by the logic of the local infrastructure. Instead, biased views about the residents, what they are willing to accept and assumptions about their wishes and so on, are more likely to influence views on green technologies. In Skotteparken the residents did not use the technical solutions as they were supposed and expected to, which resulted in technical problems and less heat reduction than expected. Statements such as: 'If they [the residents] could get a freezer into their flat, that would be wonderful, no matter what quality' (representative from the Copenhagen Lighting Department on urban renewal on Vesterbro) demonstrate a typically biased view of the users which had very little factual evidence in the Horse Stables Block. However, the cases also demonstrate that the conflicts can lead to direct negotiations between users and network managers which might result in compromises or new solutions for flow management. This was especially demonstrated in the Horse Stables Block (change of local heat production to local electricity production and the establishment of the common central heating boiler in collaboration with the CLD), but also in TERC (reed bed plant changed to a percolation facility).

Different pathways of sustainability

The green buildings in Skotteparken, TERC and the Horse Stables Block can be said to represent three different pathways of sustainable development. The question is, however, whether they represent any new pathway. The concepts of models A and C, primarily represented by the buildings of Dagøgade/Skotteparken and TERC, in many ways reflect the differences between the strategies of 'environmental sound planning' and 'urban ecology' (Jensen, 1994). The first follows a universal technical rationality, aiming at solving one problem everywhere, while the second is based to a larger extent on intuition, with a lack of any scientific approach but typically including a wider array of environmental solutions. Traditionally, flow management and green technologies in eco-communities are regarded as alternatives to the established systems. However, the general approach represented by these communities is in fact part of a long cultural tradition (Douglas, 1992; Jensen, 1994), typically expressing a strong social protest towards existing societal values. One can argue, therefore, that both strategies represent traditional pathways but with opposite attitudes towards the network logic.

In contrast, the project in the Horse Stables Block contained a number of conflicts as the initiators were largely unaware of the logic of the networks; this can be seen as a third pathway. Unlike the other projects the technical solutions were not defined from the beginning but were shaped through negotiations between the actors of the building and the network managers and thereby can be said to contain a more dynamic element than the other strategies. Due to incompatibilities it is, however, likely that the technical solutions are less impressive than those of the other strategies and might just be of symbolic value. From this perspective the common central heating boiler can serve as a symbol of this strategy. The central boiler was developed in collaboration with the actors of the green building and the network managers and represents a compromise that satisfies both parties. For the green building it represents a basis for different common green facilities, for the network managers a lesser administrative burden and thus financial savings. The solution implies a redistribution of responsibilities between users and utilities although technically the central boiler does not include any flow reductions. However, it represents a necessary base for different green appliances to be established in the future.

This strategy might help to break down cultural biases between the actors which in all cases exist between the users and the network managers to some extent. The flow managers might discover that people may be willing to sort their waste, use some advanced water-saving devices or even pay for environmental solutions themselves. For their part, the users might discover that green solutions can be discussed with the network managers and that meaningful compromises can be achieved.

CONCLUSIONS

The case studies offer some ideas about the role of green buildings in the future and their relationship with infrastructure networks. As demonstrated in the case studies, the local infrastructure context has a strong influence on the concept of green buildings; what is possible in a rural context might be most difficult to complete in an urban context as the compatibility with the networks is totally different. Therefore a certain concept of a green building might have completely different meanings when located in central Copenhagen and on the fringe of the region.

The three green buildings can be said to contain three different pathways in the development of sustainable flow management. One pathway, primarily demonstrated in Skotteparken, represents a development of green solutions that accepts the logic of the networks and exploits the possibilities of new infrastructure technologies and logic: for instance, decentralized heat and power production and increasingly liberalized utilities. However, this strategy tends to lack user involvement, running the risk of introducing technical solutions that are incompatible with the users' needs and understanding, as partly indicated in Skotteparken. In TERC a second pathway is visible, also including technological development, but based on small-scale solutions as an alternative to the large technical systems, whose rationales are largely rejected. This strategy, however, implies to a large extent a strong bias against the infrastructure systems and network managers, which means that local solutions are not necessarily meant to be technically compatible with the existing infrastructure networks and therefore might be difficult to transfer to cities. A third pathway, demonstrated in the Horse Stables Block, is based on what could be called socio-cultural development and only to a limited degree on technological development. This emphasizes an increased environmental awareness of the users and an erosion of the cultural biases between network managers and users, thereby improving the chances of developing infrastructure solutions with collaboration from both sides. This strategy, emphasizing the process instead of the technical solutions is, however, less likely to reduce flows instantly and differs in this way from the other strategies.

The three pathways of green buildings represent different attitudes towards the logic of the networks. As the actors generally try to avoid conflicts with the networks there is also a tendency that certain types of networks will attract certain types of green building concepts and thereby develop different types of interrelationships. Lack of awareness of this logic (as in the Horse Stables Block) or unexpected changes in local infrastructure planning (as in Skotteparken and TERC) are likely to lead to incompatibilities between the green buildings and networks and therefore to conflicts and confrontation between different understandings of flow management. However, this might be unavoidable if new pathways are to be developed.

REFERENCES

Andersen, I-E, Danielsen, D, Elle, M, Drewes Nielsen, L (1993) *Byøkologiske øjebliksbilleder* (*Momentary pictures of the urban ecology*), TeknologiNævnet, Copenhagen

Balslev Nielsen, S (1997) 'Omstilling af teknisk infrastruktur' ('Changing technical infrastructure'), PhD dissertation, Department of Planning, Technical University of Denmark (DTU), Lyngby

Douglas, M (1992) 'Governability: A Question of Culture', *Millennium: Journal of International Studies,* vol 22, no 3

Douglas, M (1996) *Natural Symbols,* 3rd edition, Routledge, London

Graham, S (1997) 'Liberalized Utilities, New Technologies and Urban Social Polarization. The UK Experience', *European Urban and Regional Studies,* vol 4, no 2

Guy, S, Graham, S, Marvin, S (1997) 'Splintering Networks: Cities and Technical Networks in 1990s Britain', *Urban Studies,* vol 34, no 2, pp191–216

Hajer, M (1996) 'Ecological modernization as cultural politics', in S Lash, B Szerszynski and B Wynne (eds) *Risk, Environment & Modernity. Towards a New Ecology,* SAGE Publications, London

Haughton, G (1997) 'Developing sustainable urban development models', *Cities,* vol 14, no 4, pp189–195

Honoré, J (1997) 'Den grimme ælling. Den gode økologiske bolig' ('The ugly duckling. The good ecological dwelling'), Masters Thesis at Institute for Planning, Technical University of Denmark (DTU), Lyngby

Jensen, O M (1994) 'Ecological building – or just environmentally sound planning?', in *Danish Ecological Building,* The Danish Architectural Press, Copenhagen

Jensen, P (1993) *Hvor bli'r byøkologien af?* (*What's holding back the urban ecology?*), Dansk Byplanlaboratorium, TeknologiNævnet, Copenhagen

Jensen, Th (1996) 'Dansk byøkologi – illusion eller virkelighed? En analyse af danske byøkologiprojekter og byøkologiens aktører' ('Danish Urban Ecology – Illusion or Reality? An analysis of Danish Urban Ecology Projects and the Actors of the Urban Ecology'), Masters Thesis, Aalborg Universitet, Denmark

Summerton, J (ed) (1994) *Changing Large Technical Systems,* Westview Press, Boulder, Colorado

INTERVIEWS

TERC (Torup Ecological Rural Community)
Building technician at the Technical Services, Municipality of Hundested, 21 April 1997
Representative from the Waste Water Department, Technical Services, Municipality of Hundested, 21 April 1997
Resident and former chairman for ØLK, 26 June 1997

Skotteparken
Representative from Cenergia, technical consultants, 11 August 1997 (by telephone)
Architect at the Technical Services Department, Municipality of Ballerup, 20 August 1997 (by telephone)

The Horse Stables Block
Representatives from the Environmental Protection Agency of Copenhagen, 5
    February 1997
Representative from the Urban Renewal Company of Copenhagen, 5 February
    1997
Representative from Copenhagen Water Supply, 13 March 1997 (by telephone)
Representative from Copenhagen's Lighting Department, 13 March 1997
Representative from the Urban Renewal Centre of Vesterbro, 16 April 1997
Resident and participant in the Ecology Group of the Block Council in the Horse
    Stables Block, 16 April 1997
Engineer and consultant for the Horse Stables Block, 27 June 1997

Dagøgade
Project Manager in Boplan, 25 June 1997
Architect at Hjembæk Tegnestue, 26 June 1997

CONCLUSIONS: UNDERSTANDING GREEN DESIGN

Simon Guy

This section has questioned the view that the diffusion of proven environmentally beneficial technologies and construction techniques is simply a technical challenge. In different ways each of the chapters has argued that in order to assess the changing opportunities for design actors to put their already existing knowledge into practice, we must deepen our understanding of the competing social and technical logic governing development processes.

The case study by Simon Guy and Suzie Osborn demonstrated the contingent and contextual nature of technological innovation and building design. By suggesting a flexibility and plasticity of environmental design strategies, the analysis of differing logic of environmental innovation raises significant questions about the positivistic scientific assumption underpinning the search for a consensual definition of sustainable architectural practice. By exploring how the interplay of competing design logic shapes the techno-environmental profiles and social relations of green building development, the chapter highlighted the contested nature of environmental innovation. Seen this way, alternative technological strategies are the result not of technical superiority, but of distinct philosophies of green design. That is, the concept of sustainable building is fundamentally a social construct. In order to understand green buildings more fully we therefore have to account for the social structuring of both the identification of environmental problems and their resulting embodiment in built forms through multiple technical development pathways.

The second case study by Regine Mauruszat examined how the social organization of 'green' building developments shapes the success and failure of environmental design. By demonstrating which actors influence what stage of the decision-making process and how their motives in introducing and using environmental technologies in the housing sector differ, the chapter showed that the main restrictions for implementing green building technologies are not technical deficiencies but are rather located within the complex social processes necessary to design, construct and subsequently manage a building. For example, as design processes involve a considerable number of different actors, agreement needs to be reached between all of them over objectives and procedures before the building can be constructed or refurbished. This process of interaction occurs against the backdrop of changing regulatory structures and competing standards and conventions established by society to rationalize the activity of building. These may comprise not only government specifications – very important for building – but also in a much broader sense the patterns of actor influence and interaction established through traditional practices.

The article by Jesper Ole Jensen explored the relation between the two dimensions of flow management by using a typology of interactions between buildings and networks. Through four case studies of buildings in the Copenhagen region he demonstrates that infrastructure networks have considerable influence on the concept and location of green buildings. The study showed that the logic of the network–building relationship is very different in each case and that the actors generally try to avoid conflicts between each system. In light of this it was argued that the case studies best represent different pathways of sustainable development, each of which places different emphases on network and local flow management. Thus, the Copenhagen case study demonstrated the importance of location and existing physical infrastructure in shaping the design, planning and implementation of environmental innovation in housing.

Looking across the chapters, the first important conclusion is that a building's environmental design is shaped by the strategic priorities of the many actors involved in the planning, design, construction and use of the building. There is no definitive 'green' building or optimal technical pathway; rather, many different, competing notions of what constitutes 'greenness' exist, and not just the ecocentric or technocentric extremes. As the UK case study illustrated, a green building rarely conforms to a singular technical model or any one ecological vision; it is generally a hybrid, the product of a compromise between several, often conflicting, interpretations of green design of the various actors involved. We have seen how in Berlin, the social organization of in-house infrastructure plays a crucial part in determining the technical design of buildings and how innovative forms of social organization, involving, for instance, a redistribution of actor roles, has been shown to facilitate the application of environmental technologies. However, this does not mean that the technology is unimportant. When designing a 'green' building the choice of in-house technologies is often limited by the need to fit into the surrounding technical infrastructure. This helps to explain some of the difficulties currently encountered in establishing green building projects such as in Copenhagen; if the design rejects the logic of the surrounding system it runs the risk of remaining an isolated 'island of sustainability', if it adapts too closely to the needs of the existing physical networks the openings for innovation are limited.

Taken as a whole, the section has presented a critique of past research into the environmental impact of buildings and outlined the methodological challenges facing a new environmental research agenda. Rejecting any notion of green buildings as merely differently configured technical structures which can be more or less well designed relating to an external definition of accepted environmental standards, we should view green buildings as social expressions of competing ecological values. As a result we might begin to identify more clearly the relationship between the competing conceptions of environmental issues and the social and technical processes framing building design. In understanding green buildings we therefore have to be sensitive not only to the widely differing motivations and commitments of actors but also to the range of techniques or technical innovations employed, the variety of contexts and settings in which development occurs and the social processes involved in the definition and redefinition of the nature of the environmental problem itself. In this way, we may begin to understand how distinct logics of green design are mobilized by different, often competing, actors and framed by dynamic social and technical contexts of building development and infrastructure provision. Adopting this way of seeing building design we might better recognize both the competing pathways of innovation and the hybrid nature of green building.

PART 4

CONNECTING PLANS

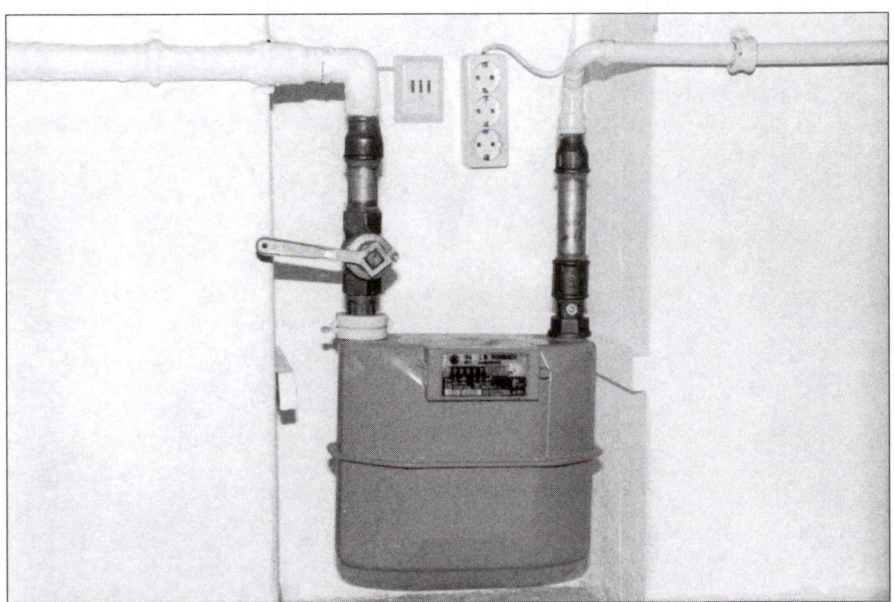

Credit: Timothy Moss

INTRODUCTION

Timothy Moss and Morten Elle

Parts 2 and 3 examined recent changes in the way technical networks are managed from an infrastructure perspective, that is, from the viewpoint of network managers and others directly engaged in providing or using utility services. A distinctive feature of the forces currently transforming urban network management is that they have emerged from outside the sphere of local planning. The changes documented earlier are not the product of local planning or policy making but of other factors such as new regulatory frameworks, changing patterns of resource use or new technologies.

The development of urban infrastructure in the past has, however, been shaped substantially by both spatial and sectoral planning at the local level, particularly in those countries – such as Germany and Denmark – with a strong tradition of municipal planning authority. Indeed, since the 1970s interest has grown in using local planning and policy to improve the environmental performance of localities. Local energy concepts and local waste management concepts are examples of less formalized, but innovative and long-term plans for minimizing resource use. Fresh impetus to the local planning of environmental flows was given by the 1992 Rio Conference on Environment and Development which, in Agenda 21, expressly targeted energy, water and waste issues as key policy fields for the sustainable management of natural resources (Chapters 9, 18, 20, 21). The call for a Local Agenda 21 (LA21) in each municipality has created a broader base for local sustainability planning, encouraging the wider involvement of the stakeholders and more wide-ranging approaches to resource management.

In other words, alongside the new agendas of the utility managers there exist parallel debates on sustainable flow management in the context of what can broadly be termed urban environmental planning. These two strands of debate can – and do – coexist in the same city. The purpose of this section is to discover how far the two levels are interconnected, what opportunities exist for linking the two in the common interest of minimizing urban environmental flows and, thirdly, how new forms of local planning can contribute to more sustainable utility services.

The UK case study investigates the degree of connection between local environmental planning or policy on the one hand and commercial and regulatory forces shaping utility services on the other. Taking the energy sector as an example, the case study seeks to demonstrate how far the changing logic of electricity management in post-liberalization UK is reflected in urban energy and environmental planning. Through analysis of an energy utility's new-found interest in demand side management to relieve network stress in the north of England, the chapter explores what shifts in energy management can mean for local energy and environmental management, indicating areas of potential reconnection between local energy planning and infrastructure management.

The second case study, from Denmark, explores interconnection from another angle, taking LA21 as an example of a new form of local planning and policy making. The interest here lies in determining how far LA21 visions for water, energy and waste management interconnect with ongoing debates among utilities on new ways of managing urban flows. This is investigated with a case study of Albertslund, a municipality of Copenhagen, where the prospects for interaction appear favourable; the region's network managers are interested in sustainable development, the municipality has several active LA21 groups and has traditionally enjoyed a high level of public participation in local planning. The case study examines viewpoints on resource use in the context of LA21, mapping resonance and dissonance between four groups of actors: grassroots groups, the municipality, the utilities and intermediary organizations operating between the others.

The third chapter is a study of diverse styles of local sustainability planning as seen through the window of LA21 initiatives in Berlin. The aim of this case study is to illustrate how new forms of local planning such as LA21 can draw on several, competing visions of sustainable flow management and that these need to be understood for connections to infrastructure management debates to be identified and exploited. Berlin lends itself to a study of diversity owing to the large number and great variety of LA21 initiatives operating within the city, each with a distinctive viewpoint on how water, energy and waste flows should be managed. The case study demonstrates how LA21 aims to reshape flow management. It seeks, further, to identify different styles of LA21 as expressed in terms of the forms LA21 can take, the visions of sustainable flow management pursued and the kinds of activities undertaken.

9 LOCAL ENERGY PLANNING AND ELECTRICITY NETWORKS: DISCONNECTIONS AND RECONNECTIONS

Simon Guy and Simon Marvin

INTRODUCTION

Cities are responsible for most energy-related environmental emissions in the developed world (Douglas, 1983; CEC, 1990). Over the last decade there has been considerable interest in the development of urban energy management strategies as a central plank of local environmental policy (Nijkamp and Perrels, 1994). There has, however, been little critical appraisal of the role of locally based energy and environmental policy. Instead it has become almost universally accepted that the mapping and modelling of the local energy economy provides the most effective basis upon which to develop local environmental policy. Consequently, there is a serious danger of local energy and environmental policy becoming 'disconnected' from the commercial and regulatory forces shaping local energy economies.

We want to critically examine the role of local energy and environmental policy from a distinctly UK perspective. In our view, considerable time, effort and resources are being directed at what has been variously termed local energy management, urban environmental management or local energy planning without a clear analysis of the changing role of energy institutions. Although privatization of the UK energy supply industries has radically restructured the energy sector, little effort has been made to critically assess what these changes mean for processes of local, urban and regional energy and environmental management. Absent from EU and locally funded studies of the urban energy economy has been any understanding of the changing contexts within which private electricity supply companies now operate. The major investment made in the development of local energy and environmental strategies and models may have increased our technical understanding of the size and intensity of energy flows through cities and regions and their associated local and global emissions, but we are concerned that policy has become increasingly disconnected from an analysis of the regulatory and commercial pressures driving these flows along private energy networks. There is an urgent need to develop a more effective understanding of the new pressures shaping the behaviour of private energy utilities and the novel logic driving the liberalized energy sector. Otherwise, local energy and environmental management is likely to remain an irrelevant technical exercise, distanced from the ongoing restructuring of local energy economies.

This chapter is structured around five sections. First, we develop a sympathetic critique of the developing concept of urban energy and environmental management from a UK perspective. Second, we analyse the changing logic in the electricity sector wrought by privatization and deregulation which is pushing regional electricity companies (RECs) into new roles in energy management. Third, we examine a case study of a new demand side management (DSM) initiative, which highlights the ways in which utilities are currently shaping local energy economies. Fourth, we review the new operational strategies that privatized utilities are developing for controlling their energy networks and the profound implications these have for the territorial management of energy resources. Finally, we conclude by examining the ways in which local energy policy may reconnect itself with the 'new energy managers' of the 1990s.

THE LIMITS TO LOCAL ENERGY PLANNING

Urban energy management is an extremely ill-defined concept. In the UK context there is no statutory basis for any form of sub-national energy-related planning. Perhaps the only exception is recent Department of the Environment advice to incorporate energy-related policies into land use planning strategies (DoE, 1992a). Although the early development of the energy sector in the 19th century provided clear opportunities for the local shaping of private and/or municipally based energy institutions, nationalization of the gas and electricity sector largely took energy issues out of the local policy agenda (Thorp and Marvin, 1995).

During the early 1970s there were alternative pressures developing at local level resisting aspects of the strategies adopted by nationalized and centralized energy institutions (see Sheldrake, 1985; Owens, 1986). Examples include resistance to the siting and development of nuclear power stations and new coal field development, local energy conservation schemes to tackle the new issue of fuel poverty, local authority interest in energy savings and new interests in the development of urban renewable and CHP/DH (district heating) energy generation technologies. Energy was no longer simply perceived as a national issue to be directed by centralized energy corporations according to their definition of the national interest. New, localized forms of resistance to key aspects of national energy policies began to develop into a much more coherent analysis of the potential for shaping key aspects of the local energy economy (see CLES, 1986; SEEDS, 1986).

Despite the absence of statutory mechanisms for intervening in the local energy economy, local authority interest in energy issues has developed over the last decade. Many local authorities have built on their role as major energy users to develop programmes of energy efficiency and conservation; innovative local authorities have developed sophisticated energy management strategies for their building stock (Sheldrake, 1985). Left-wing Labour authorities such as the former Greater London Council and Sheffield City Council developed new approaches to municipally based energy policy. These authorities introduced policies that attempted to forge links between energy efficiency, job creation and fuel poverty through the development of new energy technologies such as city wide CHP/DH (CLES, 1986; SEEDS, 1986). New ideas about municipal or cooperative control of local energy supply institutions emerged to challenge free-market belief in privatization, offering alternative modes of energy regulation. These innovative, decentralized models of local energy management were short-lived, extinguished by the abolition of metropolitan counties, restrictions on local government spending and the privatization of the electricity supply industry (Marvin, 1991).

However, as local authority environmental strategies surfaced through the 1990s a new round of interest in local energy management has developed. Driven by growing concerns over greenhouse and acid rain emissions, energy has been identified as a key component in the development of new local environmental policies. These trends have been given considerable encouragement by EU funding for energy studies, Agenda 21 and the emergence of local environmental policies, which have all fuelled interest in the role of the land use planning system as a mechanism for influencing local energy consumption (Elkin et al, 1991; Breheny, 1992; Haughton and Hunter, 1994).

Local authorities have increasingly developed new roles in the development of local energy and environmental strategies, often based on studies of the environmental impacts of local energy flows. Although there is a wide variety of development, preparation, content and participants involved in these initiatives they tend to be characterized by five key assumptions:

1 The *locality or city is viewed as a 'container'* through which energy flows can be measured and policies developed to ameliorate their environmental impacts (Owens, 1989).
2 The environmental performance of the locality could be improved if customers developed a more *rational approach to energy efficiency* (Reddy, 1991).
3 The linkages between energy use, their environmental impacts and policy options can be examined through *modelling and monitoring* (Nijkamp and Perrels, 1994).
4 The local actors involved in the energy sector such as utilities and energy users all have a *shared interest in reducing energy consumption* (Reddy, 1991).
5 The most powerful tools for the implementation of local strategies are *physical land use planning* policies and initiatives (Barton, 1988; Breheny, 1992; DoE, 1992b).

In this chapter, we attempt to demonstrate how each of these features results in increasing disconnection from the wider institutional reality of privatized energy utilities in the 1990s.

First, the 'locality' or city has an important role in energy and environmental strategy. Underpinning these strategies is the assumption that the locality is a container through which energy flows can be measured and their global environmental emissions quantified. Closely linked to this concept is the idea that strategies are more easily implemented at a local level. It assumes that the gap between production and consumption interests can be bridged by local policies encouraging the take-up of energy conservation and efficiency initiatives. The problem with this approach is that it divorces energy flows from the agencies responsible for managing energy flows. Utilities may have very different boundaries from those adopted by energy and environmental strategy. Increasingly, territorial links between the companies supplying energy and local customers, who are now able to choose their energy supplier, are being eroded. This raises questions about any idea of the locality as a container within which the most important decisions about energy management are made.

Second, local energy strategies often simply assume that local environmental performance could be improved if only users would make 'rational' decisions about investment in energy efficiency measures. Policy tends to focus on conventional information and marketing campaigns attempting to encourage local businesses and residents to take a more 'rational' approach by investing in energy efficiency. Unfortunately this simple model of overcoming the barriers to rational energy use fails to focus on the complex and often contradictory processes shaping local energy use (Guy, 1994a). In particular we are concerned that these assumptions fail to focus on the role of utilities as one of the most powerful shapers of energy use.

Third, much of the initial work on energy and environmental policy has focused considerable resources and effort into the mapping, modelling and monitoring of energy flows through the local energy economy. This has involved collecting sets of data on the intensity of energy flows through a locality, often using data supplied by private companies and utilities, which can extract key spatially differentiated information. Computer models have then been used to link information on energy consumption to assessments of the global and local environmental implications of energy use within a locality to give measures of CO_2 and NO_x emissions. The more sophisticated modelling exercises have generated scenarios quantifying the environmental impacts of different policy frameworks (see Nijkamp and Perrels, 1994). Although these exercises have undoubtedly improved our technical and scientific understanding of energy flows and environmental emissions these models do not provide much insight into the forces driving energy flows through cities. Modelling exercises have not provided a basis for helping to locate the potential for intervening in local energy economies. Privatization has meant that much of the most important information on energy flows in the gas and electricity sector has become an increasingly important commodity in competitive energy markets. Consequently utilities are less willing to release data into the public realm.

Fourth, in the absence of statutory structures for developing local environmental policy, many initiatives have been characterized by corporatist forms of organization. They have involved local utilities, interest groups, users and local authority departments for housing, planning and environmental health. They have little difficulty in cooperating in paper studies of key aspects of local energy economies precisely because there are few ways in which recommendations can lead into action. But these forms of structure also tend to neutralize conflict; such voluntary cooperation masks any conflicting interests between participants. Instead it is assumed that findings are non-controversial: surely all participants are interested in reducing the environmental impact of the locality by adopting different ways of managing energy flows! However, some of the key players may have very definite ideas about how they want to manage and shape the local energy economy. Locally based corporatist structures, with few mechanisms for implementing the findings of case studies, tend to disguise these potentially conflicting interests. An analysis of the institutional interests shaping local energy would help policy makers to identify potential conflicts of interest, thereby easing implementation of local energy initiatives.

Finally, we consider the focus on land use planning for the implementation of local environmental policy. Because of the limited powers for implementing local environmental policy, considerable interest has focused on the relationship between energy use and the land use planning process. Research has clearly demonstrated the links between key aspects of the planning systems and levels of energy use (Owens, 1986). Recently this has stimulated a significant debate about the energy implications of different types of urban form (Breheny, 1992; DoE, 1992b). Local authorities now have a statutory duty to consider the role of energy in development plan policies. Planning policy can have a significant effect on some aspects of local energy economy; all new power generation projects below 50 MW require local planning permission, creating new opportunities for planning policy to shape the development of energy generation – particularly renewable schemes – in their locality. But the emphasis on physical planning overstates the potential for land use policy tools to manage the urban energy economy. Planning can only insert ideas about improvements to levels of energy efficiency and conservation through higher building standards and the adoption of energy-efficient appliances in new built development. As the physical urban environment is renewed at an annual rate of 1–2 per cent, targeting new development will only ever have a minor impact on the overall level of energy use in cities. Local environmental policy has few powers to direct levels of energy efficiency in the bulk of existing buildings, which lie outside the remit of land use planning tools.

Consequently, we need to build up a more empirically informed, critical analysis of the provision and use of energy in particular cities to aid the development of effective policy strategies that minimize urban energy use and environmental damage. At present, environmental policy is still widely perceived as a mechanism for 'overcoming barriers to energy efficiency' (Guy, 1994b). In this sense policy is largely disconnected from the mechanisms which shape local energy economies. To date we have merely developed a set of methodologies for analysing energy flows with little understanding of what is driving these flows or how policy might be developed to manage demand. Instead we need to begin making new connections to the changing realities of urban energy decision making rather than recycling set recipe plans, blueprints and ineffectual strategies. The central task is to reinsert debates about privatization and liberalization of the energy sector back into debates about the formulation and implementation of energy-management strategies. This means that we need to develop a more effective understanding of the constraints and new opportunities for local energy management created by privatization of the electricity sector.

CHANGING ENERGY LOGICS: PRIVATIZATION AND LIBERALIZATION

Before the privatization of the electricity industry, the supply of energy to building developments was considered to be a relatively unproblematic issue. As a matter of professional pride electricity planners would quickly satisfy new energy needs with fresh supply. Of course there were always difficult technical problems to be resolved in such a complex venture. In fact overcoming these difficulties provided the defining logic of the nationalized electricity industry, the unfolding of an all-encompassing technological network embracing the nation. As the country grew, so did the network, a literal current of vitality providing the spark of economic growth. As state economists forecasted national growth, the electricity planners of the Central Electricity Generating Board (CEGB) commissioned extra power stations. With an emphasis on safety of supply, generous margins of extra capacity were built in to the network. Large, remote power stations were built to achieve economies of scale. The electricity network, integrated from generation through to supply, operated like an irrigation system, delivering 'electrons' from a large reservoir to distant customer sites (Weinberg, 1994).

The nationalized electricity supply industry (ESI) was then committed to large-scale engineering management, with the focus directly on supply capability. Whereas new generation and transmission investments represented 'visible and attractive signs of progress', distribution and loss-reducing improvements were 'unglamorous and unseen' (Berrie, 1992). Systematic DSM therefore played little part in electricity network management in the monopoly era. In the space of 20 years following the Second World War, generative capacity multiplied 17-fold (Reid and Allen, 1970, p9). This attachment to a monolithic structure driven by generative concerns has been heavily criticized. In its commitment to achieving economies of scale in the generation and sale of electricity, its monopolistic, prescribed pricing structures and its inflated capacity, the CEGB was often seen as an arrogant producer, uncaring of local demand (Bonner, 1989).

The process of privatization aims to strike at the heart of the 'production ethos'. Replacing the notion of 'public service' with a profit motive, the provision of electricity is to become more responsive to the needs of local consumers. According to the Government's 1988 White Paper, *Privatizing Electricity*, 'decisions about the supply of electricity should be driven by the needs of the customers' (DTI, 1988). To this end command of the industry has been wrested from the generators with specific responsibility for understanding and satisfying demand and handed to a new 'front line' of supply, the RECs.

The potential impact of this shift is profound. Justification for any fresh investment in supply capacity now depends upon localized demand profiling undertaken by the RECs, replacing the national, macro-economic demand modelling of the CEGB. Emphasizing consumption rather than production, the 'logic' of electricity supply is being reshaped. No longer wholly driven by supply-side engineering techniques, leaner, demand-focused network management strategies can now surface. The acceleration of commercial competition, concern about the economic and political costs of energy and environmental fears about the impact of electricity production and use is stimulating rapid change within utility industries after almost a century of relative stability. As Carl Weinberg points out, the forces driving these changes are not unique to the electricity industry. Rather:

> *'they are contributing factors to the increased emphasis on sustainability across commercial sectors and throughout society. They bring together the industry challenges (competition, growing environmental restrictions, rising costs associated with old technologies) and opportunities (new technologies and markets, and industry restructuring)'* (Weinberg, 1994, p271).

The environmental impact of these changes depends on a revised commitment to energy efficiency. While the wise owl of the nationalized electricity industry always urged the efficient use of electricity (McGowan, 1988), explicit consideration of energy efficiency as a tool of network management has been rare. However, the new, privatized regime of electricity supply is arguably providing new incentives for increased energy efficiency. As Berrie has pointed out: 'much greater emphasis is given today in electricity supply to the following: consumer response; private capital; private utilities; demand management; energy efficiency; conservation; environmental maintenance' (Berrie, 1992, p121). The signs are that RECs are questioning the 'logic of resource intensification', the maximization of kW/h supply. Instead, a more demand-sensitive approach to selling energy is appearing, a 'logic of diversification'. The aim is a 'flexible load shape', with DSM techniques employed to influence load profiles as required (Redford, 1994). These variant logics, supply versus DSM, are not mutually exclusive. A logic of diversification does not exclude the motivation to sell more electricity! Rather, the strategic point of contrast lies in the 'signals' these different logics send to network management. Different signals place contrary pressures upon network expansion, upward or downward (see Table 9.1). The resulting maximization or minimization of resource use distinguishes the opposing logic of electricity supply.

As more demand-oriented signals are sent – from regulatory bodies through revised pricing regimes, through government commitments to economic

Table 9.1 *Supply and Demand Logic of Network Management*

Supply Logic	Signal	Demand Logic	Signal
Monopoly supplier	↑	Choice of supplier	↓
Network expansion	↑	Network flexibility	↓
Prescribed pricing	↑	Dynamic pricing	↓
Fixed tariffs	↑	Real-time tariffs	↓
kW/h	↑	Energy services	↓
One-way control	↑	Interactive control	↓

competitiveness and environmental efficiency, from the novel demands for energy services from users and, critically, through more exacting market conditions – we are beginning to witness a shift in the 'logic' driving electricity provision. DSM is part of this transformation. The desire for close control of local network operations is encouraging experimentation with more sophisticated demand management techniques than hitherto practised. It is in this context that we find American-style DSM receiving wider attention among RECs.

DEMAND SIDE MANAGEMENT IN MANWEB

There have been few attempts to unpack what these new strategies may actually mean for the development of local energy and environmental policies and practices. Debates about changes in the structure of the electricity supply industry, forms of regulation and the new behaviour of privatized companies have remained curiously dissociated from debates about the importance of energy issues in local environmental policy. Here we attempt to highlight the linkages between these issues through a review of an innovative MANWEB strategy for managing a technically problematic element of its electricity network. This initiative raises new questions about the role of privatized companies in local energy management.

Holyhead Powersave project

When the branch of MANWEB's distribution network serving the island of Anglesey started to reach capacity, or become 'hot', an ideal opportunity presented itself for evaluating a DSM strategy. With only two 33 kVA substations meeting a peak demand of around 9 MW, growing at 2 per cent per year, expensive network re-enforcement, costing MANWEB roughly £1 million, seemed inevitable. By reducing demand peaks by 1 MW clear savings in infrastructure investment could be identified. Further benefits would accrue in terms of reduced refurbishment outlay and beneficial publicity. Here, it seemed, was the ideal opportunity to implement a DSM scheme.

It was estimated that £0.5 million would be spent on the project. The European Community contributed £80,000 leaving MANWEB to spend £420,000 on the scheme, leading to a saving of £430,000 by avoiding the need to invest in a new transformer. Further savings would be achieved through delaying refurbishment costs. Wear and tear on the network in Holyhead is particularly severe because of the harsh coastal environment. An electricity network runs much more efficiently and needs less upkeep where the demand curve is flat: the higher the peaks, the quicker the network will deteriorate. By reducing peaks in demand, DSM expected to reduce refurbishment costs considerably. The associated savings are difficult to quantify, but the capital costs of new equipment in an electricity supply network are immense. If the life span of equipment is increased by 50 per cent significant economic savings are possible. For instance MANWEB has 1.3 million customers and spends £50 million per year on its distribution network. If applied on a large scale, DSM holds the potential for cutting costs in refurbishment as well as in costs of new supply and transmission (Kelly and Marvin, 1995).

The Powersave project was inaugurated with great publicity. Research was conducted into the energy profiles of the island's housing stock through detailed questionnaires about current insulation levels and more complex monitoring of selected industrial and domestic buildings. On the basis of this profile energy efficiency and conservation measures were introduced:

- Two energy-saving light bulbs were offered to approximately 3500 households on Anglesey at a cost of 70 pence each (normal retail price would be around £10 each). The exercise was administered by the Holyhead Opportunities Trust, which installed the bulbs to ensure their usage.
- MANWEB installed roof insulation and comprehensive draught-proofing for £16, a fraction of the real cost. Hot water cylinders were lagged free of charge. A local installer approved by Neighbourhood Energy Action (NEA) undertook this work, again paid for by MANWEB.
- MANWEB granted £70 to customers replacing their appliances providing they chose an energy-efficient model.
- Small commercial customers received the same low-energy light bulbs and hot water cylinder insulation offers as householders. In addition a 'switch off' night was promoted, aimed at highlighting the potential for reducing evening peaks.
- Individual energy audits/advice were offered free of charge on request.

Take-up among domestic users was surprisingly high: about 80 per cent of MANWEB's customers responded to the offer of cheap compact fluorescent lights. However, much depended upon the response of the 37 industrial users. Here implementation was more difficult. Delays in take-up of energy-efficient technologies were more protracted, with investment decisions depending upon drawn out management negotiations. But success was also evident here, most notably in the adjustment to development processes effected by MANWEB's direct approach to users through free energy audits.

Building in energy efficiency: Wells Kilo

Wells Kilo is one of four big industrial plants on Anglesey, producing children's toys and play apparatus: slides, swings, prams and push-chairs. At the time of the Powersave project they were occupying a relatively small, post-war factory which was both inefficient and gloomy. Their situation was complicated by the fact that the factory was being replaced in 18 months to make way for a major new road. This meant that they were in the process of building a new factory, developed by the Welsh Development Agency (WDA) as part of a compensation deal. Wrapped up with surviving in rapidly decaying accommodation and untutored in the complexities of factory construction, Wells Kilo was following a standard development pattern, with the WDA acting as construction managers. Energy considerations were again falling by the wayside. Consultants produced a design that was costed, tendered and won by a small contracting company. Little attention had been paid to energy efficiency in the design of the specification, despite the fact that the building exceeded thermal requirements of the building regulations within the WDA's corporate environmental commitment.

Auditing energy change

MANWEB approached Wells Kilo and introduced the idea of the Powersave project. Initial contact was limited to a free energy audit, involving a couple of days of monitoring of individual pieces of equipment. This provided a profile breakdown of demand 'beyond the meter'. The results were astonishing.

The factory, dating back to the war, was typically dark and dingy. The lighting and heating system was old and inefficient. Production was labour intensive; lots of energy was used in manufacturing through energy-expensive machinery. Consumption was measured at around 300 kW, varying at different times of the year, at a cost of £57,000. Importantly, both costs and demand were expected to rise in the near future, a scenario that would not have worried a REC driven by a supply-oriented logic. But, given MANWEB's DSM criteria, this was of great concern. Walking around the factory – locating possible improvements to lighting and cooling systems and identifying the more inefficient machinery, injection moulding machines and compressed air apparatus – the potential for energy savings was clear.

Some savings became immediately obvious from historical billing data. The most stark example was the power-factor correction, designed to offset supply losses introduced by the phasing of Wells Kilo's machine plant. Wells Kilo was paying more than £2500 per year in kVar charges. Investigation soon provided an explanation. One power-factor unit was only working at 40 per cent capacity while the other was completely out of action. This had been the case for as long as anyone could remember. While evidence of technical failure existed in each bill, the necessary community of knowledge (utility) and interest (user) had not conspired to created a query. Powersave provoked this blending of interest. MANWEB concluded that these kVar charges could be entirely avoided with minimal investment, with further improvements releasing around 97 kVar to the network.

There were many other energy-saving avenues. Lighting contributed another 40 kW of demand annually, at a cost of almost £8000. Again, there was terrific scope for increased efficiency; some twenty 100 W lamps could be replaced with 15 W compact fluorescent lamps saving 1.7 kW of demand and £400 per year. The simple reduction of yard lighting from five tungsten halogen lamps (three of which were permanently off and two permanently on) to two higher efficiency lamps would reduce winter demand by 0.5 kW. At £300 the payback would only be three years. Most of the remaining lamps – conventional 38 mm fluorescent – could be replaced with 'thinner', 26 mm models (more efficient, higher light output). Savings here would be twofold. The number of necessary lamps would be reduced while the remaining lamps would consume less energy. Altogether 6.1 kW could be saved at a cost of £1700, with payback in less than a year. Improved lighting control could save a further 7.7 kW.

The list went on. Reducing leaks and stepping down the pressure of the compressed air apparatus would reduce demand by 5.8 kW, while introducing a simple thermostat to a water cooling system and cleaning the pump filters would save a further 9 kW. Adding these savings together would reduce electrical demand by some 40 kW (13 per cent) and costs by £9600 (17 per cent). Notably, none of these potential savings necessitated advanced conservation technologies. The power of the DSM strategy is the simplicity of demand measures involved in the reshaping of electrical loads. The success of MANWEB's strategy was again apparent in the electricity bill. Comparing May 1993 with May 1994 we find a reduction from £5273 to £3770. This highlights the stark contrast between supply-oriented and DSM approaches to service provision. When the meter no longer acts as the frontier of utility activity, novel energy questions arise. Electricity ceases to be taken for granted and greater attention is directed to the factory as an energy system. In the case of Wells Kilo's new development this was critical. Without the action of MANWEB it is even conceivable that the faulty power factor correction system could have been transferred, installed and forgotten in the new factory!

This new wave of energy awareness did not stop at the heating, lighting and control systems. MANWEB was particularly interested in the impact of the production process on Wells Kilo's energy profile. Most strikingly, monitoring revealed the gross inefficiency of the injection moulding machines, which were costing between £3.50 and £5 an hour in electricity charges. Some quick market research concluded that state-of-the-art machines of comparable capacity could run at 80 pence an hour. The latest machines were also quicker, safer and operated automatically, allowing overnight production runs. Interestingly, the factory manager had been aware of the operational difficulties of the machines, but lacking 'evidence' found it difficult to approach the directors. But with the capital costs of a new machine covered by energy savings over three to five years, the energy argument proved persuasive and a new machine was purchased.

Given that Wells Kilo was preparing to move to a new factory the following year, not all the savings identified would be cost effective. Each energy-saving measure had to be assessed against its payback period or transferability to the new factory and a decision made on implementation accordingly. Moreover, the long-term aims of the Powersave project depended rather more on the energy profile of the new factory. MANWEB came in late on the design of the new factory – the physical body had already been erected – but there was still time to comment on the services specification. MANWEB offered their energy consultancy services free of charge. A series of recommendations were

Table 9.2 *Comparison of the Supply and Demand Oriented Logic*

Supply oriented	DSM
Maximize supply capacity	Balance supply/demand
Separation of REC/user by meter	REC intervention 'beyond meter'
Little concern for current demand	Retrospective energy saving
Little debate over new demand	Energy audits/advice
Standardized practices	Practice locally determined
Compliance with building standards	Building standards exceeded
No social/environmental interest	Social/environmental benefits

presented to the hired contractors including the latest high frequency lighting, effective thermostatic heating regulators and magic eye energy-saving lighting controls. There was little debate and the specification was upgraded.

THE 'NEW' ENERGY MANAGEMENT?

Privatization has begun to send ripples of change through the supply-oriented strategies of the nationalized electricity sector. Whereas in the past reinforcement of 'hot' elements of the network would occur almost automatically, now the capital outlay must be closely considered. With kilowatt allowances per customer presently worth around one-fifth of pre-privatization allowances, most of the costs will be passed on to the customer. This can influence location decisions of companies seeking new space and of existing companies considering changing their production processes from gas to electricity. While the relationship between RECs and their customers is still governed by the meter as the frontier of utility activity there are signs of new network management strategies developing. RECs are increasingly venturing 'beyond the meter' in an effort to control, or at least shift, electricity demand. This gradual movement from 'supply' to 'demand' techniques is taking root only when and where it makes sense. Comparing 'beyond the meter' energy management with supply orientation reveals the impact of the DSM logic (see Table 9.2).

Although the case study is an example of highly innovative practice, it raises important questions about the relationship between the infrastructure management strategies adopted by privatized utilities and the objectives of local energy and environmental policy.

First, DSM activities push the utilities into bridging the gap between production and consumption interests by developing closer relationships with their customers, local authorities and training and local economic development agencies. Utilities are no longer simply concerned with ensuring an adequate supply of electricity up to the customer's meter. DSM strategies push the utility 'beyond the meter' as they attempt to manage demand within their customers' premises. DSM strategies can make a difference to development, opening new channels of energy-efficient innovation. Local knowledge and action can surface, as with the replacement of the injection moulding machines, at the same time as a greater commitment to energy efficiency in consideration of heating, lighting and control systems. Only through the action of an efficiency-motivated REC is this 'shaking' of the development process possible. There was no compulsion in cooperating with the Powersave scheme, but the free audit meant users had little to lose.

On the basis of this newly generated knowledge, most industrial users cooperated, introducing some demand measures. Of course, the intervention of MANWEB did not result in a wholesale reorientation of the development process. Some of the key development professionals, such as the architect, had little or no knowledge of the Powersave scheme. But this may simply suggest that effective energy-saving action is less the domain of the architect, as implied by the flood of material on 'green architecture', and more the sphere of the privatized utilities. Certainly DSM seems a more effective method of stimulating energy concerns than conventional Energy Efficiency Office campaigns. Drawing together utilities and users has a rippling impact on cultural, organizational and economic priorities shaping development practices. The retrofitting of energy appliances forces the utility into new, closer forms of engagement with a wide range of public agencies. In Holyhead MANWEB worked with local training and enterprise agencies over the fitting of energy conservation and efficiency equipment and with the local authorities in their role as a manager of properties. Consequently, in contrast to supply-oriented modes of electricity supply, DSM initiatives force the utility to form closer connections with a range of local agencies and to start to break down the boundaries between production and consumption interests, thereby encouraging the take-up of specific energy-saving opportunities that would have conventionally been missed.

Second, the territories where DSM practices are used can develop new forms of comparative advantage which may not have occurred in conventional supply-oriented modes of management. For instance, investment in energy efficiency could generate important benefits for utility customers. In particular low income households can benefit through a combination of improved thermal comfort and/or savings in the cost of energy and local businesses that introduce more energy-efficient methods of production could use the cost savings to increase profits or reinvest in the expansion of their businesses. The retrofitting of energy efficiency and conservation methods is relatively labour intensive and could contribute to local employment generation. There may also be reductions in energy use contributing to reductions in greenhouse gas and acid rain emissions. These potential benefits may be ongoing as the utility has to engage in DSM practices over long periods to manage peak demand. Consequently, those localities in areas where the REC practises DSM may be able to capture local improvements in economic, social and environmental conditions.

Third, the more widespread use of DSM practices could signal important changes in the environmental management of localities. The case study graphically charts the development of a new role for utilities in the management of buildings and localities. DSM forces utilities into closer management of the areas in which they operate; this has quite profound social, economic, environmental and spatial implications. While these impacts may find resonance with wider public policy objectives – supporting economic development, encouraging social cohesion, reducing the environmental impacts of utilities – they are also practices that are firmly implicated in the business strategies of privatized utilities. MANWEB certainly sees DSM practices as an important strategy for capturing customers and firmly embedding them within their network. Increasing competition in the electricity sector means that the utilities have to develop strategies for capturing customers and then holding on to them. DSM is certainly one response to these pressures. DSM may also mesh with other agencies' agendas. Fuel poverty pressure groups and local authorities see DSM as an important component in tackling fuel poverty, local economic development agencies are interested in employment generation and lower energy costs and environmental groups focus on the potential reduction in energy consumption.

Finally, private utilities are emerging as important managers of territory while having few linkages with conventional environmental policy processes. There were few linkages between the DSM practices on Anglesey and the type of mechanisms developed for local energy and environmental policy. For instance, there was no link to the WDA's environmental policy or the land use planning processes. Although land use changes will be important for DSM – because new development will create new demand which needs to be managed – there were no links with the planning process in the case study. While DSM strategies may generate important benefits they are not subject to any wider public debate. Alternatively, it could be argued that those areas served by RECs which are not adopting DSM principles could be disadvantaged. A situation could occur within which the interests of the electricity network and other aspects of spatial management, such as land use planning, are in conflict. Control over fundamental and basic resources like electrical power means that private companies are in a powerful position to frame the future development of the territories within which they operate.

CONCLUSIONS: RECONNECTING POLICY

There is clearly a need to start reconnecting debates about the role of energy in local environmental policy more closely to the new techno-commercial strategies of privatized utilities. Rather than spend significant resources in mapping and measuring energy flows it would be more useful if policy adopted a more effective link to the changing logic driving energy across and through utilities' own networks. Simply relying on physical powers, such as the land use planning system, is unlikely to effect major change in local energy economies. Utilities are currently developing new approaches to the management of energy flows in existing and new forms of built development. Pushing 'beyond the meter', they are engaging with consumption interests to find new ways of managing energy flows within customers' premises. These powers go way beyond those in physical planning with its limited emphasis on new development and overall spatial form. With the physical form of cities changing relatively slowly, local environmental policy clearly needs to find new ways of engaging in negotiation with local utilities over the future shape of local energy economies.

Critically, planners and policy-makers must carefully examine how the privatized utilities sector relates to processes of territorial management. Practices are highly uneven; there has been little research examining the interface between the management of what have commonly been perceived as 'neutral', 'boring' technical systems of water, waste and energy and their role in restructuring cities and regions. While there are pressures pushing some utilities into new roles as territorial managers, there are others pushing against disclosure of information on energy consumption, costs and demand patterns which are now important commodities in competitive energy markets. Utilities may have nothing to gain by cooperating with local authorities as they start to develop their own plans for the use of the territories that they serve.

Alternatively, innovative utility strategies such as DSM may create new opportunities for the planning system to reshape local energy use. The wider adoption of DSM strategies by RECs may start to generate new demands from utilities and developers for closer links with the land use planning system as the RECs seek ways of managing electricity distribution networks more efficiently. While there is the potential for new conflicts and tensions there are clearly new opportunities for utilities and planners to develop novel ways of mutually shaping the development of cities and localities. New modes of network and land use planning will require innovation in both the utilities and planning sector; without such thinking planners are likely to be left behind as utilities develop their own private visions of planned futures.

Local energy policy needs to develop a new type of agenda no longer based on neutral analysis and modelling of energy flows along networks and the development of policy options for reducing emissions. A new strategy needs to acknowledge the reality of competitive institutions of energy supply and the role of companies in developing private visions of energy futures. Understanding the institutional context which creates space for the development of new demand management logic and strategies can provide a basis for building up new ideas about local environmental policy. In sum, the shaping of local energy management demands that local authorities:

- Develop regulatory frameworks that create space for utilities to develop new ways of managing their networks that minimize resource use.
- Work with utilities to understand how they can exploit this space in their area, identifying new waves of development in relation to parts of local electricity distribution networks which are overstretched or underutilized.
- Liaise with utilities on energy aspects of the development process – consultation on proposed specifications and location of commercial/industrial buildings, etc.

While serious conflicts between the utility sectors and local authorities are unlikely to be eradicated, such an approach would begin to reconnect policy processes to vital decision making of the 'real' energy managers. Otherwise, local environmental policy will remain focused upon developing plans, studies and policies which are fatally divorced from the fast-restructuring UK energy sector.

REFERENCES

Barton, H (1988) *Is Energy-Integrated Land Use Planning Possible in Britain?*, Department of Town and Country Planning, Working Paper No.10, Bristol

Berrie, T (1992) *Electricity Economics and Planning*, Institute of Electrical Engineers, London

Bonner, F E (1989) 'The Electricity Supply Industry', *Energy Policy*, vol 17, no 1, pp15–21

Breheny, M J (ed) (1992) *Sustainable Development and Urban Form*, Pion, London

CEC (1990) *Green Paper on the Urban Environment*, Com (90) 218, Commission of the European Communities, Brussels

CLES (1986) *Local Authorities and Energy Planning: A Review*, Centre for Local Economic Strategies, Manchester

DoE (1992a) *Development Plans and Regional Planning Guidance*, PPG12, HMSO, London

DoE (1992b) *Land Use Planning Policy and Climatic Change*, Planning Research Programme, HMSO, London

Douglas, I (1983) *The Urban Environment*, Edward Arnold, London

DTI (1988) *Privatizing Electricity*, HMSO, London

Elkin, T, McLaren, D and Hillman, M (1991) *Reviving the City: Towards Sustainable Urban Development*, FoE & PSI, London

Guy, S (1994a) *The New Energy Managers: Regional Electricity Companies and the 'Logic' of Demand-side Management*, Working Paper 46, Department of Town and Country Planning, University of Newcastle

Guy, S (1994b) 'Evil Developers and Green Fairies', in *Proceedings of the 3rd IRNES Environmental Futures Conference*, Warwick University, September, University of Newcastle

Haughton, G and Hunter, C (1994) *Sustainable Cities*, Regional Studies Association and Jessica Kingsley, London

Kelly, A and Marvin, S (1995) 'Demand-Side Management, The Electricity Sector and Town Planning', *Land Use Policy*, vol 12, pp205–221

Marvin, S J (1991) 'Localization of Labour Party CHP/DH Policy – 1977–87', PhD thesis, Open University, Milton Keynes, UK

McGowan, F (1988) 'Public Ownership and the Performance of the UK ESI', *Energy Policy*, vol 16, pp221–225

Nijkamp, P and Perrels, A (1994) *Sustainable Cities in Europe*, Earthscan, London

Owens, S (1986) *Energy, Planning and Urban Form*, Pion, London

Owens, S (1989) 'Models and Urban Energy Policy: A Review and Critique', in L Lundqvist, L-G Mattsson and E A Eriksson (eds) *Spatial Energy Analysis: Models for Strategic Decisions in an Urban and Regional Context*, Avebury London, pp227–244

Reddy, A K N (1991) 'Barriers to Improvements in Energy Efficiency', *Energy Policy*, vol 19, pp953–961

Redford, S (1994) 'Management of Demand', *Electrical Review*, vol 227, no 4, pp24–26

Reid, A and Allen, K (1970) *Nationalized Industries*, Penguin, London

SEEDS (1986) *Energy, Strategy Study No.6*, South East Economic Development Strategy, Harlow, UK

Sheldrake, B (1985) 'An Energy Efficiency Programme for UK Local Authorities', *Energy Policy*, vol 13, no 5, pp485–488

Thorp, R and Marvin, S (1995) 'Local Authorities and Energy Markets in the 1990s: Getting Back into Power?', *Local Government Studies*, vol 21, pp461–482

Weinberg, C J (1994) 'The Restructuring of the Electric Utility: Technology Forces, R&D and Sustainability', in N Steen (ed) *Sustainable Development and the Energy Industries*, Earthscan, London, pp265–301

10 INFRASTRUCTURE AND LOCAL AGENDA 21: THE MUNICIPALITY OF ALBERTSLUND IN THE COPENHAGEN REGION

Morten Elle

INTRODUCTION

This chapter explores the future of technical networks from the perspective of local aspirations for sustainable forms of flow management as expressed by LA21 initiatives. LA21 has been selected because it is oriented to local planning and development, calling on local authorities to develop plans to pursue the objectives and measures laid down in the Agenda 21 document at a municipal level in a consultative process with local people and institutions. Furthermore, this document expressly targets energy, water and waste issues as key policy fields for the sustainable management of natural resources, identifying the need to 'modernize existing power systems to raise energy efficiency and develop new and renewable energy sources', to 'protect the integrity of aquatic ecosystems' and to 'minimize the creation of waste, and to ensure that wastes are re-used, recycled and safely collected and treated' (Keating, 1993).

Our interest in LA21 goes beyond these basic points of relevance, though. Several features of the rhetoric underpinning the LA21 idea would appear to resonate with some of the conclusions emerging from earlier chapters of this book. We might expect to find parallels, for instance, between the LA21 rhetoric of building a consensus of local stakeholders and our findings of growing actor engagement in network management, or over a common interest in resource efficiency or over shared recognition of the importance of socio-economic determinants of environmental change. This suggests that LA21 might be a suitable vehicle not only for promoting more sustainable forms of resource use in general, but also for exploiting the new openings for minimizing resource use created by recent changes in infrastructure management.

This chapter explores the degree of interconnection between LA21 and infrastructure management debates in a specific urban setting in Denmark where the prospects for interaction appear, at first sight, to be favourable. The region's network managers are interested in sustainable development, the municipality has several active LA21 groups and has traditionally enjoyed a high level of public participation in local planning. The case study examines viewpoints on resource use in the context of LA21, seeking to demonstrate where the visions of the professional network managers and the central LA21 actors interconnect and to explain why the opportunities for linkage are not currently being exploited to the full.

LOCAL AGENDA 21 IN DENMARK AND THE COPENHAGEN REGION

This study of interconnection between LA21 and technical networks is located in the Copenhagen region. Before exploring interconnection, it is essential, first, to gain an understanding of the national and local context of LA21 in Denmark and Copenhagen.

The process of developing LA21 had a late start in Denmark in comparison with other European countries. The national campaign was launched in 1994 by the Ministry of Environment and Energy, the National Association of Local Authorities and the Association of County Councils in Denmark (Ministry of Environment and Energy et al, 1995). Thus, until now it has been voluntary for the municipalities to work with LA21; they have no legal obligation to do so yet. However, the Ministry of Environment and Energy has made a proposal to include a chapter on LA21 in compulsory municipal physical planning.

The national campaign does not include a manual for a 'good' LA21. However, five guidelines are central to the campaign: a holistic perspective in intersectoral thinking and action, active participation by the residents and users, community thinking and acting in life cycles, a global perspective on local affairs and, finally, a long-term perspective on local affairs.

Most municipalities first started to discuss LA21 in late 1995 and early 1996. Thus, up until now, the work done is rather limited in most cases. By January 1997 most municipalities had just started their internal dialogue, but the dialogue with the citizens started even later. A survey (Ministry of Environment and Energy et al, 1997) of LA21 activity divides Denmark's 275 municipalities into four categories (see Table 10.1):

1   'The Top' – have engaged the citizens in a dialogue and follow at least three of the five guidelines.
2   'The Middle' – better than 'The Bottom' but worse than 'The Top'.
3   'The Bottom' – have not engaged the citizens in a dialogue and follow less than two of the five guidelines.
4   'Not active'.

For most of the active municipalities the work with Agenda 21 does not implicate the use of any new tools in the dialogue – it is business as usual. The focus is mostly on environmental aspects; this is reflected in the fact that most of the municipalities place administrative responsibility for LA21 with the municipal technical director (Ministry of Environment and Energy et al, 1997).

Table 10.1 *Distribution of Danish Municipalities According to Level of LA21 Activity, as of 1 January 1997*

	Denmark		Copenhagen region	
Top	25	(9%)	14	(26%)
Middle	64	(23%)	13	(25%)
Bottom	45	(17%)	11	(21%)
Not active	141	(51%)	15	(28%)

In most municipalities LA21 comprises a number of small, independent projects.

Copenhagen, as the Cultural Capital of Europe 1996, had a strong 'green dimension'. A number of local socio-ecological centres were established in the region. These centres are an opportunity for the municipalities. Often the centres are used as a vehicle for dialogue and the involvement of citizens, offering an alternative to the traditional top-down/bottom-up discussion (Kofoed and Læssøe, 1995). In theory these centres are a part of a supporting framework for the many local projects.

No initiatives have been taken by the Ministry of Environment and Energy, the National Association of Local Authorities in Denmark or the Association of County Councils in Denmark to involve the 'flow managers' in the LA21 processes (interview with Dorrit Røtzler Møller, 12 September 1997).

THE CASE STUDY: THE MUNICIPALITY OF ALBERTSLUND

To explore interconnections between LA21 and network management we focus on a particularly critical case (Flyvbjerg, 1991). The Municipality of Albertslund is outstanding with respect to LA21 in Denmark. In 1995 the municipality prepared a draft for a LA21 'plan'. There is a forum for discussion between the municipality, the utilities and the citizens in Albertslund – the 'User Group'. If one were to find any interaction between the LA21 discussion and the utilities it ought, therefore, to be in Albertslund.

Albertslund is a Copenhagen suburb, developed largely in the 1960s and 1970s. One of its nicknames is 'The Town of Plans'; it is all designed in large development schemes, nothing is left to chance. All the neighbourhoods in Albertslund have formalized local organizations, either landowners or tenant organizations. This suburb, with 30,000 residents, consists of approximately 65 'villages' – the term for the different parts of the municipality. Most of the 'villages' do not resemble an ordinary Danish village but a part of suburbia. Albertslund was the first municipality in Denmark to launch green accounting in 1992. One of the purposes was to establish a competition between the 'villages' to find out which one could save the most water, electricity, heating, etc. Hence most of the municipal green account is broken down to the 'village level', making it easy for the individual to compare his or her performance with others living in a similar kind of settlement.

Four different actor groups are active in shaping the local technical networks: the grassroots, the municipality, the utilities and the 'mid-field'.

The grassroots: new lifestyles and competing systems

Grassroots groups are seen as essential in the Danish LA21 debate. The debate has a focus on changes of lifestyle towards a 'green' lifestyle. In many 'villages' of Albertslund, in particular those with social housing, the residents have a tradition of local action, for example against high rents, bad concrete buildings and flat (and therefore leaky) roofs. These traditions have been the start of environmental groups in many of the 'villages'. Areas like Galgebakken and Hyldespjældet have been pioneers in introducing water savings. For some of the residents it is without doubt a question of forming an alternative, 'green' identity. If you cannot afford all the ordinary status symbols, you might try to shape a 'green' identity instead (Lemvig-Nielsen, 1998).

Hyldespjældet consists of 390 flats. The environmental action started in 1989 with ten families taking responsibility for a local hen house. This was followed by investments in low-flow taps, light-saving bulbs, low-energy windows and intensive waste sorting into about 40 different materials. The investments have been accompanied by a number of campaigns. This can be seen as a focus on reducing the local flows of electricity, heat, water and solid waste. It is typical of grassroots groups to try to build up systems that are competing with the existing infrastructure, just like they did in building the first green buildings, closing material flow cycles locally (see Chapter 8).

In 1994 Hyldespjældet won an award as the most environmentally correct social housing area in the Nordic countries. It has played a major role in giving the Municipality of Albertslund a 'green' image. Poul Markussen, who lives in Hyldespjældet, is one of the central innovators of many of the environmental initiatives in the municipality and in the 'village'. He has been involved in the User Group, the Cultural-Ecological Further Education Centre and the Agenda Centre Albertslund. Hyldespjældet has its own 'neighbourhood agenda' (Hemmersam, 1997).

However, most of the 'villages' are not involved in environmental activities. The municipality has a goal of 50 per cent of the 'villages' drawing up their own LA21 by 2000. However, at present, only a few have completed a 'neighbourhood agenda', many areas finding it far too academic. Furthermore, people in detached houses identify LA21 with the social housing areas (Kaltoft and Gram-Hanssen, 1997). This might be the result of the emphasis put on local organization as a key part of LA21 in the national discussion.

The traditional grassroots are used to fighting the system, including the technical infrastructure. They make their own competing systems and change their lifestyles rather than trying to change the central systems.

The municipality: sustainability is a vehicle for political change

Sustainability is a vehicle for political change in Albertslund. The chair of the Committee on Environment of Albertslund Municipal Council has become extremely important. The post is held by the mayor's son, the social democrat

Hjalte Åberg. The discussion on the decline of the social democratic welfare state has been more or less replaced by a 'green' consensus, including the conservative and liberal parties. The political dispute is not over the environmental goals but the means by which these goals are to be achieved. Environmental tasks are used to create jobs, strengthen the social networks and give some of the areas a more positive identity. The politicians have given the civil servants a very clear signal: LA21 is very important in Albertslund (interview with Hjalte Åberg, 24 October 1997). The responsibility for LA21 is placed in the Environmental Department, not the Planning Department. The Planning Department is more or less restricted to traditional land use planning.

The director of the Environmental Department is the head of the board for the utilities responsible for water supply, district heating, solid waste and waste water management. He characterizes the municipal work with LA21 as good teamwork between politicians, civil servants and others. The politicians play a leading role. Agenda 21 is visible in Albertslund's handling of the technical networks. The new water supply plan refers directly to the municipal Agenda 21 (interview with Thorvald Ovesen, 20 October 1997).

The municipality has two employees who are occupied full-time with LA21 issues. One deals with local agendas, environmental auditing and technical environmental improvements for municipal institutions, for example, kindergartens, nurseries and schools; energy saving in public buildings is one of the areas covered by this employee. The other employee deals with the introduction of a new environmental syllabus in local schools and institutions, not only teaching the children to save water, electricity and heat and to sort their waste, but giving them the skills to solve future environmental problems (Hemmersam, 1997).

Since 1995 the municipality has developed an annually revised version of the municipal LA21, describing the goals and the progress made since last year (Municipality of Albertslund, 1997a). The goals include a reduction of CO_2 emissions, renewing the sewage disposal system, preventing leakage from the water supply system and groundwater protection – a number of issues related to the technical networks.

The utilities: minor adjustments to networks

The utilities that control the flows of electricity, water, waste water and solid waste are central to sustainable flow management. In this case study the flows in Albertslund have been studied. It is important to remember that public regulation is a decisive factor for most Danish utilities. Most utilities are in theory owned by the users. However, the distance between the users and the larger utilities makes these behave more or less like private companies. Environmental regulation is strict and detailed. In the solid waste sector – to mention one example – the municipalities have to be able to determine a way of treating every kind of waste. The utilities then have to use this method of treatment; in practice the waste utilities often have to use a specific facility.

Electricity

The local (regional) electricity company NESA covers most of the Copenhagen region; it is the least 'local' utility, compared with the water, waste water and solid waste utilities. NESA has always worked with energy savings. In the early 20th century electricity was quite expensive. That made it necessary for the company to show potential customers how to save electricity as a way of creating a good relationship between company and customer. This work was intensified in 1989 as a result of a legal requirement. Electricity companies were more or less forced to engage in demand side management. Whereas radical grassroots groups talk about reducing electricity use to a minimum, the electricity companies talk about reducing the expected growth in electricity use by a few per cent.

NESA does not deal with LA21. Only two or three persons in the company know the basic ideas behind Agenda 21. Energy consultancy is, however, seen as a very important commercial activity for the company and in that respect NESA could play a role in LA21. A number of municipalities use NESA as consultants. The company offers finance for investments in energy savings to customers. NESA has a lot of activities relevant for LA21 but is not directly included in the process (interview with Gert Nielsen, 27 October 1997).

Water and waste water

The municipality plays a central role in water planning. LA21 has had an impact on municipal water planning. Sustainability is included in the following objectives of the latest water supply plan:

- reduction of water use and leakage from pipes;
- increased use of infiltration of storm water in order to replenish the groundwater;
- increased use of water of a secondary quality; and
- zoning of land use to protect groundwater.

Nature – in the form of flows in small streams – plays an increasingly important role in local planning due in part to the LA21 discussion (interview with Thorvald Ovesen, 20 October 1997). LA21 is specifically mentioned in the water supply plan. The plan includes a decrease in domestic water use from 137 litres/person/day to 112 litres/person/day in 2010. This corresponds to the municipal LA21 (Municipality of Albertslund, 1997a,b). The plan does not, however, include details of how these water savings are to be accomplished. For instance, the plan does not include a strategy for involving the households in an effort to reduce water consumption. The plan is primarily technical, dealing with adjustments to the existing technical networks.

Solid waste

VEGA, the smallest joint municipal waste company (JMWC) in the Copenhagen region, is responsible for solid waste in Albertslund. The core of VEGA is the incineration plant. The director of VEGA is very active in Danish solid waste policy discussions.

More than 60 per cent of Danish solid waste is recycled, approximately 20 per cent incinerated and 20 per cent deposited in landfills (Environmental Protection Agency, 1996). Incineration is a decisive factor in Danish waste policy and plays an important role in district heating. Recycling of household waste is based on pre-collection sorting only, primarily due to the poor results from mechanical sorting plants. Hence, the JMWCs are dependent on good collaboration with the citizens. The efficiency of household waste sorting varies a lot from municipality to municipality.

The main stated objective of VEGA is to minimize waste production (VEGA, 1997). The company has launched a number of campaigns to reduce hazardous waste in particular. To mention one example, VEGA has distributed a pamphlet on impregnated timber in order to reduce its use. Impregnated timber is hazardous waste that causes problems in the incinerator (VEGA, 1996).

Most of the JMWCs would like to be able to ban certain kinds of waste, for instance electronics built into Christmas cards and shoes. EU regulation on emissions from incineration plants is making it necessary for the plants to refuse to burn this kind of waste; action that is not popular among people who stress the importance of a single market. Another message that VEGA is trying to send to the individual households is that porcelain must not be put in containers for glass; it completely ruins the melting process.

VEGA recognizes that for most people the JMWC's main task is pure service and not to interfere with daily life. The company does not deal with LA21 as yet, but LA21 is on the company's agenda for future strategies. The vision is for better interaction between the different local areas and the company in order to find locally adapted solid waste solutions. It is, however, a problem for a joint municipal company to intervene in the affairs of individual municipalities.

It is important that the professionals have a constructive, critical attitude towards grassroots ideas. The grassroots idea that 'the more categories for sorting waste into, the better' is not regarded as sustainable. One has to be able to process the different materials afterwards. For some materials recycling can cause more environmental problems than it solves (interview with Nils Olsen, 28 October 1997).

The 'mid-field': bridging the gap?

The lack of dialogue between the citizens and the municipality is a general (and particularly Danish?) problem. There is a need for a mediator between the utilities, the municipality and the grassroots groups. These mediators have been called green centres, socio-ecological centres, agenda centres, points of democratic density, etc. They are not to be confused with environmental shops, that is, places where interested people can seek information about possible environmental improvements, water-saving devices, solar heating, etc. The centre is meant to be a link between the municipality and citizens, binding together the bottom-up movement of the grassroots and the top-down processes of the municipality. The centre should be a catalyst of local dialogue, putting sustainability on the agenda and 'chairing' the ongoing debate/process. It should be based on reaching-out activities, meeting ordinary people where

Table 10.2 *The Players in Albertslund*

Utilities	Municipality	'Mid-field'	Grassroots
District heating	Politicians	User Group	65 'villages' including:
Water	Civil servants	Agenda Centre Albertslund	Hyldespjældet and
Waste water		Cultural-Ecological Further	Galgebakken
Solid waste (VEGA)		Education Centre	
Electricity (NESA)			

they are in their daily life (Elle and Gade, 1994; Kofoed and Læssøe, 1995). In the local Albertslund context the mediators are: the User Group, the Cultural-Ecological Further Education Centre in Albertslund and the Agenda Centre in Albertslund (see Table 10.2).

The User Group

In the early 1980s, just after the second energy crisis, so-called 'heat-planning Stalinism' dominated the development of technical infrastructure. Most houses in Denmark are supplied by district heating today. In an area like Albertslund district heating became a must. Battles over fees between owners of single-family houses and tenants in more densely built-up areas arose in most municipalities. Detached houses require longer connection pipes and should therefore pay more, the tenants argued. The battles often ended in a court-room. In Albertslund the municipality created a group consisting of representatives from the 65 areas – the 'User Group'. In principle there is one representative from each area, appointed by the people living in the area. The group was told to find a compromise in the battle over fees and did so after years of discussion. It has been involved in all the decisions concerning infra-structure in Albertslund ever since.

The members of the group have learned that if they stand united no politi-cian in the municipal council will dare to oppose a proposal from the User Group. Hence, Albertslund was the first municipality to introduce extremely differentiated fees in the field of solid waste, despite the misgivings of the civil servants and the utilities that it would create too much bureaucracy (interview with Thorvald Ovesen, 20 October 1997). Now flow management is no longer a matter for civil servants alone. The User Group has brought the discussion into the open. The User Group is a central forum for discussions of changes to the central infrastructure system.

The User Group could play a decisive role in connecting LA21 and utility policies of demand side management. This is not the case yet. One reason could be that many in the User Group are promoters of a progressive environ-mental policy only if it means no change to their own daily life. They want the environmental problems to be solved by somebody else or by new technology (Kaltoft and Gram-Hanssen, 1997).

The Cultural-Ecological Further Education Centre in Albertslund

The Education Centre started in 1995 with a very active member of the User Group as the driving force. The objective of the Education Centre is to teach the citizens of Albertslund how to achieve an 'ecological' lifestyle in order to promote a less consumption-oriented way of life and to stimulate dormant cultural interests as a part of their general education. It is very much inspired by the ongoing debate on social-ecological centres. The main idea behind the centres is to interconnect the actions at the 'top' level, in the town hall, with actions carried out at the 'bottom' level, by grassroots organizations and other citizens (Kofoed and Læssøe, 1995).

The Education Centre has just one employee. The main activity is normally general education with an ecological perspective, but the Education Centre is the initiator of a number of other activities:

- the exhibition 'Sustainability Again', sustainable development in a historical perspective;
- the conference 'Ecological Space and Future Cities';
- the Nature Camp;
- the Neighbourhood Games, a competition between the 'villages' with an environmental dimension; and
- the Cultural Ecological Yearbook, 240 pages of local debate and articles on sustainability (Hemmersam, 1997).

The Cultural-Ecological Further Education Centre in Albertslund can be seen as the spiritual part of the social-ecological centre, undertaking all the teaching and awareness building. The Agenda Centre Albertslund is taking care of the more physical work, helping people to implement a number of 'green' technologies like water-saving devices and home composting.

Agenda Centre Albertslund

The Municipality, the User Group, the Cultural-Ecological Further Education Centre and the citizens of the residential area Hyldespjældet took part in the (national) Green Fund competition in 1995 on local urban ecological centres and won one of the two prizes (see the 'Urban Ecology Guide – Greater Copenhagen', Munkstrup and Lindberg, 1996). The Agenda Centre Albertslund was granted DKK 2 million to create a centre capable of assisting its residential areas in saving water and energy, reducing and sorting waste and implementing LA21 on a neighbourhood scale. The financial basis for daily operation is money taken from the utilities' funds for reducing resource use. The centre started operation in January 1996. The centre has two permanent employees and two persons on unemployment schemes (interview with Valling and Windfeldt, 14 October 1997).

The aim is to address organized groups of citizens in the 65 'villages'. The centre should contact people where they live; it should not only be a place to go to get information. The municipal administration involves the centre in a number of activities and cooperation between the centre and the municipality is good (Kaltoft and Gram-Hanssen, 1997). The centre has the full backing of the politicians (interview with Valling and Windfeldt, 14 October 1997).

LA21 on a neighbourhood scale is one of the main activities of the centre; a lot of the centre's resources are used in an effort to involve the 'villages' in making their own Agenda. One goal mentioned in the municipal Agenda 21 is that by 2000 more than 50 per cent of the 'villages' should have their own Local Agenda. However, this activity has not led to many agendas yet. Another activity is the 'organic garden' project; the centre intends to make people in detached houses interested in sustainability by involving them in organic gardening (Kaltoft and Gram-Hanssen, 1997).

The centre is very good at supporting people who contact it. However, the main problem is to reach out to 'ordinary' people, that is, those who do not contact the centre. The centre is more or less overwhelmed by the heavy burden of minor activities and has not sufficient surplus for reaching-out activities. To some extent it has become the 'environmental shop' which it should not be. As part of the effort to inspire the 'villages', the centre has written a small booklet that contains a number of ideas for the following:

- water saving: monitor the water flow and make it visible, use water-saving devices, check the installations often;
- waste water: avoid chemicals and use grey water to water plants;
- rainwater: collect rainwater, use infiltration trenches;
- electricity: monitor electricity use and make it visible, use energy-saving light bulbs, refrigerators, freezers etc, buy wind-power shares;
- heating: make the flow visible (it is in the municipal green account), use low emission windows;
- solid waste: make the flow visible, sort waste at the end points, compost organic waste, reuse and repair;
- transport: use bikes, public transport or car-sharing; and
- consumption: buy repairable goods, organic food (Agenda Centre Albertslund, undated).

It is clear that these ideas are all about reducing the flows of energy and matter in the 'villages'. It is essentially demand side management, but the connection to the people who actually run the different technical systems is not that strong.

The booklet has had success in 'villages' with social housing, but has not been used much in the single-family housing areas. Apparently these areas do not consider sustainable development a problem they have to become involved in (Kaltoft and Gram-Hanssen, 1997).

The dialogue with the local municipal administration is very positive; the centre and the administration use each other's professional competence. However, the municipal administration emphasizes the particular need for reducing the flows of water, energy and waste. They stress the utility side of the centre's work; the centre's main source of finance is, after all, the utilities. This is at odds with the main interests and skills of the employees working in 'urban nature', especially gardening (Kaltoft and Gram-Hanssen, 1997).

Concrete examples of dialogue with the utilities are over cotton buds and batteries. For waste-water treatment plants, cotton buds pose a problem when thrown in the toilet. Therefore the centre has referred to this problem in its information material. Similarly, the manager of the incinerator plant wishes people would dispose of their batteries separately (interview with Valling and Windfeldt, 14 October 1997).

Problems with sewers due to intensive water savings have not been discussed. However, it is very likely that intensive water savings could lead to severe sewer problems in some areas of Albertslund. This might be an indicator of how (in)efficient the utilities regard the centre's abilities to influence the flows. Another possibility is that the utilities are not aware of the potential of the centres.

The role of the 'mid-field'

For the time being, the 'mid-field' is not bridging the gap it is supposed to bridge. Too many resources are used to stimulate and facilitate the grassroots, creating a bottom-bottom process rather than a bottom-up process. This could be the result of the considerable emphasis put on local activities in the debate on LA21, but could also be interpreted as being the result of the high public interest in environmental matters. The fact that the 'mid-field' has not yet radically changed the way the flows are managed should not, however, lead to the conclusion that the 'mid-field' has no decisive role to play as a catalyst of change to flow management in the long run.

CONCLUSIONS

It is evident that LA21 initiatives – at least in Albertslund – deal with a number of activities related to flow management. However, many of these activities are interpreted in a very narrow local perspective. They focus on involving the citizens in creating 'small islands of sustainability' rather than transforming the technical networks. It is the small examples – like an organic garden – that are often the centre of attention. These examples are meant to be inspiring to others, the same way that a number of 'green' buildings are meant to act as demonstration projects. The local initiatives are important in the transformation of lifestyles. However, if the local initiatives continue to exist as small islands, their contribution to the transformation of society towards sustainability will be rather limited.

The very local interpretation of LA21 is largely supported by the Ministry of Environment and Energy. The ministry has not made a special effort to involve the managers of technical networks in the LA21 debate. Furthermore, the players in the 'mid-field' – the User Group, the Cultural-Ecological Further Education Centre in Albertslund and the Agenda Centre Albertslund – are under great pressure from individual citizens and lack sufficient surplus resources to address the utilities' policies.

The most 'regional' utility, the electricity company NESA, has – not surprisingly – very little interest in LA21. This may be a problem of scale; the traditional boundaries of LA21 are the boundaries of the single municipality, while NESA covers a large number of municipalities in the region. The water sector, closely linked to the municipal administration, has adopted the goals of the municipal Agenda 21 plan. However, the plan does not give any details as to how the water savings are to be made. The municipal waste company has put LA21 on its agenda for future work but has not yet made LA21 a part of its demand-side strategy.

If LA21 had been seen as an effective tool for flow management it would, beyond any doubt, have been a decisive part of the utilities' planning. But LA21 is not very visible, except in planning linked directly to the municipality. Even in an advanced municipality like Albertslund there is as yet only little interaction between the technical networks and LA21. One must remember that the Danish Agenda 21 debate is very young and the utilities have not yet got demand-side strategies 'under their skin'.

If the networks managers see LA21 at all it is as a tool for minor adjustments to existing systems, whereas the grassroots groups see LA21 as a tool for building up competing technological systems, more or less ignoring the existing structure. In social construction of technology (SCOT) terminology one can identify these as two different technological frames for sustainable flow management. The grassroots and the flow managers are thinking on quite different planes. The grassroots see the existing infrastructure as an obstacle to sustainability, whereas the flow managers see the existing infrastructure as a tool for sustainability and a structure that just needs to be trimmed.

LA21 plays a major role in local politics and planning in Albertslund. There are three important actors located in the 'mid-field' between the municipality, the 'villages' and the individual citizens: the User Group, the Cultural-Ecological Further Education Centre in Albertslund and the Agenda Centre Albertslund. One could say that the team is complete and that the municipality has an important tool for future integrated demand side management. The political will is present; it may just be a matter of time before the utilities, the municipality, the 'mid-field', the 'villages' and the individual citizens play together in a process where the flows of energy and matter become more in tune with local ecological space. Albertslund might have the key to a new kind of integrated planning of technical networks. Studies of the 'mid-field' would appear to be essential for understanding the emerging new relationships between the utilities, the technical networks, the users and other actors of infrastructure management. Furthermore, it is clearly important to study how the different actors perceive other actors' roles and potential strengths, a point illustrated well by the Albertslund case.

REFERENCES

Agenda Center Albertslund (undated) *Idekatalog – Agenda 21, Albertslunds Boligområder* (*Book of Ideas – Agenda 21, Albertslund's residential areas*), Agenda Center Albertslund, Albertslund

Elle, M and Gade, T (1994) *Lokale Byøkologiske Centre – konkurrence* (*Local Urban Ecological Centres – competition*), The Green Fund, Copenhagen

Environmental Protection Agency (1996) *Affaldsstatistik 1995* (*Solid Waste Statistics 1995*), Copenhagen

Flyvbjerg, B (1991) *Rationalitet og magt* (Rationality and Power), Akademisk Forlag, Copenhagen

Hemmersam, F (ed) (1997) *Kulturøkologisk Årbog 1996/97 (Cultural-Ecological Yearbook 1996/97)*, The Cultural-Ecological Further Education Centre in Albertslund

Kaltoft, P and Gram-Hanssen, K (1997) *Evaluering af Agenda Center Albertslund (Evaluation of Agenda Centre Albertslund)*, DTU, Lyngby

Keating, M (1993) *The Earth Summit's Agenda for a Change,* Centre for Our Common Future, Geneva

Kofoed, J and Læssøe, J (1995) *Kulturbyens 13 grønne centre (The 13 Green Centres of the Cultural Capital)*, IVTB-DTU, Lyngby

Lemvig-Nielsen, V (1998) *Strategi for et social-økologisk center (Strategy for a social-ecological centre)*, IFP-DTU, Lyngby

Ministry of Environment and Energy, National Association of Local Authorities in Denmark, Association of County Councils in Denmark (1995) *Local Agenda 21 – An Introduction Prepared for the Counties and Municipalities in Denmark*, Ministry of Environment and Energy, Copenhagen

Ministry of Environment and Energy, National Association of Local Authorities in Denmark, Association of County Councils in Denmark (1997) *Lokal Agenda 21 – Dansk Status ved årsskiftet 1996-97 (Local Agenda 21 – Danish Status 1996/97)*, Ministry of Environment and Energy, Copenhagen

Municipality of Albertslund (1997a) *Agenda 21 – Status 1996*, Municipality of Albertslund, Albertslund

Municipality of Albertslund (1997b) *Forslag til Vandforsyningsplan (Water Supply Plan, Draft)*, Municipality of Albertslund, Albertslund

Munkstrup, N and Lindberg, J (1996) *Urban Ecology Guide*, Danish Town Planning Institute, Copenhagen

VEGA (1996) *Tag trykket af træet (Take the pressure of the wood)*, VEGA, Høje Taastrup

VEGA (1997) *Årsberetning 1996* (Annual Report 1996), VEGA, Høje Taastrup

INTERVIEWS

The Agenda 21 Coordinator at the Ministry of Environment and Energy, 12 September 1997

Employees at the Agenda Centre Albertslund, 14 October 1997

Director of the Environmental Department, Municipality of Albertslund, 20 October 1997

Chairman of the Committee on Environment, Albertslund Municipal Council, 24 October 1997

Representative of the Demand Side Management Department, NESA, 27 October 1997

Director of VEGA, 28 October 1997

11 COMPETING NOTIONS OF RESHAPING FLOW MANAGEMENT: LOCAL AGENDA 21 IN BERLIN

Timothy Moss

INTRODUCTION

Planning for sustainable cities is not the sole prerogative of public planning bodies operating within the confines of a formalized local planning system. In the field of infrastructure planning an important role is played by local energy and waste management concepts, often designed in consultation with key partners, and – most recently – by LA21 initiatives, involving a much wider range of local stakeholders. As a contribution to a better understanding of new forms of local planning of infrastructure systems this chapter examines how LA21 is trying to reshape flow management in a sustainable direction. The chapter seeks to answer the following interrelated questions: what visions of sustainable flow management are LA21 initiatives currently pursuing and *how* are they pursuing these goals?

The chapter begins by asking whether we can, in fact, talk of LA21 as a common movement of local initiatives pursuing uniform objectives in a similar manner. A review of early and recent literature on LA21 traces a growing awareness of the existence of diversity within the LA21 movement. This idea is explored in more detail in the following section, in which a case study of LA21 in the Berlin region is used to illustrate multiple styles of LA21 in terms of the actors involved, the issues they address and the ways they go about solving them.[1] The third section asks how these different styles translate into different ways of trying to shape sustainable flow management. A typology of LA21 initiatives in Berlin is used to illustrate competing notions of reshaping flow management. The research findings are, finally, summarized and assessed for their policy implications.

THE CONTESTED NATURE OF LOCAL AGENDA 21

Although stemming from a single document – the Agenda 21 of the 1992 Rio Conference on Environment and Development – the concept of LA21 is today much contested, in practice as well as in the literature. The relevant Chapter 28 of the Agenda 21 document is itself very unspecific as to how its objectives should be applied at a local level. The only reference to implementation is that 'each local authority should enter into a dialogue with its citizens, local organizations and private enterprises and adopt "a local Agenda 21"' (Chapter 28.3; BMU, 1993). How this process of consultation should develop is not specified; this is deliberately left to the local communities themselves. Chapter 28 establishes only one significant organizational feature in advance: the role of local authorities in initiating the LA21 process.

Ever since, efforts have been made to set down what LA21 means, in terms of its objectives, processes and end results (O'Riordan and Voisey, 1998). There is general agreement that LA21 represents a long-term local action programme built on a broad consensus of opinion to promote the sustainable development of a community in accordance with the guidelines set down in the Agenda 21 document. It is widely acknowledged that the process of seeking this consensus requires the development of a 'culture of dialogue' between local authority, interest groups, business and residents (ICLEI et al, 1998, pp7ff). One important end product of this process is the formulation of a document – a Local Agenda – to act as a binding framework of goals, instruments and individual measures to guide the development of a community in the 21st century.

In the early literature there was a strong tendency to reduce LA21 to a simple, easily comprehensible formula. In the interest of distilling a clear message out of the complexity and openness of the Agenda 21 document and to meet the demand of local authorities for central guidance (Kuhn, 1998, p18), handbooks and guidelines were produced which were based on a rather narrow interpretation of the Rio text. Typical of some of the more common simplifications to be found among this early literature is the emphasis placed on LA21 as a written plan, on best environmental practices, on the local authority as coordinator and on the public forum as the principal means of engaging a wide range of actors (ICLEI, 1995; Deutscher Städtetag, 1995; BMBau, 1996; Forum Umwelt und Entwicklung, 1997). While being instructive and helpful in their own right, these guides to implementing LA21 have had the combined effect of suggesting that there is a 'best way' for LA21; that LA21 initiatives only have to follow the procedural guidelines and adopt a selection of best practices to be successful.

Recently, this approach has come in for some (self-)criticism and the view of the existence of a uniform path for LA21 has recently been played down. This shift in emphasis has developed out of the growing recognition of the inevitability – and even desirability – of differences in the way LA21 is interpreted in practice (cf Beuermann, 1997, p13; ICLEI et al, 1998, ppX–XI). It is increasingly acknowledged that local contextual factors, such as a specific environmental problem, administrative structures or the level of debate on sustainable development, influence the direction an LA21 process can take. This is particularly noticeable in Germany, where the prior existence of environmental pressure groups, forms of participatory planning and strong local self-government have shaped LA21 initiatives substantially (Kuhn, 1998, p19; ICLEI and Kuhn, 1998; Beuermann and Burdick, 1998). This more differentiated standpoint reflected in the recent literature on LA21 recognizes, for instance, that there is no one 'correct' form for LA21 to take, but that several paths are possible, so long as they respect the basic goals of Agenda 21, and that the path chosen is determined largely by local context and political constellations (ICLEI and Kuhn, 1998, p136). It is acknowledged that LA21 initiatives determine themselves whether they place greater emphasis on form rather than on content, on initiating fresh projects rather than on redefining existing ones or on specializing in single issues rather than on covering all policy fields. In short, diversity is beginning to be seen as a potential strength, not just as a weakness (Kuhn, 1998, p17).

This latest contribution to the debate has raised our understanding of LA21 but it poses new questions about the different forms LA21 can take. In particular, we now need to know more about *how* LA21 initiatives differ. In terms of the sustainable management of water, energy and waste flows, we need to ask what diverse visions for the future of utility services LA21 can provide and what different types of activities it can engage in to change the way we use and manage technical networks. The issue of diversity – both in general and related to flow management – is explored in the following two sections with a case study of LA21 initiatives in Berlin.

MULTIPLE STYLES OF LOCAL AGENDA 21: THE CASE OF BERLIN

Multiplicity of LA21 initiatives

Berlin lends itself admirably as a setting for exploring diversity in LA21 because it offers a large number and wide variety of LA21 initiatives existing alongside one another within a single city. There are, in fact, over 20 distinct LA21 groups in Berlin, operating at both city and borough level. Each of Berlin's 23 boroughs has its own LA21 initiative, at very different stages of development. The boroughs, however, lack the full planning authority of German municipalities; partly in response to this, there exist at the city level a further four initiatives which pursue the LA21 cause. The following overview lists those LA21 initiatives which are actively engaged in issues of energy, water or waste management, our focus of interest:[2]

LA21 groups at the city level
* *Round Table 'Sustainable Development Berlin-Brandenburg'*: This is a high-profile discussion group of approximately 35 selected representatives from different walks of public life (administration, business organizations, NGOs and research institutes), initiated in 1996 and designed to build a dialogue on sustainable development in the Berlin-Brandenburg region, drawing on experiences with round table talks in 1989/90. It has a working group (*Fachrunde*) 'Energy and Employment'.
* *BLUE 21: The Berliner Landesarbeitsgemeinschaft Umwelt und Entwicklung* was formed in 1995 by a wide range of 'developing world'

and environmental groups in order to promote dialogue on the North–South dimension to sustainable development and on the links between ecology and the developing world – aspects it feels are widely neglected in the sustainability debate in Germany. BLUE 21 operates a working group 'Materials, Land, Energy' (BLUE 21, 1996).

- *Public Working Group Local Agenda 21:* This was set up in 1995 under the initiative of borough administrations and local environmental, developing world and church groups and trade unions as a forum for exchanging information and activities between the growing number of borough groups as well as negotiating with the city Senate.
- *City government activities:* Following a poorly received report of 1995, entitled 'Local Agenda Berlin', which merely listed environmental policies and projects already being pursued by the city government (SenStadtUm, 1995), the Senate Department for Urban Development (SenStadt) has been entrusted with the responsibility for liaising between city departments on projects relevant to LA21, developing LA21 proposals for issues of city-wide importance (eg transport) and co-funding some 48 job-creation posts to coordinate Local Agenda projects at borough and city levels. In January 1998 the Senate presented a second, more comprehensive report on Local Agenda activities (Abgeordnetenhaus von Berlin, 1998). Since then the city parliament has resolved to draw up a LA21 plan for the whole city and presented a report on strategies towards a more sustainable Berlin (Enquête-Kommission 'Zukunftsfähiges Berlin', 1999).

A selection of LA21 groups at the borough level

- *LA21 Köpenick:* Germany's first LA21 initiative comprises three 'pillars': the borough administration, a public forum (approximately 100–150 participants) and an ecumenical wing. The forum operates working groups on 'Energy and Resources' and 'Waste Minimization', the ecumenical section a project on 'Energy-saving in Church Buildings'.
- *LA21 Lichtenberg:* A similarly well-established borough initiative, formed in 1994, this LA21 is run primarily by a Project Coordinating Office (*Projektleitstelle*) working in close cooperation with the borough administration. It has working groups 'Water, Soil, Nature Protection', 'Energy, Climate, Transport' and 'Waste'.
- *LA21 Hellersdorf:* Initiated in late 1995 with borough support, this initiative is strongly influenced by the environmental group *Grüne Liga*. It has a working group 'Material Flow Management'.
- *LA21 Steglitz:* Since its inauguration in mid-1995, the Steglitz LA21 has lacked public participation and political support in the borough. The principal actors are borough employees, who run a working group 'Waste'.
- *LA21 Neukölln:* Constituted only in 1997 on the initiative of the local Social Democratic Party, the Neukölln LA21 is attracting the support of a wide range of actor groups from the borough. It operates a working group 'Waste'.

Although all these LA21 initiatives operate within the same city with the same overall objective of promoting sustainable development according to the Agenda 21 document, our research has revealed great diversity in the social organization, objectives and activities of the various groups. These general differences in structure and approach need to be understood before we can explore how LA21 attempts to reshape flow management.

Diversity in social organization

There is great variety in the kinds of actor groups actively involved or influential in Berlin's LA21 initiatives. Depending on whether the original initiative came from within an administration (as in the borough of Lichtenberg), an environmental group (as in Hellersdorf), a political party (as in Neukölln), or an ecumenical group (as in Köpenick), very different actors are using LA21 to shape a more sustainable future for their neighbourhood, borough or city. Some LA21 initiatives are essentially instruments of the borough administration with consultative forums, others consist primarily of environmental groups, still others could be described as a loose network of neighbourhood action groups. The prominence of borough officials is not surprising for Germany, where local authorities have long felt strong responsibility for the environment; environmental officers see LA21 as a vehicle for strengthening their hand in- and outside the administration. The predominance of local officials in positions of responsibility within some LA21 groups has, however, contributed to the reluctance of environmental groups in some boroughs, such as Köpenick and Steglitz, to become actively engaged in LA21. Environmental groups, especially in West Berlin, have developed their own style of environmental campaigning and are sometimes unsure what they stand to gain – or even to lose – from being incorporated under the LA21 umbrella. Interestingly, East Berlin's *Grüne Liga*, emerging from the round table culture of the late GDR, appears generally less inhibited in consensus-building with other organizations.

Besides the principal actors it is worth reflecting on the non-participants. The engagement of the general public is universally low – a critical weakness of all LA21 initiatives. In particular, local business is poorly represented, apart from firms with a vested interest in environmental technologies, although there have been some notable efforts recently to seek business support (for example Round Table and in Neukölln). Of special concern to us, there is little evidence of the city's power, water and waste utilities participating on a regular basis in any of the LA21 groups. Many LA21 members view the utilities as being resistant to improving environmental quality and show little interest in their involvement, preferring to negotiate with them externally once a common position has been reached.

Organizational structures also vary considerably, ranging from the complex three-tier model in Köpenick – consisting of the administration, the public forum and the ecumenical wing – to the informal meetings of (mainly) borough employees in Steglitz. Most, however, operate some kind of public forum and working groups on key issues of concern and all borough groups now possess paid coordinators based in the borough administration. Posts financed under job-creation schemes have indeed been instrumental behind the early initiatives; they have had a major structural impact on the LA21 process in Lichtenberg and Köpenick in particular, permitting considerable work but tending to discourage voluntary participation of the public. Where the borough administration is the dominant force, as in these two boroughs, LA21 structures have become heavily institutionalized, operating – as one active member candidly remarked – as the 'extended arm of the environment department'. In general, the structures and procedures of the larger city initiatives, such as the Round Table and BLUE 21, tend to be more formalized than at borough level, emphasizing their independence from the administration.

Diverse approaches to sustainable urban futures

The various LA21 initiatives in Berlin differ not only in membership and organization but also in the issues they address and the spatial context within which they conceive sustainability. Our research confirms that there are, indeed, very different ways of 'seeing' sustainable urban development.

The central issue of concern for most LA21 initiatives is, undoubtedly, local environmental problems. These might take the form of a specific object of protest, such as the planned waste incineration plant in Neukölln, or a more general environmental deficit, such as the lack of green spaces in Lichtenberg. Alternatively, interest may be directed at defining existing environmental qualities and protecting them from development pressures, as in the suburban borough of Köpenick. A strong environmental focus is, not surprisingly, prevalent primarily among those LA21 initiatives where the environment office or environmental groups play a dominant role.

Other groups, however, define very different problems as central to sustainability. Some LA21 initiatives in inner-city boroughs with severe social problems have deliberately played down environmental issues in order to address the pressing problem of social deprivation. This is the case in Wedding, Friedrichshain, Kreuzberg and – to a lesser extent – Neukölln, where employment, public health and urban renewal take centre stage of LA21 activities. The BLUE 21 group, indeed, sees the one-dimensional environmental focus of the LA21 debate in Germany as itself a problem. It addresses, rather, the links between environmental degradation and the developing world, aiming to encourage debate on the North–South dimension to sustainability. Building a dialogue was for the initial phase of the Round Table more important than the substance of discussion. This initiative deliberately spent most of its first year just selecting suitable representatives to sit at the Round Table because it sees their involvement and support as crucial to promoting sustainable development in practice.

These various central issues are conceived of in very different spatial contexts by the LA21 groups. BLUE 21 clearly adopts a global perspective, linking local actions to global impacts. The Round Table was formed, among other reasons, to discuss sustainable development in a regional – rather than just an urban – context, covering intra-regional dependencies in Berlin and the surrounding state of Brandenburg. The Berlin Senate, in its activities in support of LA21, treats the city as a whole. Most of the borough initiatives take a borough perspective of their work, sometimes including neighbouring communities where they impinge on local environmental quality. Within the borough, however, those LA21 initiatives concerned with social issues who network with local action groups tend to operate more on the level of the neighbourhood or residential quarter. The working group 'Waste' of the LA21 Steglitz is rather unusual in focusing on a specific building. In the absence of public participation, the working group targets its attention and operations at the borough headquarters building which houses some 1000 employees and offers good data on waste flows.

Diverse modes of action

The actions taken by the LA21 initiatives to pursue these objectives also vary considerably. On the basis of experiences in Berlin, there would appear to be many different ways of delivering sustainable urban futures via LA21. In Lichtenberg and Köpenick the work of the LA21 groups is directed primarily at drawing up a draft Local Agenda document, to be revised by the borough departments prior to consultation with the general public (Leitstelle Lokale Agenda 21 Lichtenberg, 1996; Bezirk Köpenick, 1997) (see Figure 11.1). Yet this pattern, promoted by early handbooks on LA21, is not the norm. The LA21 initiatives run by environmental groups, as in Hellersdorf or Prenzlauer Berg, operate rather as a lobby for green causes, seeking debate less within the initiative itself than externally, in public meetings on specific topics. Other LA21 initiatives act more as networks, seeking to draw together existing groups and projects interested in sustainability under a common umbrella, as in Wedding. The activities of the Round Table, and to some extent the Neukölln LA21, too, are shaped by the initiatives' aim to create an open dialogue on sustainable development between key players, placing great emphasis on selecting and attracting the participants.

Further insight into the different directions of LA21 activities is gained by observing whom they are directed at. It is by no means the case – as might be assumed – that the general public is the principal target of LA21 interest. The strongly 'green' LA21 groups certainly see themselves as speaking primarily to the public, over the heads of the administration, by means of public meetings and campaigns. The more institutionalized LA21 initiatives, however, direct their proposals squarely at local government – either the borough administration or the Senate. Since these LA21 groups usually work closely with the borough environment office, this strategy is often aimed at putting pressure on other borough departments – especially those responsible for economic development – to accept measures for environmental protection. The Round Table is clearly directed at influencing decision makers in the region, in government, business and planning circles.

To summarize, the case of Berlin shows that, even within the confines of a single city, LA21 can take many different guises. Local authorities are not the only coordinating forces in LA21, environmental protection is not always the focal point of interest and there is much more to LA21 activities than drawing up a Local Agenda document. In different organizational settings and local

Präambel

Die Lokale Agenda Köpenick muß gleichzeitig Vision, Programm und Maßnahmekatalog sein. Die Aufgabenstellung weist weit über eine oder zwei Legislaturperioden hinaus und sollte deshalb weitgehend aus kurzfristigen Wahlstrategien politischer Parteien herausgehalten werden. Hauptanliegen ist, eine Entwicklung Köpenicks festzuschreiben, die sich an den Hauptanforderungen der Verbindung von ökonomischer Effizienz, sozialer Gerechtigkeit und ökologisch nachhaltiger Entwicklung orientiert.

Mit der Benennung der drei Grundparameter ist das Spannungsfeld unterschiedli... ...ger Prinzipien:

...st bevölkerungsnah

...ker an der Entwick-...tteln an Wahltagen

...sionen, die streitbar

...ung der Köpenicker

...onsensfindung mo-

...orhaben die Bürger

...ielvorstellungen der

...nsprüchen kann der ...erden. Darüber hin-

...e Diskussionen und ...werden muß. Dabei ...n Sorgen und Nöte, ...erten Programmatik

...k kann nicht an der ...ngsziele Köpenicks ... Ebenso ist auf die ...haltige Entwicklung ...können.

Bezirk Köpenick von Berlin

Lokale Agenda 21 Köpenick

Source: IRS

Figure 11.1 *Title Pages of the Local Agenda 21 Document of the Borough of Köpenick*

contexts LA21 groups define problems of unsustainability and frame ways of solving them in very different ways.

COMPETING NOTIONS OF RESHAPING FLOW MANAGEMENT: A TYPOLOGY OF LOCAL AGENDA 21 IN BERLIN

With this background knowledge we are now in a position to address the central question of this chapter: in what (different) ways is LA21 trying to reshape flow management? In particular, we are interested in discovering how diverse forms of social organization, problem-framing and action translate into different notions of how urban water, energy or waste flows should be made more sustainable in the future. Simply because these issues are environmental by nature does not mean they can only be defined in environmental terms; a variety of socio-economic, spatial or environmental perspectives on resource use are conceivable. In the following section we analyse the above LA21 initiatives in Berlin to discover how they define problems of unsustainable resource use, solutions to these problems and the processes needed to promote the solutions.

In an attempt to make greater sense out of the wide range of standpoints, a typology of LA21 initiatives in Berlin is developed. This typology is used to illustrate the existence of several distinct models for sustainable urban flow management. These models, it should be pointed out, are not based on the theoretical literature on competing discourses on sustainable development, as explored by Hajer (1995), Haughton (1997) and Sachs (1997). Rather, they are based on our empirical research in the Berlin region and represent groupings of LA21 initiatives which share certain characteristics and represent a particular interpretation of how LA21 could reshape technical networks and flow management in practice. A further point to add is that the categorizations undertaken do not, of course, exclude the possible existence of differences of opinion within individual LA21 groups or overlap between different types of LA21. Our interest is in showing how the dominant characteristics of certain types shape their approach to flow management.

Table 11.1 presents the typology of LA21 initiatives in Berlin, taking as parameters those characteristics used above to explain diverse forms of social organization, problem-framing and modes of action in general (ie key actors, organizational structure, key issues of concern, space frame, activities, main addressees) and adding to these some features of specific interest to flow management (key energy, waste and water issues of concern, preferred technology, contribution to infrastructure planning). The six distinct types of LA21 initiatives emerging from the analysis can be described in terms of their different notions of the problem, the solution and suitable processes.

Local/enviro-technocratic

LA21 initiatives of this type (eg Lichtenberg, Köpenick) are characterized by a strong focus on local environmental problems and a heavy reliance on local authority support. The ways in which they address problems of resource use are strongly framed by the administrative territory of a borough. Thus, the problems defined and the solutions sought by such LA21 groups are guided by concerns for local, rather than regional or global, environmental quality. For instance, the Lichtenberg working group on water is concerned primarily about water loss in the borough, a result of half its surface area being sealed; the Köpenick waste group addresses the illegal dumping of waste impairing the natural beauty of the borough.

Consequently, the kinds of solutions proposed relate strongly to the borough's own scope for action. These LA21 groups see their principal contribution in drawing up a Local Agenda document to act as a guideline for more

Table 11.1 A Typology of Local Agenda 21 Initiatives in Berlin

Characteristics	Local/enviro-technocratic (LA21 Lichtenberg, LA21 Köpenick)	Consensual/discursive (Round Table, (LA21 Neukölln))	Global/informative (BLUE 21, LA21 Prenzlauer Berg)	Green/persuasive (LA21 Hellersdorf, LA21 Friedrichshain)	Social/inclusive (LA21 Wedding, LA21 Friedrichshain)	Individualist/negotiative (LA21 Steglitz)
Key actors	Environment office, job-creation agencies	Balanced power (NGOs, local government and business)	Environmental and 'developing world' groups	Local environmental group	Local social initiatives and green groups	Borough employees
Organizational structure	Complex, institutionalized, high staffing level	Formalized, voluntary, institutional support	Formalized, wide support, extra-institutional	Semi-formalized, modest support from local action groups	Semi-formalized, informal, low participation	
Key concerns						
• in general	Local environment	Consensual process	North–South issue	Green lifestyles	Social deprivation	Resource use
• water, energy, waste	Focus on local problems	Employment via green technologies	Global impact of resource use	Local levels of resource use	Low priority (except social aspects)	Environmental performance of public buildings
Space frame	Borough	Region	Global/local	Borough	Neighbourhood	Public building
Technology	Small-scale green technologies	Technology benefiting local firms	Technology transfer	Small-scale green technologies	Low-cost technology	Efficient technology and practices
Activities	Formulation of LA 21 document	Dialogue between key actors	Linking green and development issues	External lobbying	Networking	Liaising with providers and users
Main addressees	Borough administration, Senate	Decision-makers, general public	Senate, general public	General public, borough administration	Local residents	Individual users of public buildings
Contribution to infrastructure planning	Making proposals to borough planners, initiating 'green' projects	Creating a forum for consensus-building	Raising awareness of global aspects to resource use	Providing ideas/arguments to borough planners	Creating projects to meet the special needs of low-income groups	Negotiating solutions to inefficient resource use

sustainable development within the borough. Issues of flow management feature prominently in the draft documents. For example, in its detailed Recommendations for Action presented to the borough administration the Lichtenberg working group on water has set out priorities for water management in the borough, established indicators for sustainable water use, called for integrated solutions and proposed initial model projects.

At the same time, this type of LA21 is engaged in individual projects within the borough to encourage a more efficient use of energy, water and material resources. The same working group in Lichtenberg, for instance, is putting pressure on the borough administration and on the major local housing associations to introduce water-saving appliances and local techniques of storm water percolation. In Köpenick the waste group is trying to establish neighbourhood composting facilities to cope with the large amounts of garden waste in the borough while the energy group organizes regular solar festivals to publicize solar technologies.

Great emphasis is placed here on promoting the application of new, often small-scale technologies, such as solar panels or waste composting, to raise the environmental efficiency of physical infrastructure at the user end. The preference for small-scale technologies can be attributed also to the commercial interests of local firms involved closely with a LA21 group. This applies particularly to the field of solar power, where the working groups on energy in both Köpenick and Lichtenberg actively promote the application of solar power technology by providing advice to house-owners and liaising between local firms engaged in solar technology and potential clients. Here there is a strong technical focus to proposed solutions; the Köpenick group, indeed, regards solar power technology, rather than reduced energy consumption, as the most realistic path to climate protection.

The way such LA21 groups envisage reshaping flow management is, therefore, to change the physical form and functions of the city at a local level, primarily via the application of small-scale, innovative technologies. Little consideration is given, however, to how these technologies fit into – or clash with – existing technical networks. The motives of various actor groups, such as the utilities or end-users, to accept the favoured technologies are also played down.

Strong trust is placed in the rationality of planning and decision-making processes. LA21 initiatives of this type display a relatively high degree of institutionalization, enjoying support within the borough administration, working closely with the borough environment department and relying heavily on staff funded by public job-creation schemes. This has eased their establishment and political acceptance, but has contributed to a loss of public support for appearing too technocratic. Jens Dangschat has criticized a similar 'technocratic/rational' model of LA21 for lacking communicative and participatory components (1997, pp185–187). Without this support, however, they lack the political leverage to persuade sceptical borough departments to adopt their proposals.

Consensual/discursive

Form, rather than content, is important to this second group of LA21 initiatives, which includes the Round Table and – to some extent – the Neukölln LA21 group. For them the Local Agenda movement is about creating a new consensual approach to development planning, drawing together a wide range of relevant actors in a dialogue aimed at overcoming obstacles of communication and understanding. The chief problem addressed, therefore, is the lack of dialogue and networking, rather than a lack of knowledge or a particular environmental issue. Consequently, these groups tend to have an open agenda, the issues of interest emerging out of a specific local context, whether it be unemployment, a disputed waste incineration plant or the need for greater regional cooperation.

As a result, LA21 groups of this type display no express preference for particular environmental technologies or for the technical style of infrastructure systems. To them, creating a sustainable city is about mobilizing local human resources to achieve optimal solutions for – among other issues – flow management, which respect ecological, economic and social concerns. One example of this is the emphasis placed on engaging small, local enterprises in promoting the application of environmental technologies. The working group 'Energy' of the Round Table addresses the specific issue of creating employment for the region through projects to improve energy efficiency. It is aiming to build on Berlin's successful model for energy-saving partnerships between energy contractors and building managers by initiating and coordinating projects which allow small- and medium-sized companies in the region to benefit from the contracts and not just the large utilities as at present.

Building up a dialogue between key decision makers of different walks of public and political life is a central characteristic of such LA21 groups. This dialogue is deliberately sought within the LA21 initiative itself, where power imbalances of the outside world are offset in order to stimulate an open discussion. In Neukölln, for instance, the working group on waste is creating a forum of mutual trust between 'professionals' and 'amateurs' following the failure of earlier mediation over a controversial incineration plant. The Round Table organized an 'Open Space' conference in 1999 to collect ideas for innovative projects. Given the weight attached to open discussion, organization and procedure are more formalized than in other groups. The political influence these LA21 initiatives seek is not through the channel of an administrative body but on the local political and business establishment via open dialogue and the dissemination of ideas by participating representatives of key local organizations.

Global/informative

A third type of LA21 takes a global perspective to sustainability, seeing in LA21 an innovative instrument to raise planetary concerns for development and the environment. The chief problems addressed by the group BLUE 21 all revolve around the so-called North–South divide. These concern the imbalance of development levels between developed and developing countries, the 'export' of environmental problems to poorer regions and global flows of material resources. The responsibility for alleviating these problems, in the eyes of BLUE 21, lies primarily with the industrialized regions of the North. The group sees its principal task in raising public awareness of the global impact of local resource use in an industrialized region and, at the same time, counteracting what it sees as a trend to interpret LA21 in purely local terms.

The kind of sustainable city envisaged by BLUE 21 is, therefore, a globally responsible city, acting with regard for the global impacts of its production and consumption activities. To this end the solutions for flow management favoured by BLUE 21's working group 'Materials, Land, Energy' are directed at reducing the North's use of resources, optimizing the flow of material between North and South and developing appropriate technologies to help the South meet its needs with minimum resource use. In terms of reshaping technical networks there is a general interest in introducing resource-saving technologies and a particular focus on the transfer of appropriate technologies to developing countries. Improving technical infrastructure in a locally sustainable form is an important component of this vision.

The ambitious task of BLUE 21 is to build bridges of understanding between local and global concerns as well as between environmental and development issues. This the group does by networking its large number of member NGOs and disseminating information through public discussions and publications rather than through administrative or political channels.

Green/persuasive

Where environmental groups are predominant, as in the boroughs of Hellersdorf and Prenzlauer Berg, the LA21 initiatives pursue a 'strong green' agenda, advocating radical changes to current patterns of resource use. The principal issue at stake, for these groups, is environmental sustainability; that is, protecting the functioning of the natural environment against threats from the human exploitation and pollution of natural resources. These damaging practices, it is argued, are rooted in well-entrenched systems of production and consumption which give little consideration to environmental costs. From this perspective, technical networks which distribute water, energy and waste flows bear a major responsibility for today's high levels of resource use. Centralized infrastructure systems are themselves viewed as part of the problem for encouraging high consumption levels and relieving individuals of a sense of responsibility for their use of natural resources.

This ecocentric approach to LA21 demands fundamental changes to conventional flow management to solve these problems. The first is to restructure the technical systems used to regulate material and energy flows such that resource use does not exceed the carrying capacity of a local ecosystem. This ultimate objective is pursued in the immediate future by creating 'islands of sustainability' of small-scale, green technologies existing within or alongside the centralized networks. LA21 groups of this type express a clear preference for small-scale, resource-saving technologies, especially those which can be operated by the end-users themselves (for example waste composting, solar heating). They are, however, sceptical of a technological 'quick-fix', attributing equal importance to persuading individuals to change their patterns of consumption and their lifestyles – the second major shift demanded.

To achieve these ends LA21 groups of this type see their task as putting pressure on both the public and the local administration to alter their practices accordingly. Hence the preferred modes of action are campaigns, public meetings and the lobbying of borough politicians, although in some cases good contacts exist to the local environment department. Debate between differing viewpoints is sought less within the LA21 groups themselves than through their external activities. Here, LA21 acts more as an action group, promoting the group's particular viewpoints in dialogue with those outside the LA21 process.

Social/inclusive

Pressing social problems are the focus of several inner-city LA21 initiatives, as in the boroughs of Wedding, Kreuzberg and Friedrichshain, shaping a very different approach to LA21. Here, environmental issues are often deliberately played down in deference to social concerns; they are pursued – if at all – in terms of their impact on living standards. A central problem of flow management from this perspective is the dilemma facing low-income and disadvantaged groups who are having to pay more for utility services yet lack the means to invest in resource-saving technologies which could help offset the higher unit charges.

Thus LA21 groups of this type want environmental technologies and infrastructure systems to be low-cost, encourage local employment and suit the means of the socially deprived. They pursue this objective in part with demands for more socially responsible infrastructure management, a concern which has heightened recently with the privatization of key utilities in Berlin. However, they feel that self-reliance is a more promising path. Their principal work, indeed, is directed at building up self-help initiatives for low-income groups. For example, LA21 groups in Friedrichshain and Kreuzberg have responded to problems of waste and the cost of its disposal by operating a system of exchanging unwanted material goods for labour services, similar to the LETS scheme in the UK (Grüne Liga, 1997, pp38–40).

An important component of this strategy is the narrow spatial focus on the neighbourhood. Whereas other LA21 groups envisage sustainable flow management spatially in terms of administrative boundaries, urban functions or resource flows, the social/inclusive groups are interested in improving the well-being of residential blocks and neighbourhoods. This they do by networking, rather than creating new organizational structures, using the Local Agenda movement as a vehicle to bring together existing social initiatives which address different aspects of the sustainability debate.

Individualist/negotiative

The case of the Steglitz LA21, where borough employees seek to reduce resource use in a single building, may appear unique at first sight. It does, nevertheless, reflect a common practice among smaller groups with low public participation to concentrate their efforts on individual actors (providers and consumers) in their immediate surroundings. The issues raised and activities engaged in depend largely on the personal preferences of those few individuals actively involved.

In the case of the Steglitz LA21 the interest is in improving the environmental performance of public buildings. Borough employees active in the LA21 working group on waste have identified, with the help of available data and personal knowledge, practices of poor waste management in the main administrative building. Using their personal contacts they are seeking to persuade other employees, particularly in the acquisitions department, to reduce waste and improve waste sorting. Here, persuasion or negotiation is conducted usually on a one-to-one basis, between an LA21 representative and the person deemed responsible, to achieve small improvements in an informal manner.

It would be inappropriate to try to ascribe a particular vision of sustainable flow management to such an individual, minor case. Even so, it is worth noting that isolated actions of this kind are seen by the protagonists as part of a larger story. In this case, the LA21 participants viewed their efforts to reduce waste in the context of a general process of administrative reform, designed to make the public sector more efficient. The Steglitz case is more important, though, for illustrating a particular style of LA21 characterized here as 'individualist/negotiative'.

CONCLUSION AND POLICY IMPLICATIONS

This chapter has examined the ways in which LA21 is trying to reshape urban technical networks and flow management. Using an empirical study of several LA21 groups in the Berlin region it has demonstrated that LA21 can take many different forms, thus substantiating similar observations emerging in the recent literature. In practice as in theory there would seem to exist no single model for a sustainable city.

We have taken the argument further here by explaining how LA21 initiatives can differ, offering explanations for these differences. The principal areas of diversity lie in the social organization of LA21 groups, the problems and solutions they define and their modes of action. For example, while some LA21 groups focus their activities on formulating a Local Agenda document, others emphasize the creation of discussion forums or better networking between existing action groups. The reasons for these differences would appear to grow out of a specific local context. By this is meant not merely a locality; the existence of so many diverse LA21 initiatives within a single city – Berlin – clearly indicates a wider range of contextual factors at work. These factors include: the origins of an LA21 initiative, its membership and level of participation, the way it is organized and whom it is designed to target, the existence of pressing environmental, social or economic problems and the way these are addressed by the relevant actors.

In the main section of this chapter we have demonstrated how these multiple styles of LA21 translate into different and competing notions of how to reshape flow management. Focusing attention on water, energy and waste flows, it was found that visions for the sustainable management of resource flows also differ substantially, depending on how existing problems of resource use are defined, where solutions are sought and what modes of action are preferred. The focus of interest can vary from finding technical solutions to local environmental problems to raising awareness of the global interdependency of resource flows or linking environmental protection to the social and economic development of a community. To make sense out of this diversity a typology was developed, pinpointing six distinct strategies for managing material and energy flows in a more sustainable way. These six types have been termed according to their thematic focus and mode of action: local/enviro-technocratic, consensual/discursive, global/informative, green/persuasive, social/inclusive and individualist/negotiative. Developing this typology has contributed to our understanding of sustainable flow management by attempting an initial categorization of the multiple visions for sustainable futures in existence and explaining these types in terms of their socio-technical determinants.

The implications of these observations for policy-making, with respect to Local Agenda, are threefold. Firstly, rather than encouraging each LA21 initiative to follow a common path, it would be more effective to build on the existing strengths of an LA21 group, understanding how it works. Expectations of individual LA21 initiatives should be levelled at what they each can contribute, rather than at what the Local Agenda process as a whole is intended to achieve. It follows that there is little point in pursuing the argument over what constitutes a 'true' LA21 initiative when it can come in so many different guises. Consideration needs to be given instead to what is widely missing in all LA21 groups, such as representation of the local business community and thus of an important market-oriented perspective of sustainability. The absence of the water, energy and waste utilities in any of Berlin's LA21 groups – even those with a specific focus on resource use – has limited the extent of consensus-building and the impact of LA21.

Secondly, more thought needs to be given to the suitability of transposing best practices to different settings. Trading successful examples of sustainable development without adequate consideration of how they fit into a specific regulatory, political and socio-cultural context has caused many promising ideas to be abandoned as unworkable. Understanding how urban infrastructure systems work, socially as well as technically, and what pressures they respond to in a localized context is an important prerequisite to selecting suitable best practices from other cities or regions. LA21 groups would appear well placed to make this assessment and to suggest ways of adapting best practices to their unique, local environment.

Thirdly, understanding Local Agenda merely as a planning document overlooks the existence of LA21 initiatives which place greater emphasis on LA21 as a process, either building a dialogue between local actor groups, raising public awareness of sustainability issues or networking between existing local action groups. This suggests that we should not seek to measure LA21 solely in terms of its end products, but of its wider influence on policy making. A wider interpretation of Local Agenda as a process would open up greater opportunities for it to link with parallel discourses on urban flow management and local environmental planning, seeking out and exploiting communities of interest around specific objectives.

NOTES

1 I would like to thank Dr Ursula Krause and Corinna Kennel for their help in researching the case study.
2 In most cases, being 'actively engaged' means operating a working group specializing in one of the three sectors energy, water and waste management.

REFERENCES

Abgeordnetenhaus von Berlin (1998) *Mitteilung – zur Kenntnisnahme – über Lokale Agenda 21 für Berlin*, Drucksache Nr. 13/2395, 21 January, Kulturbuch-Verlag, Berlin

Beuermann, C (1997) *Local Agenda 21 in Germany (I). Five years after Rio and it's still uphill all the way?* Wuppertal Institute Papers, no 68

Beuermann, C and Burdick, B (1998) 'The German response to the sustainability transition', in T O'Riordan and H Voisey (eds) *The Transition to Sustainability. The Politics of Agenda 21 in Europe*, Earthscan, London, pp174–188

Bezirk Köpenick von Berlin (1997) *Lokale Agenda 21 Köpenick. Arbeitsentwurf*, Berlin

BLUE 21 (Berliner Landesarbeitsgemeinschaft Umwelt und Entwicklung) (ed) (1996) *Konzept für das Projekt Berlin 21. Umwelt- und entwicklungspolitische Bilanz einer Metropole*, BLUE 21, Berlin

BMBau (Bundesministerium für Raumordnung, Bauwesen und Städtebau) (ed) (1996) *Lokale Agenda 21. A: Stand und Perspektiven der Umsetzung von Kapitel 28 in Deutschland, B: Übersicht über internationale Programme und Strategien*, Schriftenreihe Forschung, vol 499, Bonn

BMU (Bundesministerium für Umwelt, Naturschutz und Reaktorsicherheit) (ed) (1993) *Umweltpolitik. Konferenz der Vereinten Nationen für Umwelt und Entwicklung im Juni 1992 in Rio de Janeiro. Dokumente. Agenda 21*, Bonn

Dangschat, J (1997) 'Sustainable City – Nachhaltige Zukunft für Stadtgesellschaften?', in K-W Brand (ed) *Nachhaltige Entwicklung. Eine Herausforderung an die Soziologie*, Leske & Budrich, Opladen, pp169–191

Deutscher Städtetag (ed) (1995) *Städte für eine umweltgerechte Entwicklung. Materialien für eine 'Lokale Agenda 21'*, DST-Beiträge zur Stadtentwicklung und zum Umweltschutz, vol E, no 24, Köln

Enquête-Kommission 'Zukunftsfähiges Berlin' (1999) *Zukunftsfähiges Berlin*, Abgeordnetenhaus von Berlin, Drs 13/3800

Forum Umwelt und Entwicklung (1997) *Lokale Agenda 21. Ein Leitfaden*, Forum Umwelt und Entwicklung, Bonn

Grüne Liga Berlin (1997) *Berliner Beispiele. Gute Nachrichten zur Lokalen Agenda 21*, Grüne Liga, Berlin

Hajer, M A (1995) *The Politics of Environmental Discourse. Ecological Modernization and the Policy Process*, Oxford University Press, Oxford

Haughton, G (1997) 'Developing sustainable urban development models', *Cities*, vol 14, no 4, pp189–195

ICLEI (International Council for Local Environmental Initiatives) (1995) *European Local Agenda 21 Planning Guide*, European Sustainable Cities and Towns Campaign, Freiburg

ICLEI and Kuhn, S (1998) *Handbuch Lokale Agenda 21. Wege zur nachhaltigen Entwicklung in den Kommunen*, Bundesumweltministerium / Umweltbundesamt, Bonn

ICLEI, Kuhn, S, Suchy, G and Zimmermann, M (eds) (1998) *Lokale Agenda 21 – Deutschland. Kommunale Strategien für eine zukunftsbeständige Entwicklung*, Springer, Berlin/Heidelberg

Kuhn, S (1998) 'Kommunales Mosaik – Entwicklungstrends der Lokalen Agenda 21 in Deutschland', in International Council for Local Environmental Initiatives (ICLEI), S Kuhn, G Suchy and M Zimmermann (eds) *Lokale Agenda 21 – Deutschland. Kommunale Strategien für eine zukunftsbeständige Entwicklung*, Springer, Berlin/Heidelberg, pp13–20

Leitstelle Lokale Agenda 21 Lichtenberg (1996) *Lokale Agenda 21 Lichtenberg – Diskussionsentwurf*, U & A Consult, Leitstelle Lokale Agenda 21 Lichtenberg, Berlin

O'Riordan, T and Voisey, H (eds) (1998) *The Transition to Sustainability. The Politics of Agenda 21 in Europe*, Earthscan, London

Sachs, W (1997) 'Sustainable Development. Zur politischen Anatomie eines internationalen Leitbilds', in K-W Brand (ed) *Nachhaltige Entwicklung. Eine Herausforderung an die Soziologie*, Leske & Budrich, Opladen, pp93–110

SenStadtUm (Senatsverwaltung für Stadtentwicklung und Umweltschutz) (1995) *Lokale Agenda 21 Berlin*, SenStadtUm, Berlin

INTERVIEWS

Representative of the Round Table Sustainable Development Berlin-Brandenburg, 3 July 1997

Representative of BLUE 21 and Berlin 21, 9 July 1997

Representative of Project Coordinating Office of LA21 Lichtenberg, 10 July 1997

Representative of Senate Department for Urban Development, Environmental Protection and Technology, 15 July 1997

Representative of borough administration Steglitz, head of Working Group 'Waste' in LA21 Steglitz, 21 July 1997

Representative of Working Group 'Energy and Resources' in LA21 Köpenick, 30 July 1997

Representative of Working Group 'Waste' and chair of support group in LA21 Köpenick, 1 August 1997

Representative of Working Group 'Waste' in LA21 Neukölln, 5 August 1997

Representative of Public Working Group LA21 and *Grüne Liga*, 5 August 1997

Representative of BUND (Berlin) and working group Local Agenda 21, 14 August 1997

Representatives of *Grüne Liga* Hellersdorf, Working Group 'Material Flow Management' in LA21 Hellersdorf, 20 August 1997

Representative of Working Group 'Water, Soil, Nature Protection' in LA21 Lichtenberg, 21 August 1997

Representative of Working Group 'Waste' in LA21 Lichtenberg, 21 August 1997

Representative of Working Group 'Energy' in LA21 Lichtenberg, 3 September 1997

Representative of LA21 Köpenick and environmental adviser in Köpenick, 9 September 1997

Representative of the project 'Energy saving in parishes' in Köpenick, 18 September 1997

Representative of Senate Department for Labour, Vocational Training and Women, head of Working Group 'Energy' of Round Table, 27 October 1997

Conclusions: Planning for Sustainable Urban Flows

Timothy Moss and Morten Elle

This section has explored the contribution and response of local environmental planning to the new logic of infrastructure management emerging in response to regulatory, commercial and technological changes. Three case studies have documented in different ways how these shifts in infrastructure management are being reflected and considered in the arena of local planning, from formalized activities of spatial or sectoral planning to Local Agenda 21 initiatives. Focusing on the issue of interconnectedness between local environmental planning and infrastructure management, the section has identified how and why connection is currently limited, what new opportunities for linkage are emerging under the new conditions and what knowledge is necessary to improve linkage to the benefit of urban environmental performance in the future.

The case study of the north of England revealed how local energy planning oriented around measuring and modelling energy flows as well as spatial planning directed towards new development both failed to connect to an electricity utility's emerging interest in limiting electricity consumption via DSM in order to relieve network stress. This example illustrates the need to 'reconnect' debates on the role of energy in local planning to the new techno-commercial strategies of privatized utilities. As the chapter points out, new approaches to managing energy flows in which energy utilities are going 'beyond the meter' offer a number of opportunities for linkage with local planning processes. In the interest of a more efficient and effective use of their technical networks utilities are seeking closer relations with their customers (including local authorities), they require better knowledge of local factors affecting energy use, are becoming more sensitive to land use changes and their impact on energy consumption and are offering services which link in to the agendas of public agencies (eg creating employment). As a result, utilities are acquiring new roles in the environmental management of a locality – a development which local planners need to exploit better than at present.

The Copenhagen case study demonstrated that, even in a municipality where the conditions seem favourable, debates on sustainable flow management within the LA21 movement and within the infrastructure management community have been largely unconnected. The main players on either side – the grassroots groups within LA21 and the network managers – are both interested in resource efficiency but are talking on different planes. The network managers see the existing infrastructure systems as a tool for sustainable development; for the LA21 groups they are part of the problem and need to be replaced with alternative technological systems. The localist approach of many LA21 groups, more interested in creating 'islands of sustainability' than reconfiguring whole networks, does not relate to the utilities' agenda of optimizing their networks. Interestingly, actor groups have been created in Albertslund to act as intermediaries between the grassroots initiatives and the network managers but they are currently not able to bridge the gap. Connecting the two isolated, but related, strands of debate on sustainable flow management, the case study concludes, requires potential communities of interest to be actively sought and cultivated.

The case study of LA21 in Berlin demonstrated the great diversity of visions and pathways for reshaping flow management which can coexist even within the confines of a single city. This diversity, our research suggests, springs from unique combinations of local contextual factors comprising not just the prevalence of a technical or environmental problem but also the social organization and modes of action of each LA21 group. These factors shape the way LA21 groups define a problem and where they seek sustainable solutions, resulting in different – even competing – styles of sustainable flow management. The different styles observed in the empirical analysis were developed into a typology of six distinct approaches, ranging from the localized/enviro-technocratic to the social/inclusive and consensual/discursive. Developing an awareness for such diverse approaches and an understanding of their roots, it is argued, will be important for identifying and building linkages between LA21 initiatives and the agendas of the network managers.

Looking across the case studies, it is possible to identify a number of common themes and general conclusions. The first clear message is that local environmental planning is as yet largely disconnected from the new agendas of network managers. Local energy concepts in the UK are drawn up with little consideration for the new regulatory framework within which the privatized utilities now operate. LA21 initiatives in Copenhagen are more interested in changing lifestyles than in reconfiguring existing technical networks. As a result it is quite possible for two different, but complementary, strands of debate on sustainable flow management to be pursued in isolation from another within a single city.

Secondly, it is equally clear that both local environmental planning and urban infrastructure management could benefit from greater cooperation and interaction. The aim of utility managers to strike a better balance between supply and demand in different parts of their network creates interest on their part in land use changes and spatial planning which the planning community could meet by helping to direct development to areas of free network capacity.

The practice of measuring and modelling local environmental flows for whole localities could be applied more usefully to establish under- and over-utilized sections of an infrastructure network and thus encourage the more cost- and resource-efficient use of existing infrastructure. In other words, the emerging new logic of network management is creating new communities of interest with local planning.

Thirdly, to identify and exploit these communities of interest requires an appreciation of the diversity of interests shaping local planning. The case studies of LA21 have demonstrated that a wide range of visions for sustainable infrastructure systems can coexist within a single locality. They have illustrated further that the process of planning sustainable forms of flow management is neither as straightforward nor as linear as is often assumed. The complex interplay of diverse visions and different modes of action makes the process unpredictable and the outcome ambiguous. Planning for sustainability under these circumstances is, therefore, not well served by the search for a blueprint for sustainable flow management, designed to be superimposed on existing structures and processes. More promising would appear to be the search for 'windows of opportunity' which present themselves when, in the course of shifting pressures, there is an overlap of interests between two or more parties.

Finally, this section has helped to enhance understanding of the importance of context dependency in determining which path or paths are taken. The case studies have all shown how the interests and activities of key actor groups are framed to a substantial degree by local contextual factors, whether it be a particular environmental problem, an existing infrastructure network or a strong culture of public participation. Understanding these local social and technical forces and their interaction is, it is argued, an important step towards selecting appropriate practices of urban infrastructure management and local environmental planning.

PART 5
RE-INTERPRETING URBAN INFRASTRUCTURE

Credit: Morten Elle

12 CONCLUSIONS: CONTESTING NETWORKS

Simon Guy, Simon Marvin and Timothy Moss

Utility services for water, energy, sewage and solid waste shape the flow of a substantial proportion of the material resources used in cities. They draw on external water and energy resources, distribute these in the required quality and form to consumers and dispose of waste products in and beyond the urban region. The re-ordering of urban technical networks creates the potential to develop new styles of management that keep a downward pressure on resource use and its associated environmental impacts. Past strategies to improve the environmental performance of these infrastructure systems have focused on technological efficiency and innovation, encouraged by state regulation and market incentives. While acknowledging the progress already achieved by these strategies, this book has highlighted the importance of recognizing different styles of infrastructure management shaped by locally specific social and technical contexts.

EUROPEAN URBAN INFRASTRUCTURE IN TRANSITION

The need to understand the importance of new styles of infrastructure management is particularly evident today. Utility services across Europe have to adapt to a variety of new challenges. Among these liberalization and privatization are the most familiar but there are many other concurrent pressures, including stricter environmental regulation, heavy infrastructure investments and growing public concern for service quality and costs. These forces for change are challenging established strategies and practices that have underpinned the management of infrastructure systems. It is becoming increasingly difficult, in particular, to maintain the conventional supply-driven logic of building up network capacity to meet constantly rising demand now that the old regulatory structures – such as territorial monopolies – are being eroded.

The transition of urban infrastructure systems in Europe is, at the same time, giving valuable insight into the forces that shape environmental innovation. The task of limiting the environmental impact of utility services has usually been seen by urban planners and network managers as a technical problem to be addressed through the application of new technology. However, today's pressures are suggesting that addressing the environmental problems of utility services has much to do with different styles of utility management. The challenge is to develop our understanding of how conducive the social organization of traditional network management is to resource conservation and pollution prevention.

Assemblage of signals

The book has progressively revealed the very diverse signals shaping urban infrastructure systems. These include primarily: liberalization and privatization, tighter environmental standards, shifts in consumption patterns, under- and overcapacity of networks, competition between rival technologies, reduced government funding and disputes over the price and quality of services. At any one time and place a unique set of physical, economic, environmental, social, organizational and technological signals is working to push infrastructure management in new directions. It is this blend of heterogeneous signals, widely prevalent across the case study regions, which is responsible for the ongoing transition of infrastructure management.

Places and networks

Whereas most, if not all, of these signals could be detected to some degree in each of the regions under study, their strength and influence on infrastructure management was observed to vary enormously in different spatial contexts. For example, the process of liberalization is most advanced in the UK; the problem of network overcapacity is strongest in Germany and Denmark. Water pollution is having a greater influence on infrastructure design in the regions of Berlin and Copenhagen than in the north east of England. Different traditions, structures and conditions of infrastructure management in each region give a distinct emphasis to each of the pressures creating an assemblage of signals specific to that locality. The unique interplay of these locally specific signals explains how the pace and nature of the transition process varies across Europe.

Sustainable Flow Management: a Contested Concept

The management of urban flows via infrastructure systems is therefore the product of a highly complex interweaving of forces. Furthermore, new types of flow management can take different styles shaped by their local context. It follows from this that efforts to make flow management more sustainable cannot resort to a static model of sustainable flow management. No single model would fit neatly onto such a wide variety of emerging management styles. The concept of sustainable flow management is more useful as an empty concept that provides a framework for conceiving sustainable futures but is filled with objectives suited to a specific local context. This is not merely a logical deduction: our research shows that sustainable flow management is a highly contested concept in practice. Different actors within a single locality interpret sustainability in diverging ways, holding very different opinions on how technical networks should be managed more sustainably in the future.

Emerging logics of infrastructure management

New pressures on infrastructure management and diverse opinions on how to respond to these signals are seriously challenging the conventional logic of service provision. The flow managers in utility companies and regulatory bodies are having to rethink how resources and networks are managed. The prevalent logic of build and supply, characterized by territorial monopolies, physical networks centred around a single, large-scale technical system and a techno-centric approach to problem solving, is being undermined. Our research identified a number of emerging logics being developed by utility managers:

- Commercialization: improving competitiveness and efficiency to withstand market liberalization and meet rising investment costs.
- Demand side management: providing extended services to (select) customer groups in order to maintain customer loyalty and use existing network capacity more efficiently.
- Technology mix: introducing new decentralized technologies to complement existing centralized systems.
- Spatial differentiation: devising new spatial contexts of operation to attain a more efficient use of resources.

Reconfiguring infrastructure networks

As the pressures for change mount and new logics open up in response, the question remains how these influences are currently being translated into the practice of infrastructure management. This process of reconfiguration of selected infrastructure networks was examined in each of the case studies conducted in the three urban regions.

Networks

The three case studies on reconfiguring water supply and sewage disposal networks explored competing solutions to a regional water resource problem as an illustration of the new signals and logics currently changing the way water and sewage services are supplied. Three emerging challenges to network management were explored with the case studies: adjusting existing systems to accommodate shifting contextual factors through water recycling in the Berlin region; incorporating decentralized technologies into centralized networks through rainwater percolation technologies in Copenhagen; and responding to a resource crisis in the case of the Yorkshire drought.

Three broad conclusions can be drawn from the research. The first is that infrastructure networks can become destabilized as a result of changed environmental conditions, requiring a fundamental shift from the established style of network management. Second, a key feature of the reconfiguration process is the increasing complexity and heterogeneity of infrastructure management as users are given new roles, new technologies are added to existing networks and a wider set of social actors become involved in the network. In response, flow managers are developing new techniques for engaging and shaping the socio-technical development of the network. Third, there is little evidence of the old logic being simply replaced by a new one. On the contrary, in this time of planning uncertainty it is evident that several logics can coexist within a single infrastructure system, indicating a degree of flexibility in styles of network management not usually associated with utility services.

Buildings

The buildings case studies investigated what factors shape the application – or non-application – of environmental technologies and practices at the micro-level of design. This views reconfiguration from the perspective of a network's end-points or node. The interest here lay in determining what social contexts assist or hinder the creation of green buildings and how in-house infrastructure and urban technical networks shape one another, thereby creating or blocking openings for environmentally sensitive design.

The first important conclusion is that the strategic priorities of the many actors involved in the planning, design, construction and use of the building shape a building's environmental design. There is no definitive 'green' building of optimal technical structures. Instead competing notions of what constitutes 'greenness' exist, and not just the ecocentric or technocentric extremes. A green building is rarely a model for any one of these visions; it is generally a hybrid, the product of a compromise between several, often conflicting, preferences of the various actors involved. Consequently, the social organization of in-house infrastructure plays a crucial part in determining the technical design of buildings; innovative forms of social organization, involving for instance a redistribution of actor roles, have been shown to overcome obstacles to the application of environmental technologies. Finally, it is often overlooked when designing a green building, how the choice of in-house technologies is limited by the need to fit into the surrounding urban infrastructure. This helps to explain some of the difficulties currently encountered in establishing green building projects. If the design rejects the logic of the surrounding system it runs the risk of remaining an isolated island of sustainability, if it adapts too closely to the needs of the existing physical networks the openings for innovation are limited.

Plans

The final three case studies explored the contribution and response of local environmental planning to new logics of infrastructure management. The purpose was to discover how far recent shifts in infrastructure management are being reflected and considered in the arena of local planning, ranging from formalized activities of spatial or sectoral planning to LA21 initiatives.

The findings revealed, firstly, that local environmental planning is as yet largely disconnected from the new agendas of network managers. Despite a common interest in the efficient use of natural resources in urban contexts, the two arenas of debate are largely unconnected, running in parallel even within the same city. The energy, water or waste management concepts of local authorities commonly fail to take into consideration the altered regulatory and commercial framework within which utilities now operate. LA21 initiatives have a tendency to view utility companies and their technical networks as part of the problem, rather than essential players in strategies for more sustainable flow management in cities. Our research has revealed, though, that the emerging new logic of network management is creating new communities of interest with local planning. The growing commercial interest of utilities in the impact of urban development on their technical networks and the new locally based services they provide or encourage (eg demand side management) are creating contexts for mutually beneficial cooperation between local planning and urban infrastructure management directed at a more efficient use of natural resources. To tap these emerging communities of interest, it is argued, will require more fine-grained knowledge not only of the utilities' viewpoints but also of the wide range of actor interests and innovative approaches to sustainable flow management which exist within a particular locality. Linking infrastructure management to local planning in future will entail a more flexible approach to planning with a strong emphasis on seeking out 'windows of opportunity' for pursuing particular policy objectives.

RETHINKING FLOW MANAGEMENT

Previous research on technical networks has tended to focus on issues of technological efficiency and innovation, state regulation, market incentives and information campaigns for consumers. Studies of urban technical networks that aim to explain the socio-technical factors shaping new styles of network management remain rare. Successfully assessing the potential of infrastructure networks to improve environmental quality will depend increasingly on understanding how infrastructure management is shaped by the interaction of social and technical signals in a specific local context.

There is, then, a clear need to take forward debates on sustainable urban development, material flow management, the liberalization of utility services and the development of large infrastructure systems. In this book we have demonstrated this process by highlighting the importance of local context in creating 'windows of opportunity' for environmental innovation. Rather than offer a further definition of sustainable resource use in cities, we have examined the potential for more sustainable forms of resource use to be derived from understanding how contextual forces shape infrastructure management. We have shown how the interaction of complex economic, spatial, environmental, social and regulatory signals in a specific locality can open or close spaces, or opportunities, for environmental innovation in technical networks. Being able to recognize the emergence of new openings or windows of opportunity is, it is argued, becoming increasingly important at a time when utility services in Europe are undergoing major transformation. Focusing on local context has also contributed to our understanding of the very different visions and pathways of sustainable urban development pursued by local actors.

Complementing recent research on material flow management, which has been directed primarily at quantifying flows and establishing targets for sustainable levels of material flows at national and regional levels, we have also examined the problem of implementing more sustainable forms of resource use in urban regions. We have examined the motives and scope for action of key actors in the water, sewage, electricity and solid waste sectors to introduce – or reject – environmental technologies. In doing so we have identified how interactions between the physical or technical side of service provision and the socio-cultural dimensions of resource consumption powerfully shape the context for environmental improvements.

Research on the liberalization of utility services has, in the past, tended to focus on the issues of ownership and/or regulatory structures for a single sector. In contrast, this book has broadened the perspective of debate around the reconfiguration of networks in three ways. Firstly, we have set liberalization in the context of other major forces currently reshaping utility services, including stricter environmental regulation, shifts in consumption patterns and growing competition between technologies, thus explaining change in the utility sectors in terms of regionally specific combinations of these multiple new pressures. Secondly, we have reintroduced debates about environmental issues, illustrating how liberalization, as well as undermining some existing environmental policy objectives, can contribute to creating new communities of interest for efficient resource use. Thirdly, using analytical approaches from science and technology studies, we have demonstrated how the major transformation of utility services today is revealing large infrastructure systems to be more flexible and adaptable to change than they appear to have been in the past.

The social construction of technical systems

The underlying message of the book is that if the enormous potential of technical networks to improve environmental quality is to be realized, it is necessary to view infrastructure management as a socio-technical issue. Technological innovation in the utilities sector is driven by a complex web of economic, social, technical and environmental signals that can be shaped only partially by isolated regulatory pressures, financial incentives or information campaigns. We have argued the importance of understanding how social and technical systems interact in a specific local context.

An important first step is to map the social organization of infrastructure management. This entails mapping the social interests involved in the planning, provision and use of utility services, the influence each group possesses and how they interact with one another. The need to understand the social organization of utility services is, indeed, growing more urgent as new technologies, new commercial pressures and new institutional arrangements are rearranging conventional roles and engaging new actors. This applies in particular to consumers who, as targets of customized services or as operators of decentralized or in-house technologies, are now playing a growing part in infrastructure management.

Secondly, there is a growing need to rethink the spatial scales of flow management. In the past the boundaries of technical networks were determined largely by the area served by the sole service provider, often corresponding with the territory of a political-administrative unit. Today the spatial homogeneity of utility services is giving way to more complex spatial relationships. On the one hand the external boundaries are becoming more fluid as territorial monopolies are eroded and utilities begin to define their spheres of commercial interest rather according to physical networks and resource flows. In other respects the spatial scale of operation is decreasing as a result of the more widespread application of decentralized technologies and the growing spatial differentiation of service provision. Together these recent changes are requiring policy makers to seek the most appropriate spatial level of action for specific measures.

Thirdly, there is increased recognition of the importance of local context in understanding and managing flows. Examples of environmental 'best practices' are exchanged internationally often without much consideration of how they might fit into an unfamiliar institutional setting. As a result many promising ideas run aground when put into practice if they have not first been dismissed by planners as unsuited to local conditions. This project has emphasized the local embeddedness of infrastructure networks, demonstrating how the development trajectory of a technical network is framed significantly by local or regional contextual circumstances. By this is meant not only the social organization, mentioned above, but also the existing physical and technical structures of the networks. These need to be taken into consideration when adapting appropriate practices from elsewhere.

Fourthly, there would appear to be a range of competing pathways along which infrastructure management is capable of developing in response to recent pressures for change. What we are witnessing is not the replacement of one dominant logic by another, but the emergence of several new competing logics that are, nevertheless, capable of coexistence. The policy significance of this observation is enormous. In terms of technology innovation policy, it implies departing from notions of a simple 'technology switch' and seeking, instead, an optimal combination of mutually compatible technologies. In terms of long-term objectives for sustainable development, it undermines the rationale of seeking the definitive version of sustainable flow management, calling on policy makers to be sensitive to different styles of flow management and different pathways to achieving more sustainable forms of resource use.

Finally, these different styles of flow management will involve a new approach to planning infrastructure systems. The notion of a linear planning process from conception to implementation – already challenged in other policy fields – is becoming increasingly inappropriate for technical networks. Infrastructure planning today is highly complex and subject to greater levels of unpredictability than in the past. This is placing a strain on infrastructure planners, who are professionally ill equipped to meet this challenge. They will require new management skills to help them to respond flexibly to changing circumstances and to link together the technical and social worlds of infrastructure management.

CONTESTED URBAN FUTURES

This book suggests the urgent need for a fresh approach to understanding urban infrastructure based upon a different image of sustainable cities. Rather than the bounded container defined by physical resource flows and populated by socially anonymous individuals encountered in much sustainable cities literature, we envisage a rather different city. In the contested city a heterogeneous mix of actors and agencies shape city development, framed by their social, organizational, temporal and spatial contexts of action. The voices of private utility companies, environmental groups, transport providers, local authorities, housing associations, technology manufacturers, architects, developers, investors, all types of building occupiers and other urban actors all shape the debate on sustainable cities. This cacophony of voices, sometimes heard in harmony, more often in discord, has forced us to engage with changing structures and processes of urban development which tend to escape the conventional sustainable cities debate.

Structural shifts such as the privatization, liberalization and globalization of resource provision and the changing social organization of urban design and development has served to radically reorder the social, regulative and commercial constraints on, and opportunities for, environmental innovation. New actors and institutions have become influential, new assemblages of political, commercial and environmental concern and new forms of formal and informal governance now shape processes of resource management and building design. Within this image cities represent a theatre of competing voices, each contributing to the ongoing social construction of sustainability.

This way of seeing stresses the critical importance of recognizing different styles of infrastructure management, shaped by locally specific social and technical contexts. Different traditions, structures and conditions of infrastructure management in each region give a distinct local emphasis to environmental innovation. It follows from this that efforts to make resource management more sustainable cannot resort to a single, static model. Different social interests within a single locality interpret sustainability in different ways, holding very different opinions on how technical networks should be managed more sustainably in the future.

This dynamic, contextual debate about the sustainable city means that we need to recognize the emergence and coexistence of a variety of environmental logics, each reshaping cities in a myriad of ways, some overlapping, some conflicting. Commercially driven smart technologies, community inspired recycled design, private utility sponsored resource management strategies, local authority environmental planning and central government regulatory practices all stumble over each other, variously prioritizing ecological, technological, aesthetic, health and community issues, all in the name of the environment. Even within such apparently technical initiatives as DSM programmes, the design of greener buildings and the use of recycled materials, we found a shifting perspective on the use of alternative technologies, the role of consumers, the need for information, the necessity of advanced computer modelling techniques and the effectiveness of market and regulatory delivery systems.

The notion of a set of best technical practices is simply too narrow and static to capture this multiple reordering of the city. Instead, a notion of competing environmental logics is required to acknowledge the variety of pathways of innovation, in turn reflecting the diverse contexts of urban environmental action. Rather than focusing on technical or economic constraints, an alternative approach would acknowledge that action is shaped by a multiplicity of factors and cannot be reduced to a simple view of a 'barrier' to change (Guy, 1999). Instead, there is a multiplicity of local contexts within which individual and organizational behaviour is shaped. This way of seeing views social action not in terms of individualized and manageable behaviour, but rather as the capacity of socialized actors to innovate within highly constrained and dynamic contexts of action that may sometimes enable and sometimes inhibit environmental innovation. We must, therefore, seek to understand how the changing social organization of environmental innovation structures the potential of different coalitions of actors to shape sustainable cities. Accepting the multiple rationalities for action, the policy task becomes one of identifying windows of opportunity arising from the coexistence of different social, political and commercial interests in alternative forms of environmental innovation.

The promotion of sustainable infrastructure and cities must start with a contested vision of both network management and the city. Here, new and sometimes unlikely partnerships may be formed in the pursuit of alternative urban futures. In the pursuit of new forms of environmental value, windows of opportunity may emerge that allow utility companies to help their customers to reduce energy demand by investing in low-energy light bulbs rather than new power stations, property developers and investors to collaborate with architects and clients to promote low-energy buildings, water companies to help developers redesign water systems to reduce network stress and local authorities and community groups to work with network managers to promote environmental technologies and practices. The research challenge is to map the multiple constructions of the sustainable city, to understand the changing social contexts that produce them and to build an understanding of the multiple logics emerging to reorder social relations, resource flows and urban form.

RESEARCH AND POLICY CHALLENGE

Adopting this way of seeing networks, it soon becomes apparent that the sustainable city cannot be reduced to a simple standardized definition or vision. There is growing consensus among sustainable cities researchers that the search for the sustainable city needs to be reoriented to the search for pathways towards different types of sustainable city. Competing visions of the sustainable city each embody a different analysis of the problem and alternative attempts to reorder socio-technical relations along very different pathways in order to create quite different urban futures. There are three important implications of these observations for sustainability research.

First, we need to be much more modest in the claims we make about what the sustainable city might represent. Rather than search for a consensual definition, the task of research should be an attempt to understand the broader nature of city development, of which environmental innovation continues to be only one element. We need to recognize how the sustainability question gets caught up, reinterpreted and recast in a whole range of debates about the future development of cities. Out of the mangle of the diverse practices, multiple rather than singular visions of what the city can be are emerging.

This, second, has important methodological implications. The role of research should be to identify and unpack the competing claims for what the sustainable city might become. With a much enlarged and active group of social interests competing to promote their own notion of the sustainable city, research needs to map the social, political and commercial assumptions, forms of socio-technical reordering and alternative visions entwined in different initiatives, plans, policies and strategies deriving from a whole range of private and public sector interests.

Third, we need to be sensitive to the potential for a particular pathway to dominate policy debates, squeezing out alternative environmental logics which do not enjoy wide support. Conventional experts and policy makers may tend to prefer the development of particular pathways, ignoring those embryonic pathways representing marginalized social interests. In this context the role of research is to keep alive a multiplicity of pathways by opening a wider discourse and dialogue about the types of future we might be able to create.

Overall, such a project would produce a fertile research context. Rather than seeking to limit the sustainability debate to a relatively narrow set of parameters and actors we should seek to widen the debate by linking the sustainability agenda to broader questions about the future of cities, to consider the role of particular socio-political interests in shaping urban development and to identify the tensions and resonance between powerful and marginalized pathways of development (Guy and Marvin, 1998). In this way we would begin to respect the highly contested nature of the search for a sustainable city that expresses the diverse perspectives that will compose the city of tomorrow.

REFERENCES

Guy, S (1999) 'Evil Developers and Green Fairies', in B Fairweather, S Elworthy, M Stroh and P Stephens (eds) *Environmental Futures*, Macmillan Press, London

Guy, S and Marvin, S (1998) 'Electricity in the Marketplace: Reconfiguring the Consumption of Essential Resources', *Local Environment*, vol 3, no 3, pp313–331

INDEX